IN THE SHADOW OF
ANGKOR

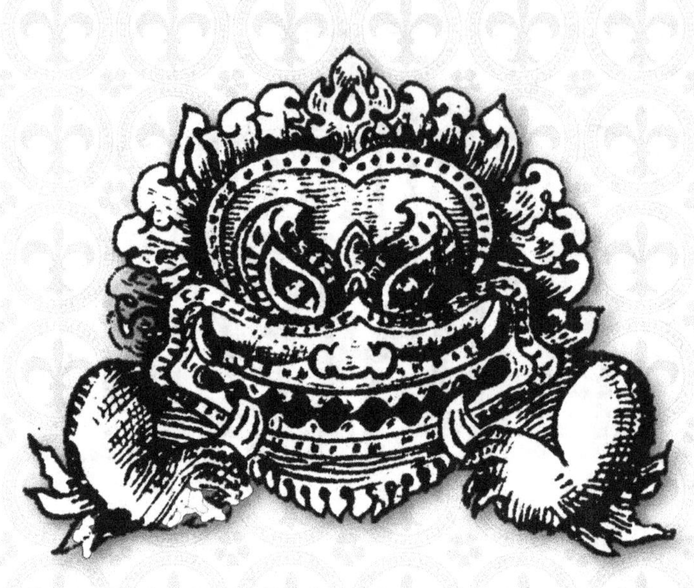

IN THE SHADOW OF ANGKOR

Unknown Temples of Ancient Cambodia

Notes and Impressions by

George GROSLIER

*Project Manager for the Mission to Cambodia for
The Ministry of Public Education and Fine Arts*

1913–1914

Foreword by **Milton OSBORNE**

Edited by **Kent DAVIS**

Translated by **Pedro RODRÍGUEZ**

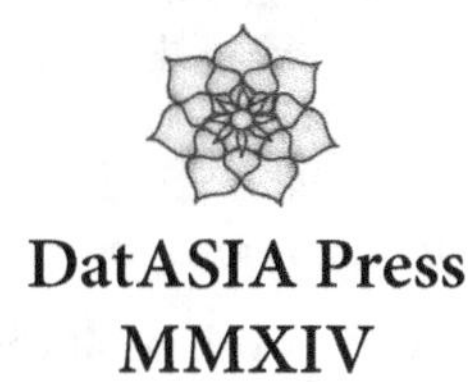

DatASIA Press

MMXIV

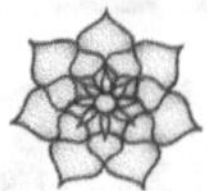

DatASIA Press — www.DatASIA.us
© Copyright 2014. DatASIA, Inc. Holmes Beach, Florida

First Edition
ISBN 978-1-934431-90-0
Library of Congress Pre-Assigned Control Number: 2011943381
Printed simultaneously in the United States of America and Great Britain.

Production Credits

Edited by **Kent Davis**

Translated by: **Pedro Rodríguez**

Cover design: **Rebecca Klein**

Text design: **Surendra Gupta**

Archival and photo assistance:
The National Museum of Cambodia, Darryl Collins and **Joel Montague**

Acknowledgements

With gratitude to **Nicole Rea Groslier** for her guidance and inspiration
in reissuing her father's works.

With the editor's special thanks to the Groslier family, and to Sophaphan Davis,
Jon Dobbs, Meng Dy, Tom Kramer and Duffy Rutledge for their special contributions.

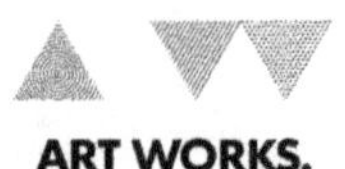

A **Translation Fellowship** from the **National Endowment for the Arts** (**NEA**) awarded to Pedro Rodríguez helped this effort. Established in 1965 by the United States Congress, the NEA is an independent government agency that has awarded more than $4 billion to support artistic excellence, creativity, and innovation for the benefit of individuals and communities worldwide.

To join the discussion on how art works visit the NEA at **www.arts.gov**

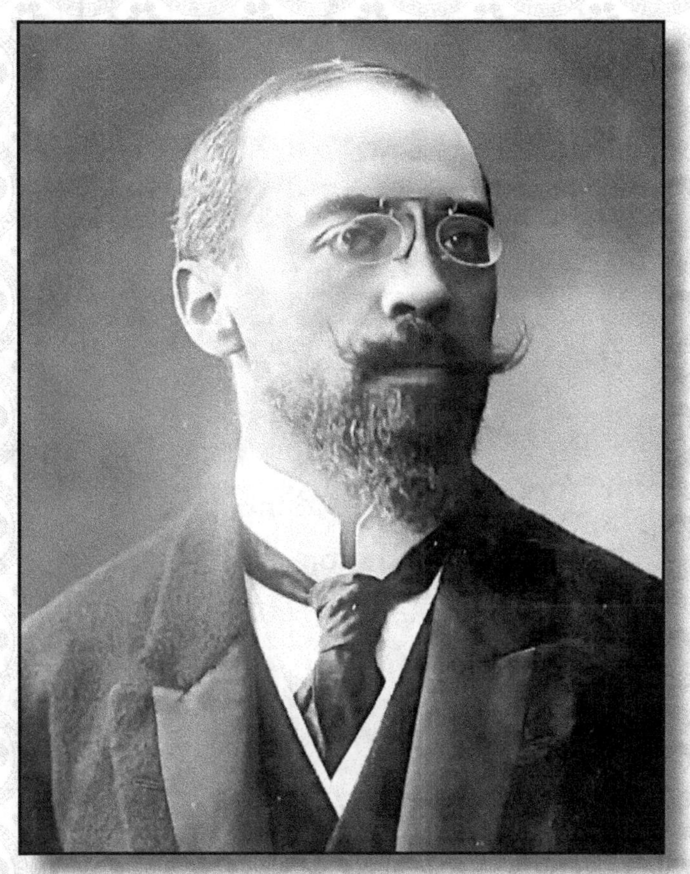

A Monsieur Albert SARRAUT

Ancien Ministre de l'Instruction Publique,
Ancien Gouverneur Général de l'Indochine.

Très respectueusement,

G. G.

To Mr. Albert SARRAUT

Former Minister of Public Education,
Former Governor General of Indochina.

Most respectfully,

G. G.

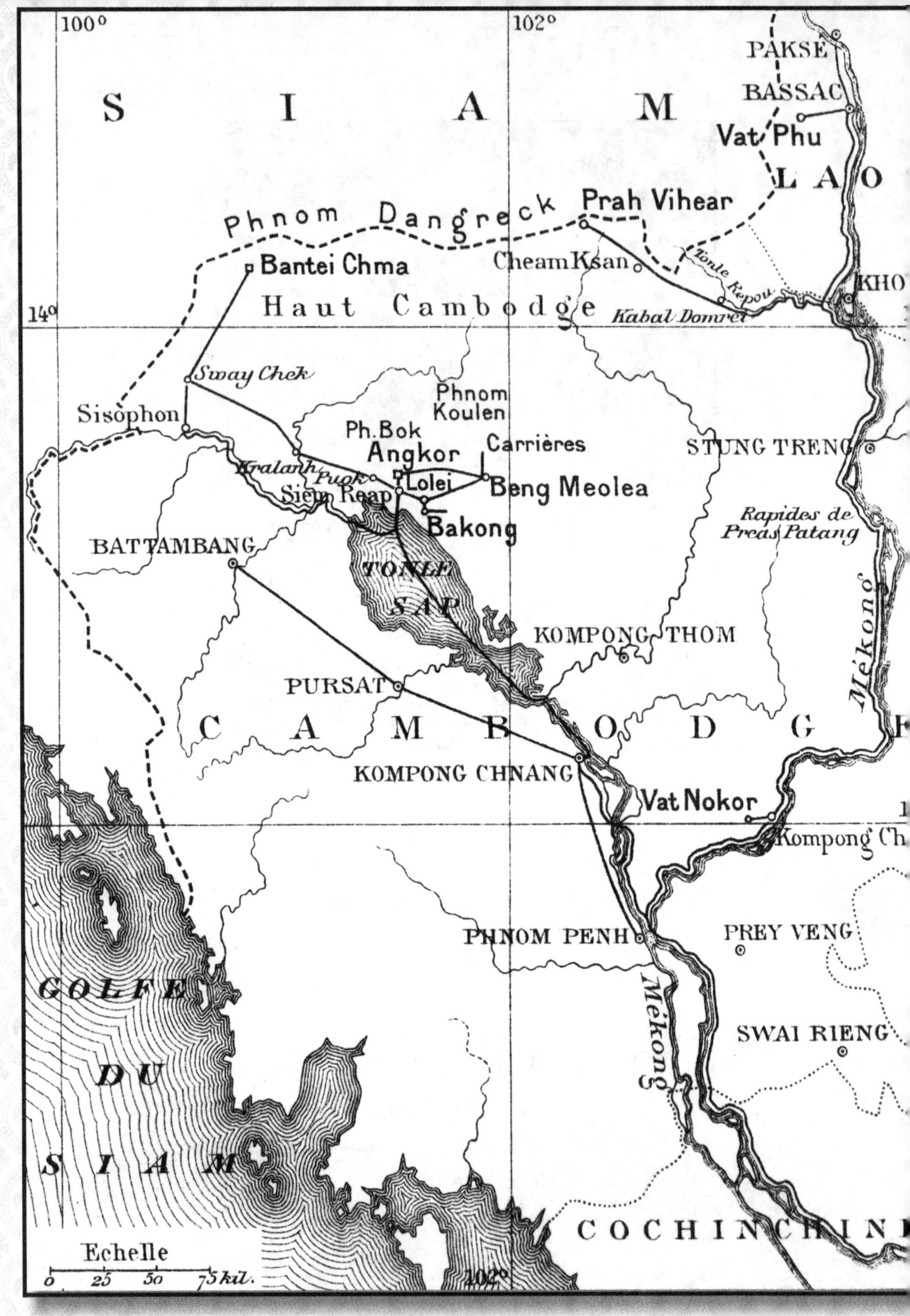

Groslier Mission Itinerary – April 1913-January 1914

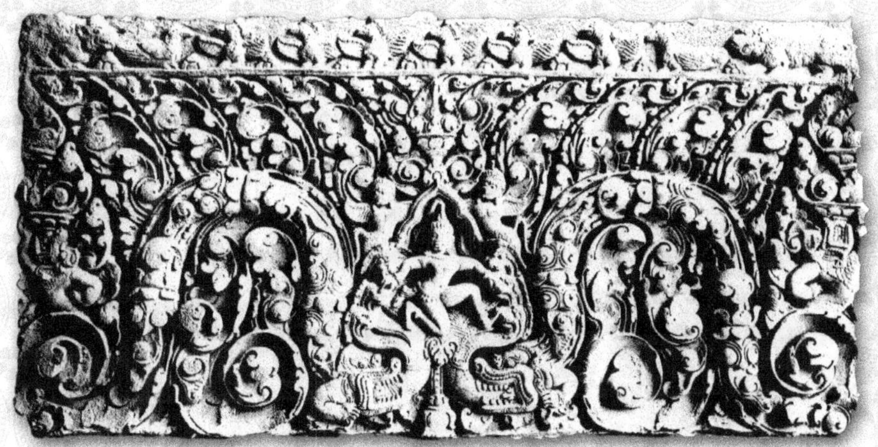

Table of Contents

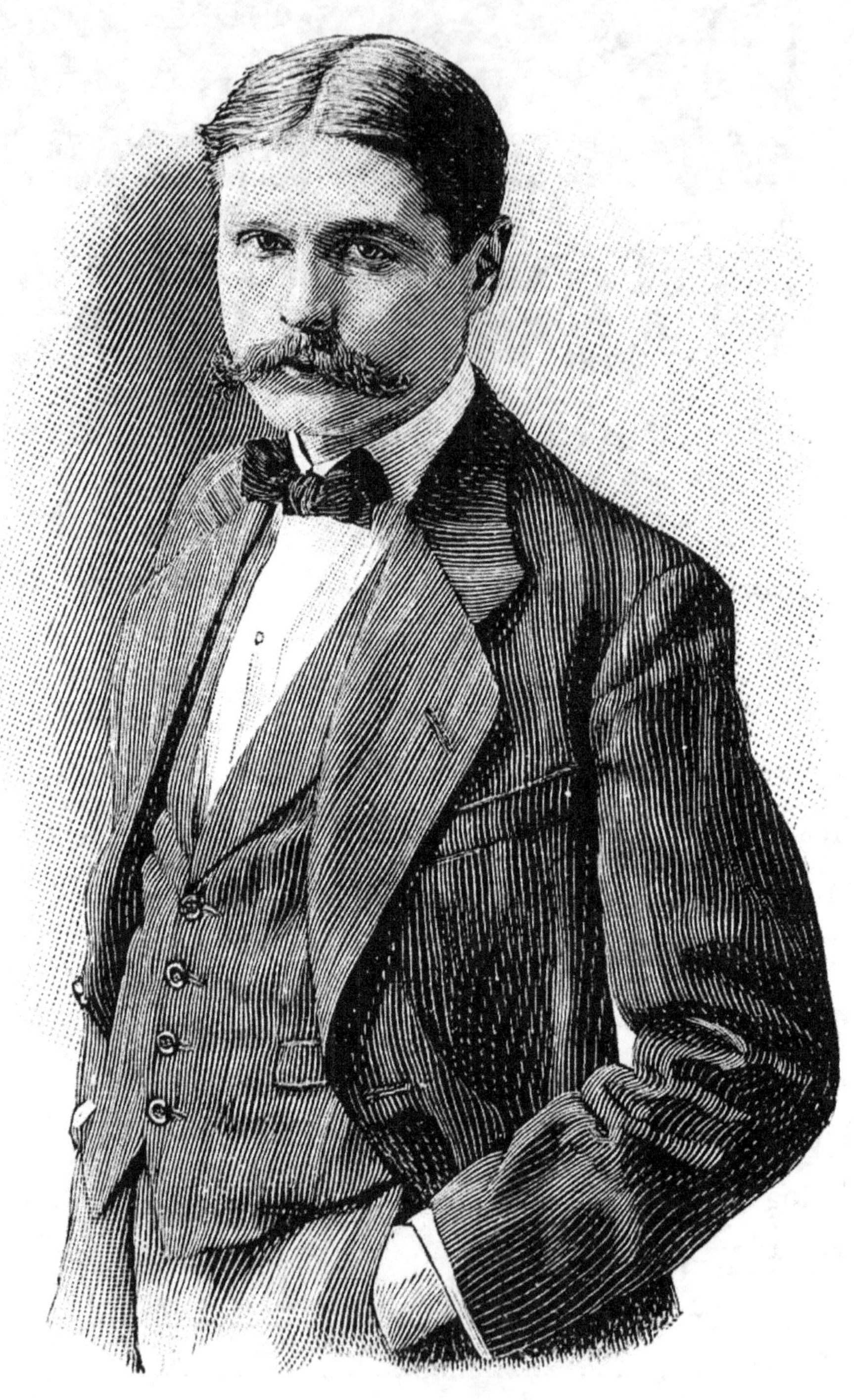

George Groslier

February 4, 1887 — June 18, 1945

Foreword

For anyone with an interest in the great temples of the ancient Angkorian empire, whether as a tourist or scholar, the publication of George Groslier's wonderful book, *A l'Ombre d'Angkor: Notes et impressions sur les Temples Inconnus de l'Ancien Cambodge*, is a cause for real celebration. Now made available in a sensitive English translation as, *In The Shadow of Angkor: Unknown Temples of Ancient Cambodia*, this bibliographically scarce book is a great deal more than an extended catalogue of what were once little-known, Cambodian temple ruins—temples such as Preah Vihear, Banteay Chhmar and Wat Phu, located far from the main Angkor complex sited close to the modern provincial town of Siem Reap. But while much of the interest in the book stems from the description Groslier provides of these temples as he saw them in 1913, when they were indeed virtually unknown to more than a few western scholars, there is much more to be found in this book of lyrical, and at times poetic, writing.

At its most fundamental, the book is an account of a young man's journey through a Cambodian and Lao landscape into which the West had barely penetrated. We rest with him after he has climbed to the upper shrine at Wat Phu and share his exertions as he clambers to reach the summit where Preah Vihear looms above the northern Cambodian plain. The immediacy of his descriptions in this book do more than hint at his later ventures into the field of fiction, a field in which his sense of landscape is richly present. For those who know the areas through which Groslier travelled, what is striking is the extent to which much of what he describes has remained unchanged to the present day. At the same time, and emphasising the author's humane personality, the book, is also a sympathetic account of the peasant Cambodians and Lao whom he encountered in his travels. It is, as well, a penetrating reflection on ancient Cambodia's art and architecture and on the Hindu and Buddhist religions that were the wellsprings of its beliefs.

As is already clear, George Groslier was a man of many talents, and one with a distinctive personal background. His contributions to our knowledge of Cambodian arts in their many forms remains important to the present day. It is fitting, therefore, that he is remembered today through his greatest monument, the remarkable Cambodian National Museum in Phnom Penh, of which he was both architect and for more than two decades its director after its inauguration in 1920. The first child born to French parents in Cambodia in 1887, Groslier had grown up in France with a deep awareness of the country in which he had been born. Apparently, this did not lead to his initially having any great interest in returning to what was then French Indochina, where his father had continued to serve as a colonial civil servant while George, his siblings, and his mother lived in France. His talent as an artist led to study at the Ecole nationale supérieure des Beaux-Arts in Paris and to short-listed participation in the Prix de Rome competition. But his failure to win the prize was the catalyst for his being selected to be sent on a mission to Cambodia by the Ministry of Public Education in 1910, an assignment that led to his first important publication, *Danseuses cambogiennes, anciennes et modernes* (*Cambodian Dancers: Ancient and Modern*), now happily available under Kent Davis' editorship and which provides a detailed account of Grolier's life. The book is illuminated by Groslier's own illustrations.

By 1913, and as an approbation by the Ministry of Public Education for his earlier mission, Groslier returned to Cambodia to begin the travels that are the subject of this book. One hundred years after the book was written, it is difficult to imagine just what an undertaking travel in Cambodia away from the capital and a few provincial towns was like. Groslier's account vividly conjures up the nature of this travel, by *pirogue* or oxcart, with the need at times to float the cart across swollen rivers or to endure slow, bumpy progress over rutted tracks under a merciless sun. It is surely not too much to imagine Groslier reflecting on an earlier French traveller who encountered similar difficulties, Francis Garnier of the French Mekong Expedition in the 1860s when he made his epic overland journey from southern Laos to Siem Reap.

Groslier's book is very much a document of its time so far as some of the detailed archeological information he offers is concerned. His dating of some temples, both large and small, has subsequently been revised, and his suggestion that the ancient Khmers lacked mathematical ability is certainly not accepted nowadays. Despite his genuine sympathy for the Cambodians and Lao he encounters it is evident that he is a man of his age in some of the judgments he makes of them. But none of these minor aspects of the book detract from its importance and its basic humane appeal. This fact makes Groslier's death during the Second World War after torture by the Japanese then occupying Cambodia a tragic counterpoint to his richly productive life.

It was my privilege to know George Groslier's son, Bernard-Philippe Groslier, the distinguished *conservateur* of the Angkor temples. To have the opportunity to write this brief introduction to his father's book is a further privilege for which I am deeply grateful.

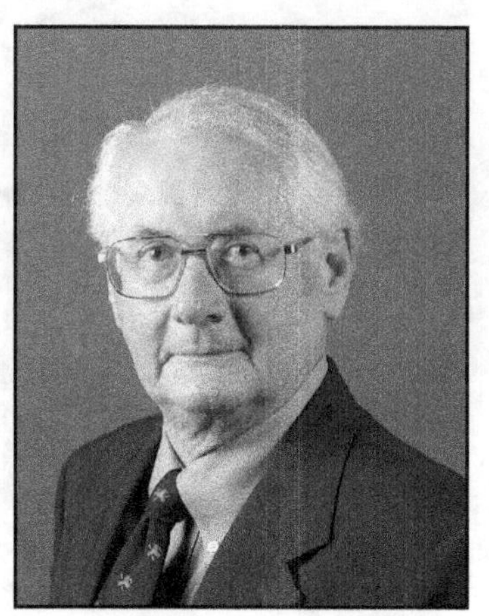

Milton Osborne

Milton Osborne is a Visiting Fellow at the Lowy Institute for International Policy, Sydney, and a long-time observer and writer on Cambodian politics and history. His books include, *River Road to China: The Search for the Source of the Mekong; Before Kampuchea: Preludes to Tragedy; Sihanouk: Prince of Light, Prince of Darkness;* and *Phnom Penh: A Cultural and Literary History.*

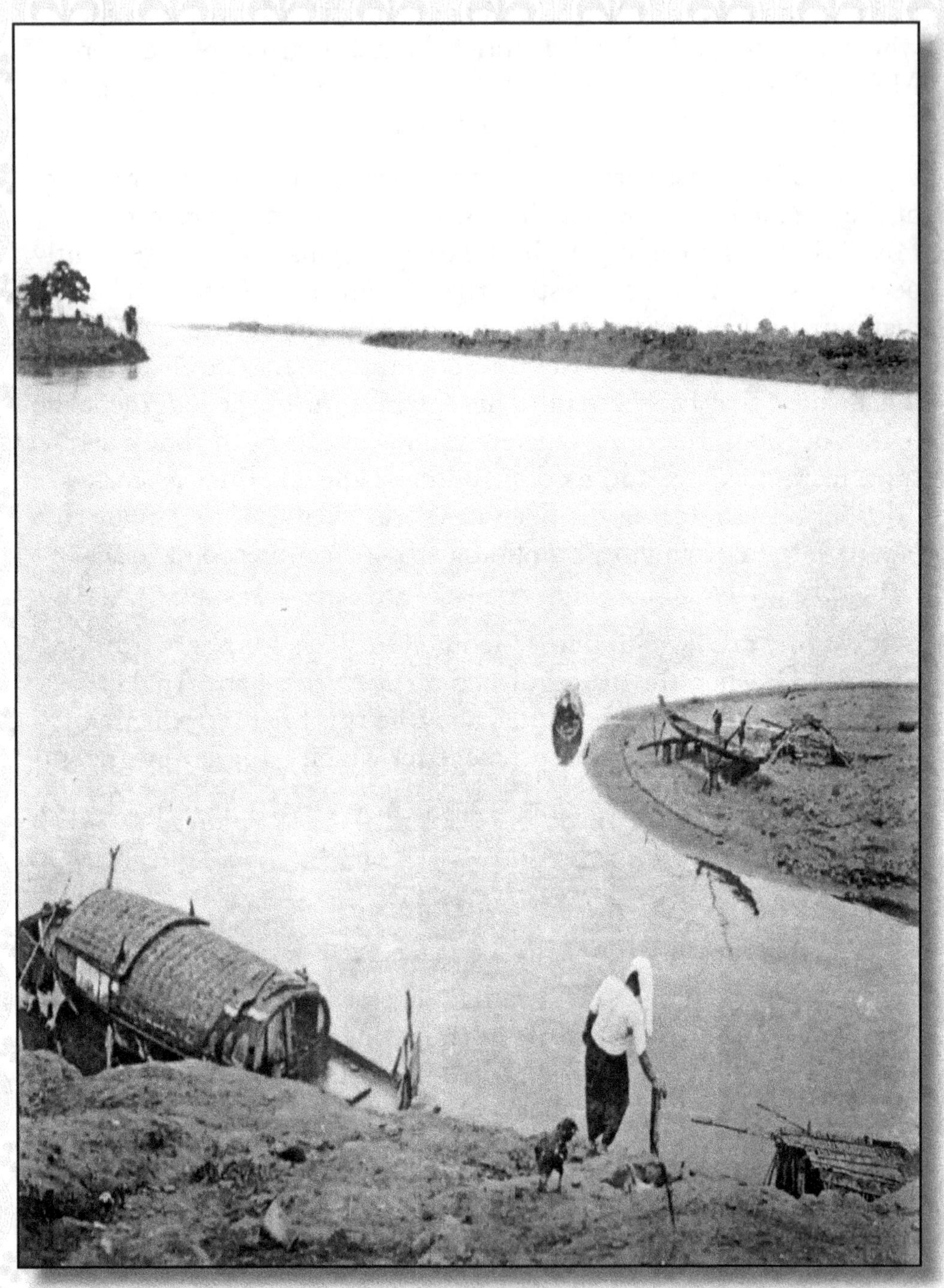

The Mekong at Kampong Cham.

1.
On The Mekong

1

Friday, June 6, 1913

t is low water, the river's time of great poetry, with the steep banks cut sheer in the fleshy red earth. All the trees there grow vigorously. There are teaks, with broad leaves of tender green; sugar palms and their fruit; bamboos like spurts of water, green and slender at bottom, tumbling up top with a delicate flourish; huge banyans sheltering pagodas; black mangos. There are bony-white cadavers of great trees, their twisted branches gesturing desperately at the passing waters. Since nothing in this country is completely dead or completely sad, even the skeletons sport plumes: luxuriant creepers.

Often a little island will emerge, like a great vessel in mid-celebration, entirely bedecked with verdure, and lying at anchor in the current. And always the mauve-flowered, floating weeds; the blue birds; cormorants black and motionless in the sunshine, wings spread; a pirogue sleeping under a tree and gradually filling with leaves; a naked child bathing; the scintillating leap of a fish; saffron bonze habits, tossed up on the bank to dry.

The sampans curve up at the ends. Standing on each end, held aloft, a paddler, and seated in the center, often, a woman, dazzling in her scarf, and set there like a great flower. Sampans ride high, on the very surface of the water. They skim past like narrow black crescents, and the water repeats them upside down. There are thus two crescents: one gliding, one trembling.

The pirogue by itself, dug out of a single tree trunk, nearly exhausts the riches of the riverside dweller. He fishes from it, transports fruits and provisions in it, under the protective cover of leaves, and often lives in it. When tired he crouches aft and showers himself with the exquisite water. He sings refrains to aid in his rowing. In his pirogue he lies down to sleep and dreams, rocked by the river in the shadow of bamboo. In his pirogue he carries his wife, "set like a flower," while his children play at handling the paddles.

Here a tree trunk, formerly rooted at the water's edge and rocked only by the wind. Now both wind and water have at it, and the trunk pursues its double existence, still bound to the same old bank.

All of it stirs my emotions as I watch the native sampans pass. An intimate poetry in the rocking of a wake on the calm, wide waters of the river. The whole world beyond is grand and solemn: the burning sky, the distant, mysterious banks, the silence.

II

The banks fade off to the horizon, and rocks emerge here and there. The trees, battered yearly by waters rising to meet their first boughs, display white roots reaching into the current. A thick, enduring foam swirls. Everywhere reddish eddies trace out some treacherous spot, a peril, an abyss. The great white sky is implacable. The water makes a dulcet sound. Rapids ahead.

Perched on the gunwales, those skinny planks encircling the craft, the paddlers speed up their maneuvers, their tense, bare feet striking in rhythm.

They lean far out, in defiance of gravity, backs rounded and streaming under the sun, paddle ends in their armpits, and they engage in battle. The junk goes nowhere. It rocks from side to side, tips up at the prow, grinds on branches at the water's surface. The bamboo poles bend to the breaking point and vibrate like the strings of a viol. Men pant and cry out. Then all ceases. The obstacle is past.

Broken with fatigue, the paddlers push the junk under a leaning tree. They leap with delight into the water, drink it down in long drafts. It is a beautiful thing, this repose, this freshness, this replenishment of strength from the very element that moments ago — at a spot still within view, and where a fallen man was a dead man — had sought to wrest away their lives.

A tranquil, civilized man stretched out under the pirogue's roof can observe these successive tableaux of violence and peace, and the matter of life thus quickly come into focus, especially when it suddenly depends on nothing but a bamboo pole that a man might break over his knee, or when the vague gaze and sunken cheek of the opium smoker are writ plain on a paddler's face.

To me, as I am none too certain of my tranquility or my civilization, the danger seemed quite illusory. I was concerned more with the how than with the why of the men's efforts. That, and not the rapids, is what made an impression.

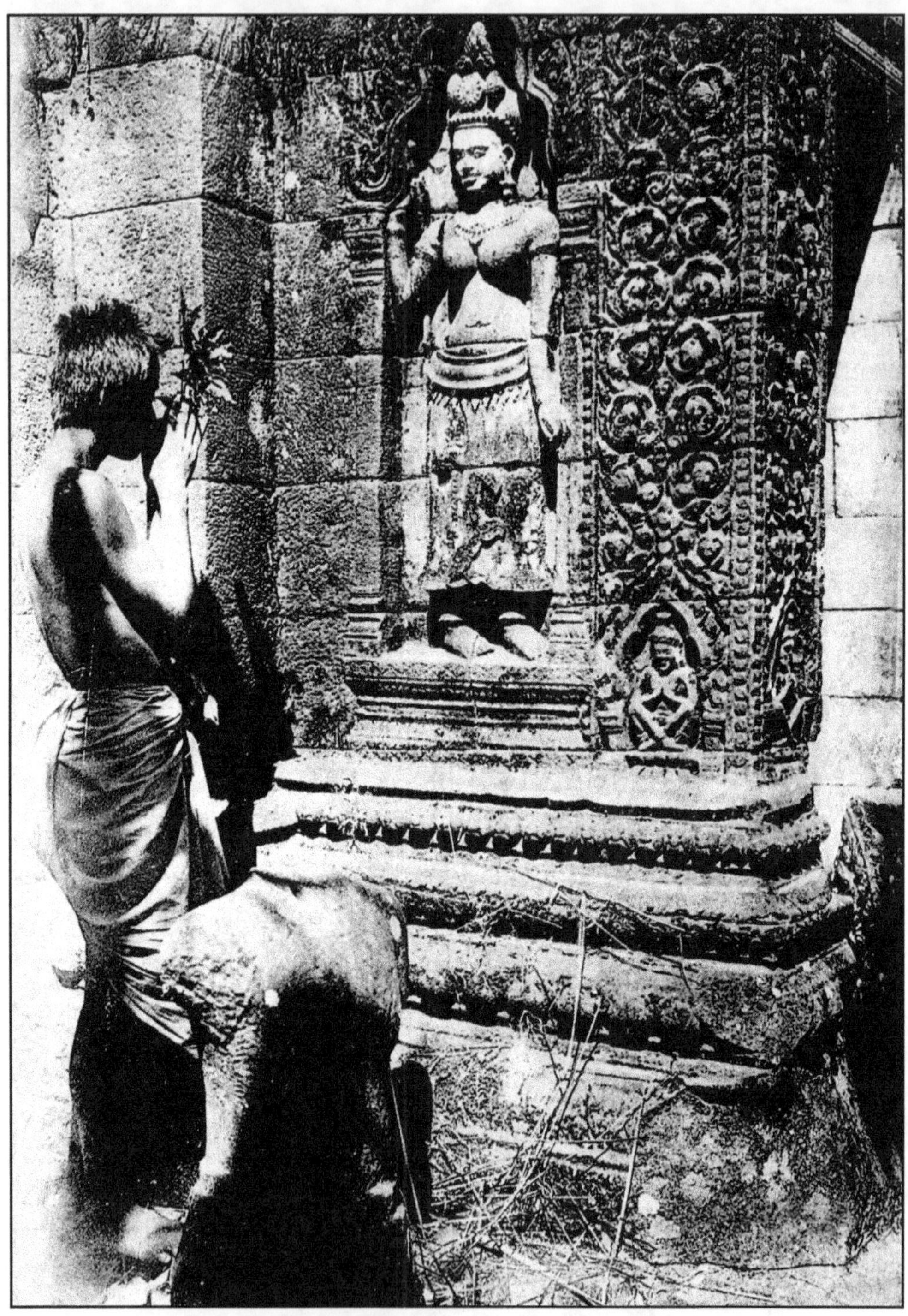

**Early photo of a young Laotian man making an offering
to one of two *devata* (goddess) images at Wat Phu.**

2
Wat Phu

III

Sunday, June 15, 1913

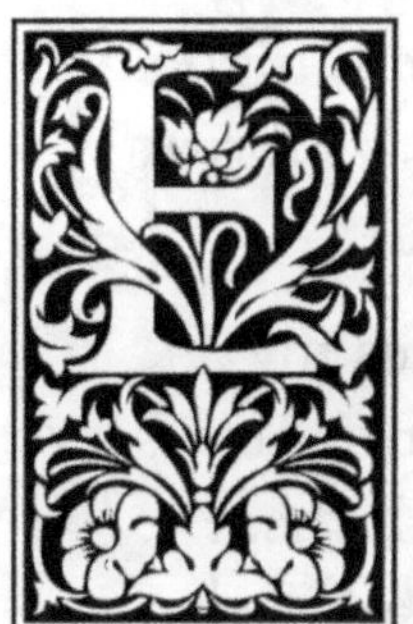ach of the two structures on the first foundation of Wat Phu is low and long and rests on a vigorously molded sub-base. The roofs have collapsed. Four leaning columns rise from a perron at the center.[1] Crowning the great, undecorated walls is a frieze of exceptional richness, however delicate. The whole displays a noble elegance.

There you have a cold, exact description. Now consider the pains I would have to have taken to express it in paint. Would I have managed to transcribe that "noble elegance"? Moving on…

Rain-washed and sun-baked, the sandstone blocks have taken on infinitely subtle tones over the centuries. Would my brush prove supple enough to render the "infinitely subtle sandstone" that my pen need only mention? Wonder no more why painters sometimes dabble in writing.

Farther on, the hillside against which the temple was built rises into perpetual cloud cover. Cool water dribbles drop by drop from rocks overhanging the sanctuary. A bonze crouches at the entrance to a grotto, his psalmody falling to my ear. A light breeze ripples

---

[1] An outdoor stairway leading up to a building entrance, often at the building's front.

the waters of the great lake at the foot of the hill and carries with it, from who knows where, the scent of lemongrass and frangipani. The eye roams freely over the plain, the Mekong valley, and the blue horizon of the Bolaven Plateau.[2]

Our edifice now has its setting. But have we yet conveyed the charm of its simplicity, the eloquent character of its leaning columns at dusk? How comfortably this temple sits, overlooking the land, blending a bit with the verdure as it turns blue!

Now from the plain comes the jingle of buffalo bells. The horizon turns purple. The bonze's psalmody has vanished with his yellow robe. The breeze has fallen. The lake sleeps under a veil that tears on trees of its shore. Everything fades: the edifice, the great stairways, the sentinel monsters, and the sanctuary itself, high amid the blooming trees, the hill, and the plain. And above it all rises the shrill song of the cicadas, calling from the horizon.

Need I say it? At such moments a joy absolute invades my tranquil soul. Beyond the lake, in this lost, remote setting, I descry the fire of my camp. I have come to beg the secret of all these things, if possible to uncover it, and then to tell it. As a traveler brimming with enthusiasm, passing where my countrymen do not pass, should I not exert my faculties to their maximum, and retain some trace of these generous hours? Stumbling upon a brook during my journey, I make a bundle of my clothes, get off my feet, and take to the water. I try to reach the far bank.

IV

Monday, June 16, 1913

From my seat atop the grand staircase, I watched a crowd of Laotian women depart. They had come with offerings of pineapple, bananas, rice, and small candles for the bonzes.

---

[2] Located in southern Laos, east of Pakse, the Bolaven Plateau is approximately 50 km wide and rises to a level of 1,000-1,350 m. The area was formed millions of years ago by a volcano. Today it is best known for its dense jungle, dramatic waterfalls, and diverse population of hill tribes.

Today was a religious feast day. Hence the white flowers carefully set out on the ancient boundary stones and grimacing monsters of the avenue.

The women descended the great staircase in bunches and were gradually channeled into the avenue toward the unfathomable verdure. Their empty baskets swung on the ends of poles. All made the same gesture, a folding of the arm, the graceful curve standing out against the sky.

Four little girls passed by. Two wore a scarf of white, the third of a vibrant, acidic pink, the fourth of blue. Their baskets were similar, their bodies charming, and all four wore a flower over the ear. They gazed upon the steep staircase, with its tall, fragile, crumbling steps. Then, dazzling, adjusting their scarves over their young breasts, they climbed in turn onto grey stones, into the sunlight. Other women piously tore out weeds around the sanctuary.

Smoking, the bonzes watched the show. They had found themselves a spot in this place of dreams, at the foot of a wall of great rocks wrapped in leafy garlands. The air there is always cool. The river spreads in the distance. Under the blooming trees stands a small, ancient sanctuary, home to the Buddha. It is carved like a reliquary, having formerly streamed with the water of lingas.[3] Nothing — not the barking of dogs, not the words of men, not the vain noises of the earth — disturbs the airy tranquility.

The sunny day drew to a close under grey skies. Mount Lingaparvata[4] displayed its mass in profile, like a lion at rest, head

---

[3] A Sanskrit word, meaning "mark" or "sign," applied to phallic objects that are worshiped as representations of the Hindu deity Shiva, or more generally as symbols of male creative energy. The male lingam almost always rests on a base representing its counterpart, the *yoni*, symbolizing Shakti and Devi, the female creative energies that move through the entire universe. The union of lingam and yoni represents the indivisible oneness of male and female from which all life originates. (Various sources including Wikipedia.)

[4] The mountain itself has a natural lingam on its peak and has been worshiped since ancient times. The city of Shrestapura, at the base of the mountain on the Mekong River, dates back to the fifth century. Later the temple became part of the Khmer empire.

partly raised. A transparent fog blurred its flanks of tragic blue. A pewter sky shone in the still water of the rice paddies.

V

Wednesday, June 18, 1913

Just past the monumental perron on the shores of the lake begins the long avenue to the sanctuary. Aligned with the path of the sun, it begins with a slight slope, follows the hillside, and leaps by great staircases from one platform to another before finally reaching the small sanctuary, some six hundred meters from the lake.

The forest ends on either side, allowing the sun to devour the ruins. Elegant boundary stones stud the ground crookedly or lay strewn over the stone slabs. Formerly the great serpent Naga[5] could be seen there. Its stone body once bordered the avenue, the hoods of its heads spreading at the perrons. There were also basins and gardens down below, to the left and the right.

On the first foundations rest the two buildings already mentioned. A few young trees have sprouted since the clearing of the land but cannot yet provide the proper shade for decaying matter.

The avenue continues beyond, lined with a now-toppled double colonnade. It passes successive foundations between the ruins of *aediculae*[6] and finally reaches the foot of the final staircase, that of the sanctuary, whose eighty steps rise eighteen meters.

Aside from the sanctuary, around which the trees either have not been destroyed or have grown back, the Wat Phu group does not make much of an impression. False archeological ideas led to the felling of trees centuries old and the removal of creeper garlands,

---

[5] Author's Note: Naga is a divinity in the form of a polycephalous snake, worshipped in Cambodia..

[6] Small shrines. The Latin word is the diminutive of *aedis* or *aedes*, meaning temple or house.

that confident finery from which the soul draws such sweetness for its dreams. Naked and grey, the monuments that without the sanctuary have no real character of their own are somber and sad. They bake in the sun. One's gaze does not wander from leaf to ornament, from toppled statue to the vine that clutches and weeps over it, from wall to vault, from window to nearby horizon. Instead it passes brusquely from shadow to burning sky, from vacant earth to bare wall.

To remove the finery is to summon chaos. The error has a long history. Roots and branches have completed the devastation begun by men. But over these cadavers tremulous trees spread their shade and fragrance, and mosses their polychromatic cloth. Vegetation has slain the victim, the better to entomb him. Clear water slumbers in the hollows of the stones, and orchids shine in the green shade. Lest there be a little detour, lest the walk be prolonged another step, these slow, miraculous labors, the serenity and great, ineffable peace of centuries, are undone in a day.

VI

Thursday, June 19, 1913

Villages lie hidden at the foot of the hill behind a thick wall of slash: spiny bamboo to make their entrance invisible, for fear of the tiger. At the gates are little altars with dried flowers and propitiatory rice, for fear of spirits. From there one enters a vault of banana trees.

First the dogs bark, frightened by the *casques blancs*,[7] and small, naked children flee. Then one smells the stink of buffalo hides drying in the sun, under fly swarms of metallic sheen. Then, at last, the picturesque and the exotic make their appearance.

Huts, facing every cardinal point and open to the winds, huddle here and there, under guava trees with tortured, twisting trunks,

---

[7] *Casques blancs* literally means "white helmets": i.e., pith-helmeted colonialists.

amid frail and slender arecas and the blooming tufts of bamboo, or in the shade of a century-old banyan. They are built on stilts as tall as a man, covered with thatch, and shuttered with panels of woven bamboo. Water jugs stand before them, under young trees or on the jutting plank floors. These jugs are often kept in harmonious arrangement, by a basket of rice or a frayed creel, in the sun-speckled shade. In certain places the most insignificant things illuminate one another or are set down in such a way that their volumes, or the spots of light and shade that they filter, commingle in perfect harmony.

Beneath the huts are rattan pack saddles; troughs of split bamboo; freshly dyed cotton set out to dry; round, varnished baskets, with which to draw water.

Women were weaving. One wore a *champa* flower over her ear and metal beads on her wrist.[8] Her lovely, heavy breasts blossomed in the grey shade. She turned as I approached, and a slender sunbeam illumined the ivory cone adorning her ear. Atop a long stake beyond the hut where she dwelled was a pigeon house with the peaked roof of a pagoda. Farther on, two men watched over chunks of butchered meat, broiling on a grill over a fire. The men, bloody to the elbows, were seated on a rice pestle. Their wolf-headed dog lay asleep on the blond bed of the mortar.

As I wandered the village, and aptly rustic feelings coursed through me, I tried to recall the distant villages of France. In vain I tried to imagine great trees, a sweltering July day, a wheat mortar in the barnyard, a pigeon house at the courtyard entrance, and an ox cart under the walnut tree. I could not juxtapose the two visions.

Here in the bush (which is not the countryside — our countryside), in this bitter, scorched brush, where only rice and a few squash can grow, the village is no gathering round a belfry. It is an oasis only slightly more hospitable than the jungle. It is

---

[8] Champa refers to the fragrant *Plumeria* or Frangipani, common throughout Cambodia.

shelter from big cats. Those who live here are not poor workers but wretched men. They harvest their rice in the mud. They are stalked by evil spirits. Mosquitoes whine around their nakedness. The slightest wound leaks pus, and they poison it again with the unguents of their witch doctors. There are six months of drought. The earth cracks, the granaries empty, and water runs short. Then come six months of rains. The land floods, and everything rots. Fevers reawakened rise from the ground, and their miasmas linger under the trees.

Yes, the forests are superb, the flowers enormous, and the evenings magnificent! But was it not a Westerner, unable to bend *rustic* to fit his meaning, who coined the term *exotic*?

Rice, the sole crop, does not rise like a promise in the manner of our wheat and ryes. For those who sow it, rice is not an emblem of prosperity, a reason to expand the barn, or a dowry for their daughters. It is the necessity of necessities, the indispensable thing, the object of the labors of every man hoping to check starvation.

At harvest time the hillsides are peppered not with joyous groups but with sullen savages knee deep in mud, who howl lugubriously in the night to defend their meager foodstuffs from birds and big cats.

We should not be led to believe that in countries like these, where the journeys are endless and the traveling hard, one is always passing through magnificent places. There are rides between walls of grass that extend far overhead. There are endless days in glades, where the big, dry leaves of small, stunted trees litter the ground and crunch metallically underfoot. There are hours without end under sampan roofs, with blinding water all around.

Fatigue is the name of the game. Sweat streams down your body. The sun burns your eyes and skin. You are broken by the hesitant trot of your little horse, the pitch of your elephant, the jolt of your cart. Horseflies by the swarm provide escort. You cannot sit on the ground in the shade, for the red ants are everywhere and the mosquito, herald of fevers, is king.

Perhaps you are in the forest. Now terrifically armed brambles dangle in thin filaments. The bamboos are covered with sharp thorns as long as daggers. The way often has to be cleared by axe, and it closes behind you in stifling, humid shade.

What about the water? In it sleep the gharial[9] and the long-necked, eagle-beaked turtle, which likes to rip chunks of flesh out of passers-by. Then there are the long grasses, sharp as a falx.[10]

The quinine you consume daily causes buzzing in your ears. Your forehead wrinkles up under your heavy, heavy helmet. Out in these solitudes you spend whole weeks under such conditions. And it is under such conditions that you must keep all your wits about you. However repulsive you might find it, you must cling to this savage, hostile world with all your strength if you hope to solve a few of its mysteries, elucidate a few of its beauties. It is an uneven match-up, but beautiful and invigorating.

Back from the village, I told a coolie to go into a pond and pick some pink lotus. Big as two fists, bloody, heavy, the flowers gleamed strangely under the trees and on the black water. A fleeing bird cried out through the branches. I watched the man emerge filthy and ugly from the stinking water, which clouded up with mud and rose to his thighs. In hands held out from his body lay the divine flowers.

---

[9] George Groslier probably did not encounter gharials (*Gavialis gangeticus*), which are native to India, but Siamese crocodiles (*Crocodylus siamensis*), a species now endangered and under the protection of the Cambodian Crocodile Conservation Programme (CCCP).
[10] Latin word originally meaning sickle, but later used for other curved blades.

3
Tonle Repou

Saturday, July 12, 1913

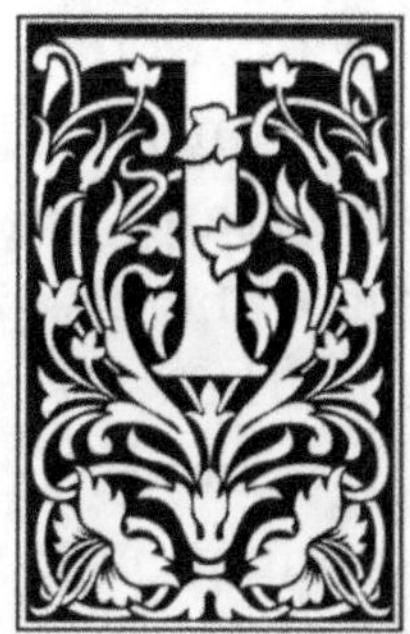he Tonle Repou is a sad, calm river. The banks are but fronds moving in uniform majesty. It is four o'clock, and I have seen no human being, no sampan, not a trail of smoke since this morning. Even bird calls are rare. The sole living creature I have glimpsed was a great serpent swimming upstream, head up out of the water, trailing a long triangular wake.

The bonzes of Kampong Sralau have lent me their sampan. Taking up the center is a loggia, covered with a woven, domed roof, decorated at its four corners with airy, sculpted *naga*s. It has five small, square windows to air it out.

Yesterday at dusk my convoy stopped at a bend in the river, under leafy vault, and tied up at a gnarled tree. This tree had fallen into the water, but the trunk, reviving, had curved up again, white and round, like the neck of a swan.

From the bank I could see the Cambodian wife of one of my men. She was inside the cabin and illuminated by the flame of the tea light she had just lit. Mirror in hand, legs crossed, she was combing out her short hair. All day long she had been sticking flowers into it for their scent. Her meticulous hand shuttled back and forth between light and shade. A few gleaming utensils defied identification, and an orange scarf still hung in front of a window, so as to block out the sun.

Framed by the door of the junk, this scene fit into two square meters and seemed suspended in the landscape. Beyond lay the night-like shadow of the tree in its vault-like droop; the water, glinting with the last of the daylight; and the far bank, now deeply black.

Many Angkorean bas-reliefs depict, either in a boat or under the roof of a palanquin, a princess, mirror in hand, who whiles away the time on long journeys by maintaining and adding to her beauty.

One thousand three hundred years ago, on this same river, on the way to the same temple, perhaps even on this very spot, a prince stopped his convoy. The sampans and their ornaments were exactly like these. One of the women in the cortege, round mirror in hand, doubtless carried out her ablutions. She was of the same physical type, and similar in loincloth and gesture. Perhaps there were menacing clouds in the sky, just as there are tonight. The old sculptures show the same curtains in the windows. To guard against the evening cool, moreover, the ancient princess might have draped over her chest — women otherwise left their chest bare at the time — the same orange scarf.

Between three stones, as in the era of Angkor, the coolies light a fire. These are inhabitants of that high Cambodia whose heights our civilization has not yet reached. They are naked but for a short *sampot*[11] over their loins and speak the old language. I recognize them from the bas-reliefs, where I saw them wield the same knives and cook rice in the same pots.

And thus with every moment that goes by you convince yourself that nothing about these people has changed. The carts have the

---

[11] *Sampot* is Khmer for the long, rectangular piece of cloth, often made of silk, that is traditionally worn around the lower body by all classes of people in Cambodia. It can be wrapped, draped, and folded in many ways. In Thailand and Laos it is called the *pa-nung*, and is similar to the *dhoti* in India, the *longyi* in Myanmar, and the *sarong* in Malaysia.

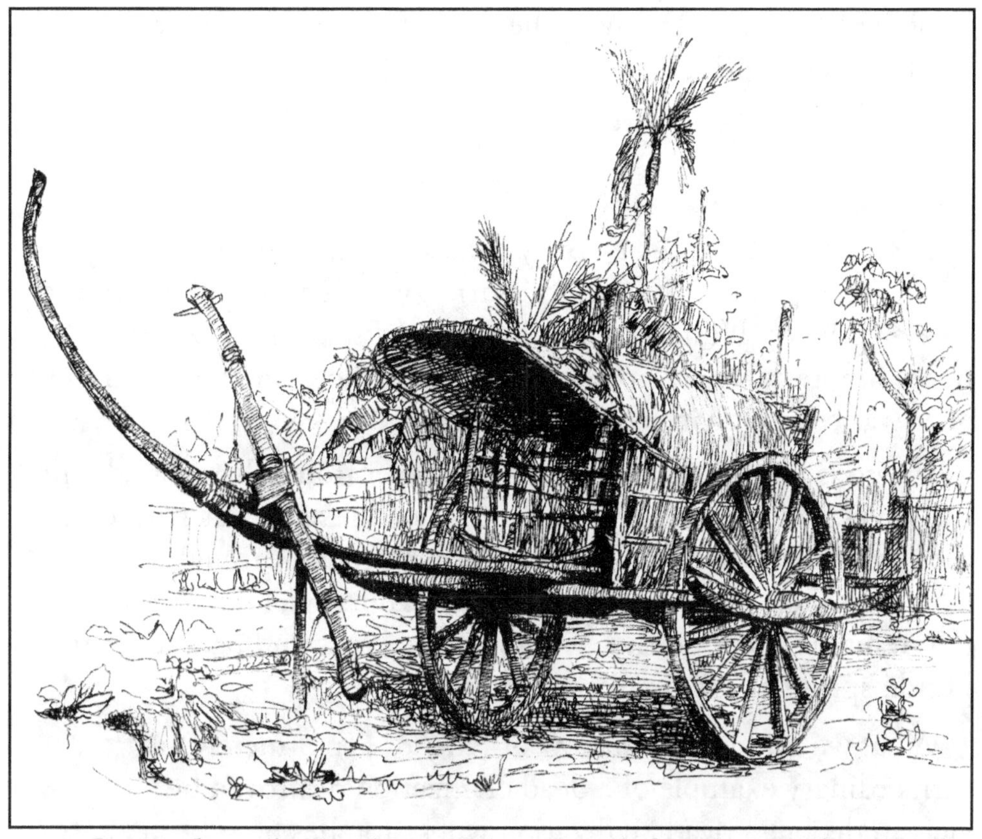

Ox cart drawn by Groslier on Feb. 6, 1911, before this expedition.

same number of spokes on their wheels. The wooden huts are the huts on the sculptures. The weapons and fish traps have not varied. The jewelry of ages past adorns the ears and throats of the women of the rice paddies. The same jesters precede the corteges. Rice is weighed with the same weights and on the same scales. The eight-hole flute, the cymbals, the conch shells, and the tam-tams of ten centuries back still sound at every feast.

But, like a great reptile caught in an eternal cold spell, these people are stuck in a torpor, and their temples crumble. It is all unwitting. They give the matter no thought, never bother with their chrysalis, hardly recognize the buildings built for ritual adoration. They drag themselves blindly along age-old paths, but they have grown stiff. It is all they can do to follow the ruts. The woman combing her hair yesterday in the sampan, looking for all the world like the ancient princess whose daughter she is, has only the barest notion that she is traveling toward the ruins of her own past.

VIII

Every place in the country is historic. The Mekong valley was tramped over by the emissaries of civilizing and destroying princes. Hundreds of kilometers of roads have left their traces in forests where no one ventures anymore and whose ground once was covered with men.

The gods have vanished, and Death, ever ironic, has spared only the slaves. Power proved vain, and the void reserved its respect for the savage man's utensil. The Hindu spirit sailed through this land like a vessel on the sea, and capsized in all its splendor. Now all that remains afloat on these waters is the boats and paddles that the Hindu spirit had originally encountered.

What we find in the shadow of Angkor is not merely an extraordinary example of a dead civilization destroyed by vicissitude, but a dead civilization whose torches have been kept alight and shine on. Rome and Greece endure. Their children no longer live like their forefathers, but they have preserved their philosophies and immortal arts, or live off their echoes.

Here everything is dead. All the spirits have foundered on savage man. Invincibly apathetic, closed in eye and ear, passive, and less malleable than the stones he was made to carve — the stones have at least held an impression! — savage man, in his serenity, has over centuries and upheavals preserved his natural poise. Though enslaved, woman and man, before death could claim them, have always let fall the essential seed of the race and of species. And here they are again, despite fire, iron, language — just as they were in times of old — together on the ruins, one offering up the same flowers, the other making the same gesture.

Sunday, July 13, 1913

I am subject to inexplicable enthusiasms. Is it perhaps because my weary, dozing faculties awaken with a start from time to time? Is it perhaps because my faculties sometimes respond in unison to the environment and the thoughts it stirs up. I don't know. But need I really know whence come the waves of perfume that pass over the water, from bank to bank?

A great rain has fallen, and the rainy season begun. The river was spiky with rebounding droplets. Like shiny bronze sculptures, heads down, the paddlers steered to hug the trees. They had protected their cargo with great sugar-palm leaves, pleated and spread like fans.

My Annamite boy, nearly naked and arching up at the fore of the sampan, raised his arms and head to the sky to receive the refreshing shower. He seemed a continuation of the pirogue's prow, like the statue of some young god, sculpted in ivory and placed there to cleave wind and wave.

He gave long shouts, further to frighten the monkeys on the bank. The coolies cried out in turn, and the growling, joyous cries of all these men rose through the rain up to the treetops. Amplified by these sonorous solitudes, they reflected off the water like a thunder from below.

A tree had fallen into the river. The creeping vines that it had dragged down still clung to vines on the bank, like long, swinging, rain-pelted tentacles. The storm died down. Silence followed hard on the noise of the water. A pearl lay on every leaf, and in the freshness of all that wet vegetation I felt one of those ineffable jolts, the utter joy of being alive.

As master of the fifteen-odd men with me, with my house following in tow, and our schedule set by me alone, I judged that my life was mine, all mine, to command; that I needed answer to nothing, to nobody. At night I make my bed at the most beautiful spot en route, wherever it seems to me that I shall awaken to the river's most beautiful dawn. And if in some such place it so please me to erect my house, live there, and die there, I require only the will to do it.

In places like these money no longer counts for anything and vanity has no reason to be. The fallen tree's exemplary disaster forbids all pride. Life, death, and the watchful horizon are eternally joined. Rot and the flower, their symbols, are powerless to inspire a petty, base, narrow, or vile thought. I am the center of this solitude, the soul or heart toward which all things converge. The flowing water, the wind, the trees, the sky are all mine and — because I am alone — mine alone.

Could it be so in the countryside of France? There man is everywhere and claims everything in sight. A field of wheat calls the harvest to mind. The forest belongs to somebody. Propellers beat the river. And one's spirit always comes up against the iron circle of civilization's necessities.

Nothing of the sort here. From the nest of leaves where my sampan is tied up I sally forth to the treetops on the horizon. Not once on my path, however long it might be, will the idea of man spring to mind, for here the human being is completely bound to nature, and no act or aspiration can unbind him.

Having traced great circles at the height of its powers and youth, my spirit, free, may now dissolve or settle down softly on any spot whatsoever, and no obstacle will prevent it from keeping its vigil or sleeping beneath folded wings.

4
Preah Vihear

Friday, July 25, 1913

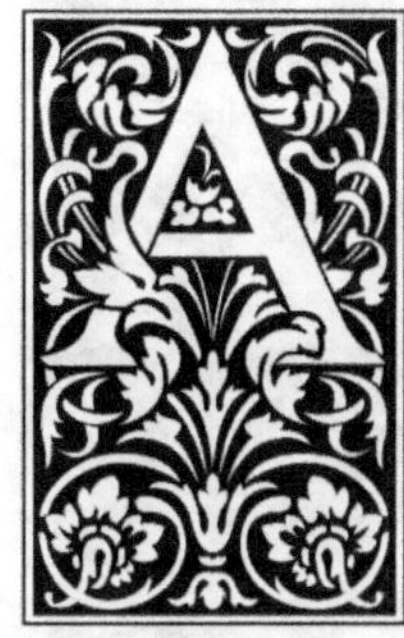fter tomorrow I shall arrive at Preah Vihear. I feel the darkest premonitions. For more than three years I have dreamt of studying this temple. From Angkor, when the weather was fine, I would often look far to the north and could barely make out the Dangrak chain. I knew the temple was perched atop like an eagle's nest, and I would feel both an irresistible desire to go there and a sort of irrational fright.

Every time I thought of the temple two ideas — like quarreling sisters: one superb, one tragic — would rise up in my mind. I knew how hard it was to reach the spot, high on a peak, at the edge of an abyss. I would imagine its desolation and the bitter, lashing wind that had already passed over all of Cambodia and Siam. I knew, too, that the trails leading up to it were the trails of wild elephants, that they served as gathering places for Siamese rebels, that the tiger was king of that land. Divided as I was between desire and fear, the first word written on my mission's itinerary was Preah Vihear.

In my long journey there not a day has gone by without incident or accident. Continual storms have brought continual trouble, cutting off paths. New provisions have not reached me, and I am condemned to eat rice morning and night. Four days on a junk, two

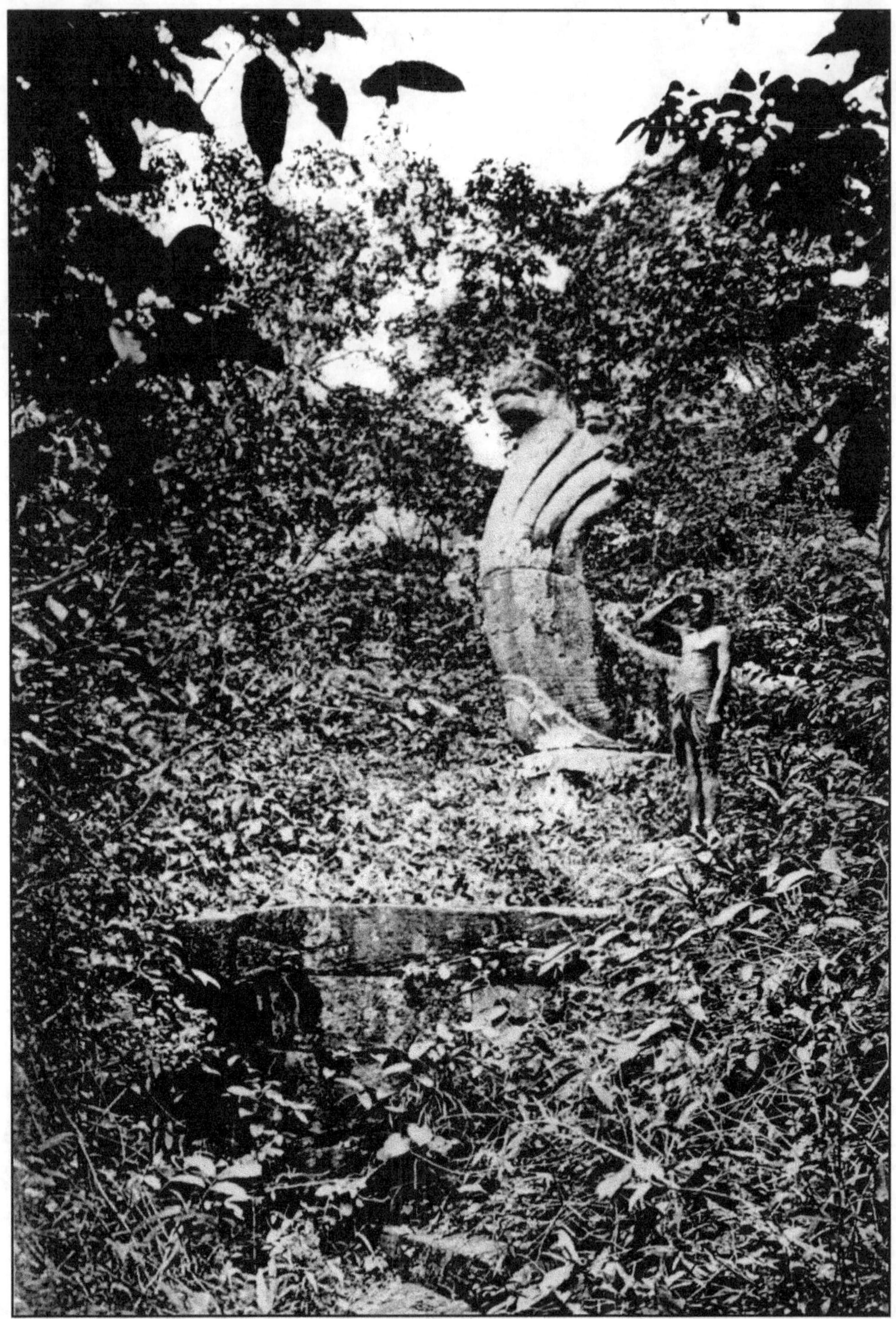

A naga at Preah Vihear. (height: 3 m 78; width: 1 m 50).

days on a cart, camping in a village abandoned after an epidemic of cholera, broken-down vehicles, clouds of horseflies keeping us perpetually frantic: it has all exhausted my crew.

After two days' march, under pouring rain, through sullen glades, with nothing picturesque or hideous to delight my eyes, I reached the farthest outpost of Cheom Khsan, hoping there to restore myself and replenish my supplies, for a French delegate is stationed there with a handful of militiamen. I found him dying of fever and dysentery.

<h1 style="text-align:center">XI</h1>

Tuesday, July 29, 1913

Three days to make fifty kilometers! But I have reached the foot of the peak. It rises from the south, little by little, and at the end of a long ridge at about seven hundred meters it breaks off suddenly, into a sheer drop. Beyond lies Siam. It is raining.

Though I was harassed by horseflies under the moaning hoop of my cart, my premonitions waned as the blue of distance faded from the mountains. Yet the number of accidents increased after Cheom Khsan. Ten times daily we had to unload the vehicles so as to float them across torrents, and we reached the end of each stage by torchlight.

Thus I am now nine days from the Mekong, twelve from Angkor. On the way I came across only four, wretched villages, each with just a few houses. Before us lies the impassible chain of forest-covered mountains. To the north, a sea of Siamese savannas. To the south, a sea of Cambodian savannas. Everywhere, uninhabited land — or, if one prefers, the earth's monstrous life. Terrific rain showers veil the nearest horizon and crackle on the tall grasses. In that place a temple was built, that it might stand alone, reigning over the surrounding immensity, deploying its long galleries amid the clouds.

Is there a lighthouse lost at sea whose pride can compare with that of Preah Vihear? Does a lighthouse not meet some necessity? What we have here is but an altar surrounded by galleries.

XII

On the mountain's eastern flank, in the green shadows of the forest, are to be found the remains of a road about a kilometer in length. For every convulsion of sandstone in the flanks that it scales, the road rises in a crumbled stair, reaching a height of forty meters. Right and left, monstrous blocks of stone, white as flows of molten wax and ringed with creepers, form steep escarpments, hemming in the road and raising it up. Steps carved into the mountainside alternate with steps made of blocks added to the mountain. Elevated slopes take up where chiseled steps leave off. Everywhere water flows down in torrents and rivulets. In the humus one finds traces of big-cat droppings. Monkeys howl in the trees.

Our ascent took three hours, and the morning fog closed in at my heels. I would raise my eyes in vain, for the grey rock was a wall before me. The motionless trees formed a dome, in whose shadows the white trunks gleamed. With this dome always reforming, the rock always upright, and behind me the fog always sealing off the path, I felt as if I were climbing up out of the world.

Nowadays we have gunpowder and machines to penetrate the mountains with. The Khmer had their chisels and their hands. And if it is true that the eagle and the elephant live for centuries, what a show, what a stampede of builders the old solitary beings populating this region must have witnessed!

One arrives at the vast plateau believing that the goal has been reached, only to discover a new avenue, to the south, more than six hundred meters long and at right angles to the first. This leads, at last, to the promontory atop which the temple rises.

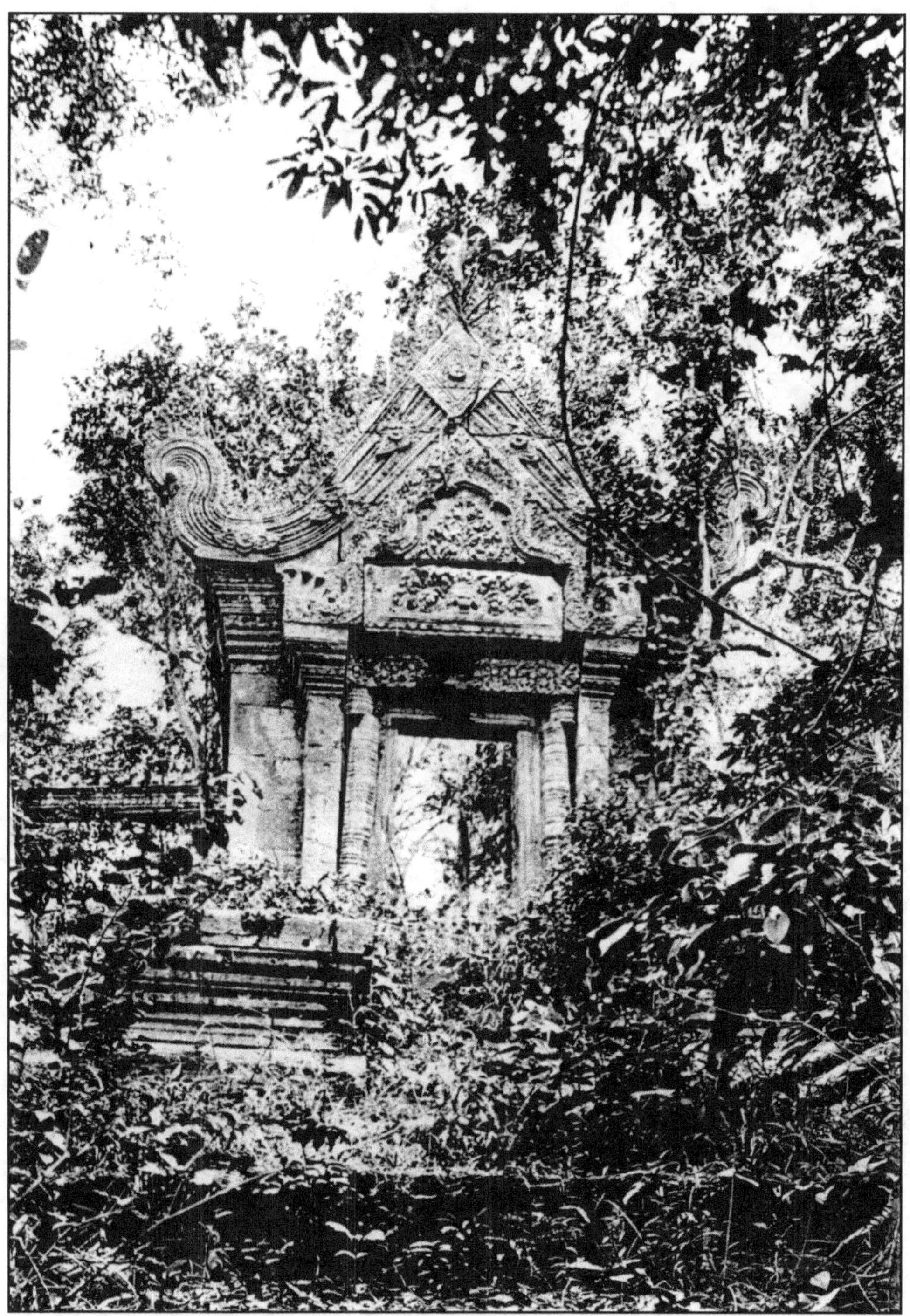

**Preah Vihear. East pediment of the first monumental gate
(doorway height: 1 m 30).**

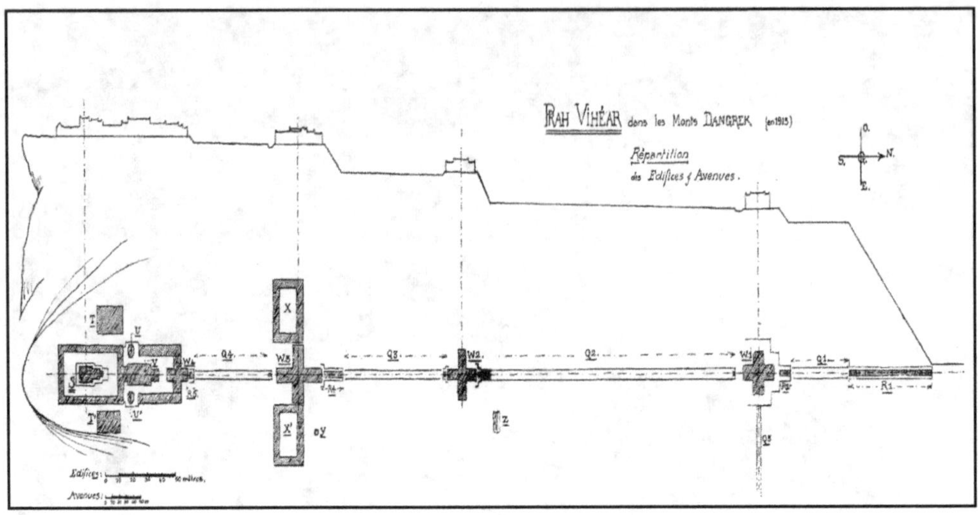

Groslier's original 1913 Preah Vihear site plan with elevations.

This second road begins with a monumental staircase of
twenty-five courses, decorated with lions. There one finds a first
gopura,[12] of incomparable elegance. Built of sandstone in the
manner of a wooden colonnade, it survives in this airy place as a
charming ruin. At the corners the pediment frames become great
seashells. Adorning the frames are violet flowers and broad, scarlet
umbellifers. To the east and west, sinking into the abyss, are the
sandstone of the plateau and the tops of the first trees. To the
south, the road begins and slips beneath copses between a double
row of toppled pillar-milestones.

The whole site has thus a north-south orientation. The sanctuary
is preceded, along the new, six-hundred-meter road, by five
monumental entrances, each at a stage atop a staircase. All have the
same cruciform design and once had the same broad, wooden doors,
of which only the hinge mortises in the threshold slabs remain.

We are as yet still outside. Illuminating the dark depths of a
tall copse is a green shimmer, from the sacred basin dug into the
sandstone. And suddenly the wonderful *naga* rises up. But here the

---

[12] Monumental entrance gate to a Hindu temple, frequently found in South Indian and Khmer
architecture.

sculptors conceived the largest and noblest of their *naga*s, its heads raised to a height of three meters above the slabs. In the mists one mistakes it for a great god's hand spreading in some grave gesture.

Man the profaner has carved in vain within the tremulous green of the forest. Too distant, too dangerous, the place has healed its wounds without delay. But we have yet to reach the summit, and the bitter, perpetual winds are as yet just brushing past. Also, the roads, the sacred basin, the toppled perron, the stairways like torrents of stone, the secondary structures, the outer walls, the columns, the gables, the subtlest leafy flourish — all display their moss, their orchid, their blossom, their creeper, the glory of the fallen.

Only down below, on the rocks that form the very point of the granite vessel, at the edge of the abyss, have the raging gusts and the rains forbidden the big trees to climb, leaving only vetiver and a few brambles to hide the traces of man.

XIII

Saturday, August 2, 1913

My mood is serious. The wind blows lugubriously. Big swifts fly by at extraordinary speeds, whistling past like whips. The gallery where I have set up camp surrounds the sanctuary, forming a rectangle of about forty meters per side. Small, square windows open onto the interior.

There are five structures forming the successive entries, there are two exterior structures, and the sanctuary has two colonnades — yet nowhere in this massive temple does a window open out onto the vastness! I mean not a one, because the two narrow, rectangular bays that do exist, each closed off by five little stone colonnettes, were cut horizontally under the gutters and are out of reach.

This temple was erected on one of the highest summits in a mass of mountains. The sanctuary is a bastion, an observatory, a torch.

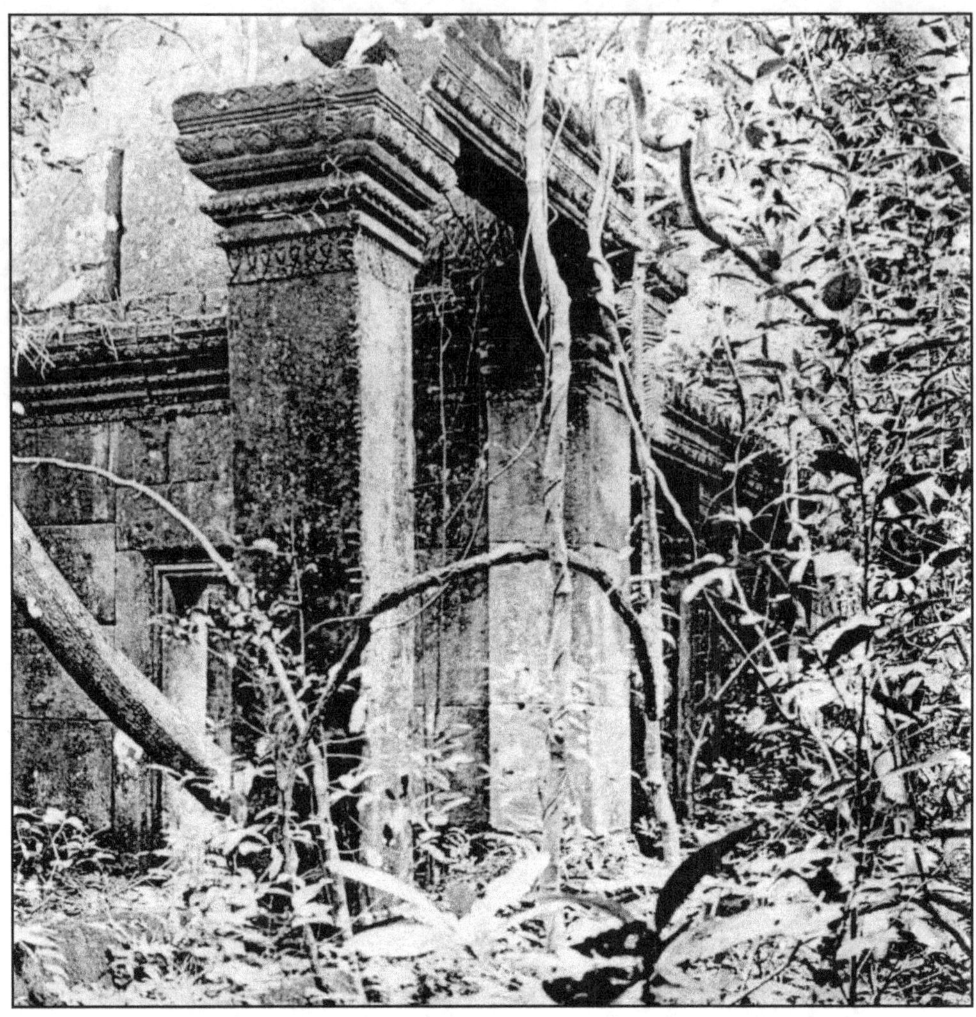

**Preah Vihear. Colonnade of the second monumental gate
(column height: 2 m 55).**

To the north it dominates Siam; to the south, Cambodia until to the Kulen Mountains, near Angkor; and to the east and west, the surrounding mountains, which advance like enormous junks in the green water of the jungles. This triumphant temple — to which thousands of beings once raised their eyes — is blind on all sides, showing nothing but walls.

"Let us climb the rocks," the builders must have said, "and lower our eyes no more. Down below, all is but dust. Let us dwell deep in the sky, with our thoughts and prayers. Let us glorify the gods, and fix our gaze on their images. The adoration of men and the incense of their altars shall rise to us just as they do to the gods."

In this lofty, rain- and storm-battered asylum for reflection, prayer, and bodily mortification, over which only birds pass, and which still exudes a somber, bitter austerity, the architects opened windows, galleries, and colonnades exclusively onto interior courtyards.

And so despite height, logic, and beauty, in full awareness of the emerald land and grandiose horizon that lay at their feet, the thousand hermits and sacred women of Preah Vihear could better feel the hand of their god weighing on their hearts and the cold of the stones pressing on their foreheads.

XIV

Saturday Night, August 2, 1913

It is night. Never did so sepulchral a calm reign during my nights at Angkor, near faces of Brahma smiling under the moon, or at little Preah Khan, where panthers prowl. Not a star in the sky. The wind has died down.

The trumpeting of wild elephants have risen through the mists at sundown, echoing through the mountains, to meet us from below.

Does the *naga*, bordering the avenues on these empty heights, not still crawl about after nightfall, stirred by the formidable churning?[13] Will it not come into these galleries, where my weakness keeps vigil, and notice the light of my lamp?

Here I am lighter than the smallest stone of its temple, less lively than the least of the creepers that have vainly set their graceful creep against its weighty crawling.

---

[13] Here, Groslier alludes to the *naga* Vasuki's participation in the legendary Churning of the Ocean of Milk, as described in the Hindu epic the Vishnu Purana. The Khmer depicted the churning on many of their temples, even modeling their capital city of Angkor after it. The east wall of Angkor Wat displays the world's largest artistic depiction of this legend.

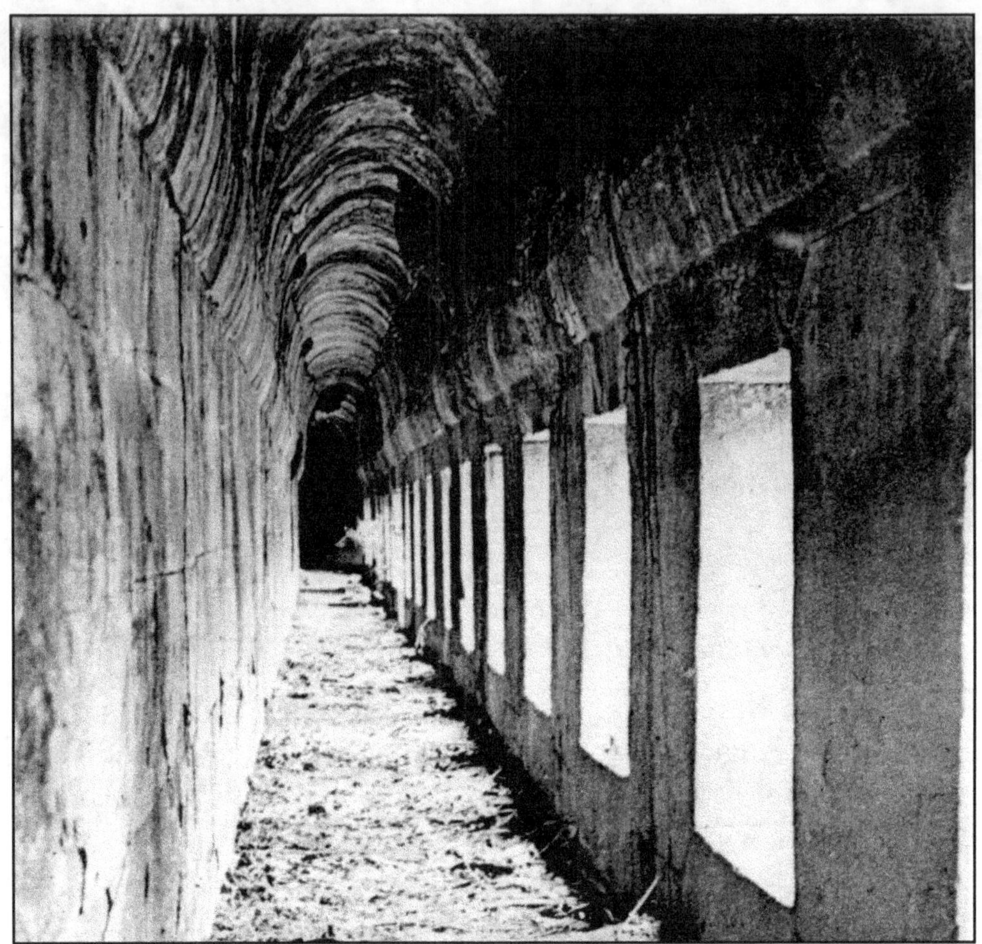

**Preah Vihear. Sanctuary's surrounding gallery
(width: 1 m 40; north-south length: 42 m).**

Solitary traveler, I come to these old grey stones in search of secrets for which civilizations have shed their blood and spent their genius!

A man will chase another man whom he catches skulking through his garden. And here nothing chases me out. Chance has brought down on my head none of the wall blocks, which nevertheless crumble daily. Death is here. All I hear is the sob of water somewhere seeping. Cambodia has fallen into shadow at my feet, and my candle is a laughable parody of the sacred fire.

Watching alone from these nocturnal heights, over the land and men, should I summon a smile or sink into sadness?

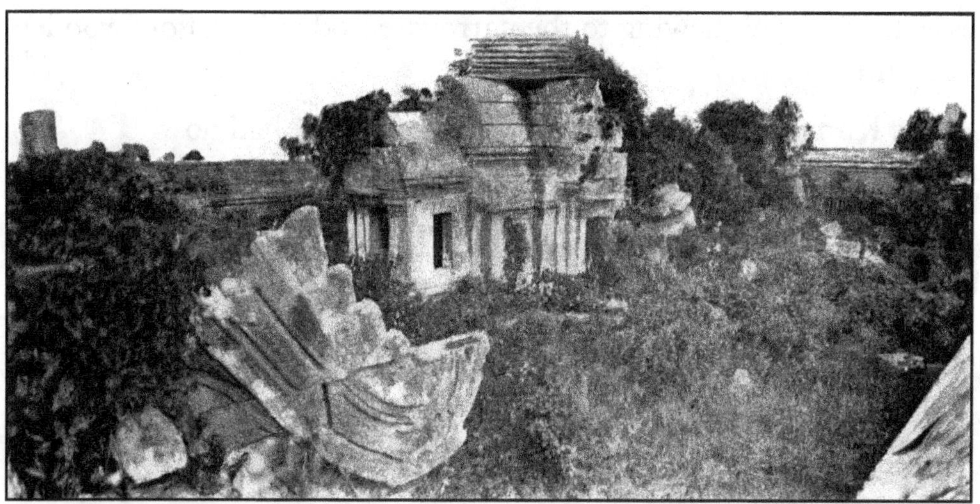

Preah Vihear. Northwest view of the sanctuary and surrounding gallery.

XV

Sunday, August 3, 1913

One thousand four hundred years ago the Hindu initiators, day by day stoking the religious fire they had kindled on Khmer land, and watching it grow, decided to shelter their idols in durable monuments. Being themselves too few for the work, they requisitioned the people.

The people had until then worked only wood. In substituting stone, the artisans of the time were unable to imagine that the means of construction and the design of the buildings ought to have changed. All Khmer temples have stones assembled by mortise and tenon, windows built as frames and set into walls, turned colonnettes, gables as thin as boards. Certain stone lintels (in groups of the first period) were scooped out and reinforced with a wooden framework, as if the builders had doubted their new materials and deemed it necessary to reinforce them with a strong, rot-resistant wood whose durability they had long known of.

Better than any other place, Preah Vihear displays this instinctive, specifically Khmer architecture, never straying from its essentials, always hewing to the narrow reproduction of old wooden structures.

The Khmer lacked all mathematical principle, had no experimental past, used no formula and committed the same errors in every wall. From the first monument to the last, they always used the same cruciform plan and the same combination of galleries. They built as one might sculpt or erect a scaffold.

Though deplorable architects, they were great artists. From the very beginning they managed to achieve majesty and superlative order. Stacking enormous blocks at random, with nothing but ingenuity to guide them, they managed all over the country to erect monuments whose sole architectural quality is their layout but that in allure and effect rank among the world's most beautiful.

Developing no further, this inspired multitude moved inexorably toward death. They fell with one blow, just as they had arisen, along with their buildings.

Was this weakness? Was it not, on the contrary, a sign of unparalleled strength?

What other people has managed for ten centuries to keep an idea intact, a religion sovereign, an ideal pure, an art immobile in its beauty, despite all possible developments, and then fallen all at once?

Is it possible with the changing aspirations of civilized man to evaluate the extraordinary vitality of that flame passed from sanctuary to sanctuary, a vitality that on the eve of its extinction completed the towers of Angkor Wat?

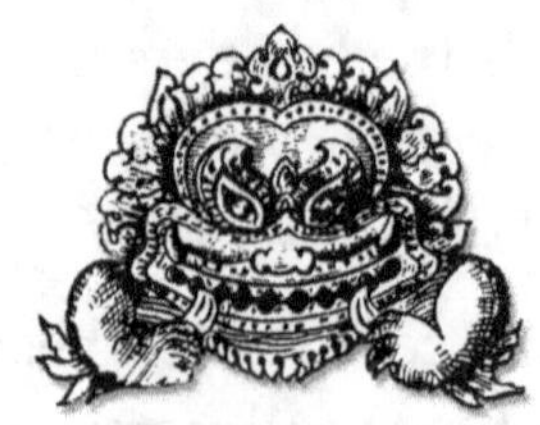

5
Angkor

Tuesday, September 2, 1913

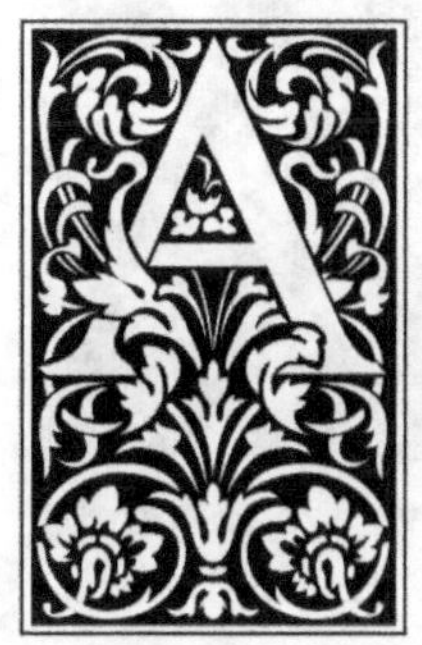s I approached Angkor I could not quell a certain apprehension.

For two years I had seen it only in my mind, recalling my first, nearly three-month stay. In the interval I had lived the active life of youths who seek their way, eyes fixed on their goal even in the midst of Paris and all its temptations. It was Angkor that I had fought for, Angkor that had held my gaze through the window of my atelier, and its wonders were always on my lips.

But now, as I approached it, before I saw the great stone lotus rise above a sea of treetops, I wondered whether long exaltation had not, day by day, imperceptibly denatured my memory, and day by day embellished it, changing towers of stone into towers of gold.

Formerly I had seen only Angkor, so dazzling to my eyes that it had remained an unparalleled revelation. If all that one has seen can be focused at one point, a point to which one turns in times of reflection, Angkor was certainly my point, my crowning experience.

I was almost there, yet it seemed to me that I was still breathing the winds of Preah Vihear, which had made such deep impressions. I felt as if that gloomy monastery still held captive some of my

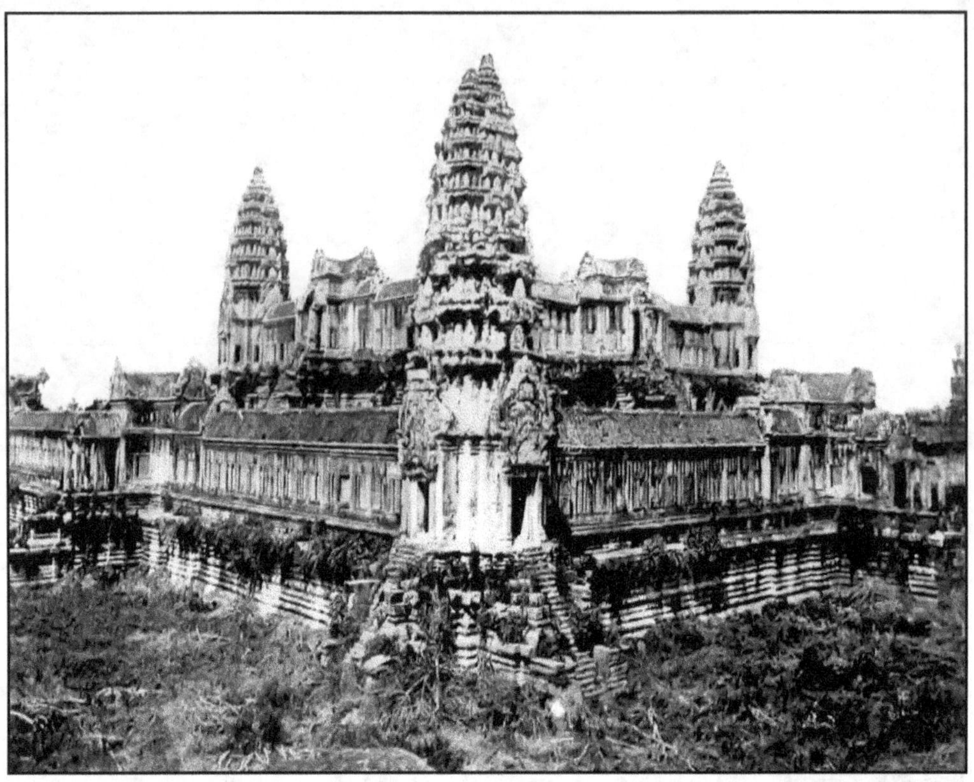

"It was Angkor that I had fought for, Angkor that had held my gaze through the window of my atelier, and its wonders were always on my lips."

admiration. Other famous, subsequently studied temple groups came to mind in turn. I was moved with all these newly discovered idols, while the other, the first, only gleamed in the distance. I was moved with many new enthusiasms that I had believed impossible. I thus doubted that my old admiration could last.

Wondering whether Angkor would look as beautiful as ever, I advanced toward the great lakes, where marabou storks linger as if in meditation. The foundation of a man's love is not always the beauty and quality of his love's object but the ideas that he develops about it in its absence, and the colors in which he clothes it for his dreams.

I have just seen Angkor Wat, temple of the royal city, once more.

I had awaited the most advantageous hour, when the sun is low and about to vanish. The air was extraordinarily limpid, the sky mottled with little white, cottony clouds.

First, from afar, the five towers seemed closer than they had previously, and their foundations more marked. The mass took on a grey-green hue so fine that the stone attained a vague transparency. The great bamboos to the sides were doubled in the still waters of the moats.

The whole road had already been cast into shadow, and the shadow soon reached the esplanade, beyond the monumental entrance, uniform, green, dominating the two, vaguely defined sacred basins; the well where bonzes, their yellow robes laid out on the grass, carried out their ablutions with clear water of an apparent violet tinge. Oxen passed by. And beyond all that, at the center of the immense horizontal line of galleries on the first foundations, above motionless palms and rising shadows, the staggering mass and its five conical towers — bathed in sunlight.

There was no shadow to underscore jutting stones, the thousand *naga*s of the tympana, the fabulous scenes of the pediments. The antefixes on towers of the lightest-colored stones gleamed like topaz. At the finials the round profiles of great lotus flowers were etched on the sky with an incomparably dulcet lightness. And the blazing sky, seemingly so close, lay gently upon them. An odor of fruit wafted through the air.

I wanted to be at the sanctuary for sunset's final sparkle. I ran. But in the courtyard on the first floor, amid the columns of the noble, cruciform gallery, where ancient vermillion mingles with the green of moss and fades into the night beneath the vaults; when the still waters of the four basins reflecting the foundations appeared before me, and the mystery, shadows, and memories stirred by my steps roiled in the hollow of every statue, I came to a stop, set aside my quest for eventide crimsons, and turned to the temple's soul.

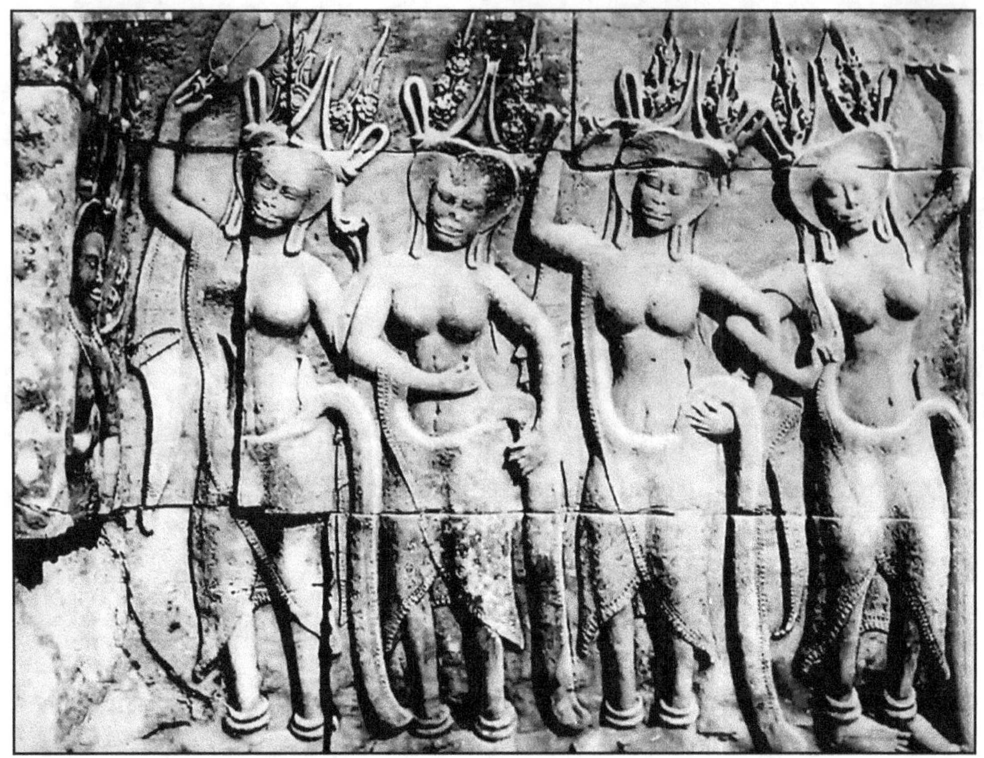

"Overhead, I knew, a cortege of dancing, bejeweled *devatas*, foreheads encircled with tiaras, undulated along the friezes."

Before the hundreds of Buddhas amassed at the south, before those poor, rotten intruders, worm eaten but still noble, the propitiatory incense sticks left by daily pilgrims were still burning. A few lotuses were withering. Overhead, I knew, a cortege of dancing, bejeweled *devatas*, foreheads encircled with tiaras, undulated along the friezes.

I recognized all the stones, all the hues: pearl greys, silver greys, leaden greys, greys of green, red, mauve. Beneath the galleries there still reigned the beauteous, ardent shadow that swallows all: the still movement of the sculptures, the monsters and the flowers, the lacey walls — and thoughts.

High in the increasingly violet air storks passed in slow flight. At times one could vaguely make out the litany of distant bonzes. At regular intervals rang out the tremulous, prolonged cry of a bird.

Darkness fell suddenly, and I quit the temple. From the vast, cruciform perron I watched the sunset. Sunlight was still piercing the gathering dark clouds and bleeding through in spots. Water gleamed from the hollows of certain slabs. In the moats bull frogs took up their metallic song. Beyond, beneath its smoke, the village of Trapeang Sre was dropping off to sleep.

XVII

Friday, September 12, 1913

The temple's chief course of stone rests on an entirely sculpted foundation two and a half meters high. A colonnade stakes out the perimeter, crossing four chambers, one per corner, and four systems of gates, one per side. It is more than six hundred meters long.

It always lies in green shadow, because of exterior trees blazing in the sun. One's gaze follows the interminable vault far into the distance and escapes only through a little rectangular hole, about as big as a hand: the corner gate. A second vault with a pitched roof doubles the colonnade, and the walls facing the four cardinal points swarm with bas-reliefs.

At this refuge, in its cool air, far from the noise of the world, one bathes in legend and the past. On the stony surface, a crowd of heroes, warriors, and princesses, bustling, strolling, or killing one another. The sandstone has the color of flowers or bronze. Here and there the rub of pilgrim fingers has made them shiny and black, like marble or ebony. Vestiges of red remain in the hollows of statues. The polychromatic appearance subtracts coldness and mass from the stone, making the already countless and fantastical scenes all the more incredible.

Like the Egyptians, like all primitive makers of ornament, the Khmer superimposed the foregrounds and backgrounds of their scenes. All the characters of the Mahabharata and the Rāmāyana parade by, escorted by their music, or do battle, as in the literature, with epic fury. Here and there amid the chaos and fury appears the beloved hero, calm, charming, wearing a diadem on his forehead, guided by the power of a symbol or a god. And the melee begins again.

The spaces one perceives between the square column, the sunlit trees, and the sky, white with water vapor, are less vast than the world carved into the wall. A hundred artists labored over it. Some were masters, to whom were accorded the honored surfaces and the places most often seen. The others were unskilled students, but moved by the same ardor. The architects lacked for talent but not for men.

A temple would scarcely be erected before another was begun. Preah Vihear was unfinished when the Bayon appeared. The Bayon was unfinished when work began on Angkor Wat.[14] It was madness to raise and decorate stones, but everywhere the halt was sudden and the workers just stopped, setting down hammers that had been set for the next blow.

What happened so suddenly to those incomparable sculptors? There remain sheltered under the architraves chiseled lotus-flower petals that seem to have bloomed yesterday. Their stamens are visible. Their lacy leaves swell with the gentle, mauve air of the shadows.

What slight, filiform tools carved the stone so that not even a pencil lead can probe the groove of a leafy flourish? The door jambs and the bottoms of walls and columns seem decorated with embossed leather. There is a slight protrusion from the chevron of a pilaster, and from it juts a tiny god in prayer, the size of a fist, adorned with bracelets and a diadem. Climbing the forty steps of the stairs feels like climbing on flowers and pearls. Whether in a courtyard or at the peak of a tower, the curls, rosettes, and garlands

---

[14] When Groslier wrote this book, in 1913, the Bayon, because of its poor condition, was thought to be much older than Angkor Wat. In fact, Angkor Wat was built ca. 1115-1150 AD, while the Bayon was begun about fifty years later.

end only to give way to sacred women, smiling, arm in arm, or in mid-dance.

This sort of abundance was given free rein throughout the kilometers of galleries and on the sides of stone mountains. The central tower of Angkor Wat is sixty-five meters tall, and the temple alone is two hundred fifteen by one hundred ninety meters. Banteay Chhmar is larger. The Bayon, Ta Prohm, Preah Khan, Beng Mealea are of about the same dimensions.

And there are more than six hundred structures in the country!

The stones were polished, rubbed against one another until the joints were perfect. The architects' inexperience brought infinite complications. To transport a stone, it was necessary first to dig holes for pegs. What sort of work could compare with this?

The builders of our European Middle Ages could apply an already perfected science. Once the plans were drawn up, their authors could vanish, and various corporations, each with its own means, could get down to work. But here?

If ever there was an instinctive body of works, untouched by craft, science, or the past; if ever there was a grandiose ensemble conceived and completely created by the human brain, with no account taken of material, or even possibilities, is it not Angkor, whose very shadow shelters titans?

XVIII

Monday, September 15, 1913

Before closing this topic, I would like to convey a clear idea of the decoration at Angkor Wat, and of Cambodia's great monuments in general. This time I shall require some figures.

Besides the eight hundred meters of bas-reliefs and the immeasurably long friezes, along which dancers, each in an elaborate niche, make ritual gestures,[15] there are more than eighty tympana, two meters high by three at the base. Their form is determined by the flame-like undulations of *naga*s, and each encloses a legendary scene. There are more than one hundred lintels, each comprising ten to twenty leafy flourishes. Every gate has two sculpted exterior pilasters.

Sections of wall exceeding ten meters in length are covered with successions of little circles, squares, or lozenges, each enclosing a character. The door jambs, sixty centimeters thick, are carved with curling stems or rosettes containing divinities or heroes. In plurality and arrangement they form legendary scenes. The curls of each jamb may be estimated at three hundred, and there are more than two hundred doors. From here one need only multiply.

Each colonnade has more than eight hundred columns. Each column has a praying Shiva or a decorative ensemble at the base of each of its four faces. The roofs — certainly more than three kilometers long — are all ribbed, and each rib is a little *naga*, whose successive blossoms form a gutter. Along the peak of the roofs is a ridge of niches, each animated with an ascetic in prayer.

Sculpted on plinth bands three, six, and nine meters tall are motifs on escutcheons and lotus petals. Up close, one sees a *garuda*[16] at the center of each. Fifty meters up, through opera glasses, one can see all the previous motifs repeated and storks dreaming alongside smiling goddesses.

I won't even elaborate on the five hundred window jambs, which are similar to the door jambs; the bays and their turned and decorated colonnettes; the friezes, tall as a man, that run like unfurled tapestries; the four-hundred-meter plinth of the access road; the even heavier ornamentation of the monumental entrance; the ornamentation of the secondary structures; the

---

[15] Here, Groslier distinguishes himself as one of the earliest (and *only*) scholars to recognize that the *devata* of Angkor Wat are portrayed as making "ritual gestures," called *mudras*, that convey specific meanings. See www.devata.org for more information.

[16] Author's Note: Winged monster with a bird's head and a tiger's legs. Vishnu's mount.

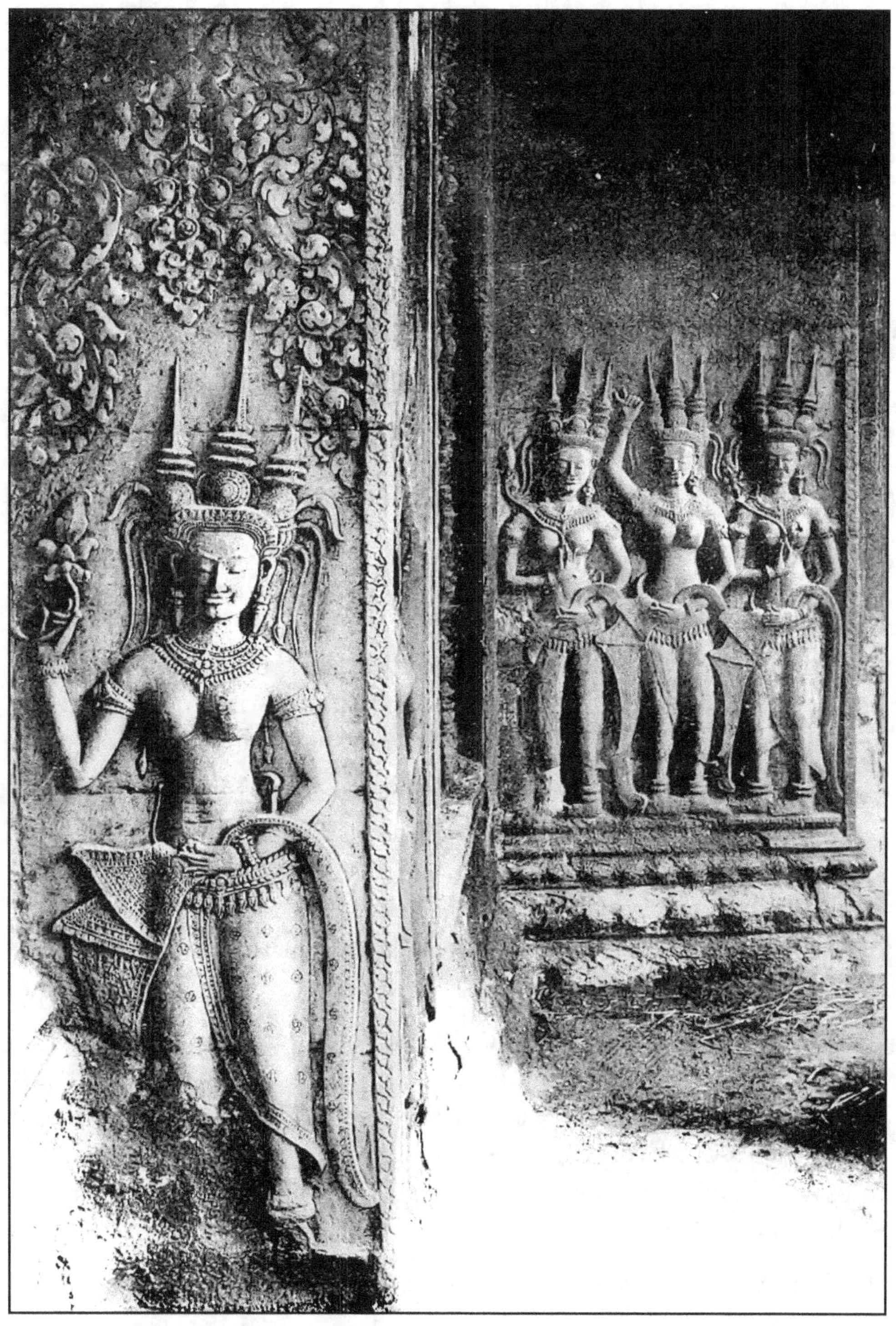

"...dancers, each in an elaborate niche, make ritual gestures..."

lotuses of the capitals and stairs; the lions of the foundations and the *naga*s of the avenues. I shall pass in silence over the tympana[17] at the corners, the decorations running parallel above and below the bas-reliefs — and thus, despite this astonishing list, I fall short of reality.

I do, however, insist on mentioning that all the gates were once shut with two sculpted, wood leafs. Since all the interminable galleries had coffered ceilings decorated with large rosettes, the area and quantity of decoration in worked wood that has disappeared from Angkor Wat alone would certainly exceed that of the stalls, chairs, and aisles of all our cathedrals in France. The number of statues, of any material, once present in this temple and that were broken, profaned, and dispersed runs into the thousands.

It is useless to go on. Neither words nor pictures nor figures can convey the magnitude of it. One has to go there, live there. One has to see it in dazzling daylight and in the bloody light of evening. One must climb the grand staircases, dominate the sea of verdure, linger for hours free of all worry, amid columns still tinged with ancient gold. One must witness the green snows of the moon.

A few, yellow-robed bonzes sometimes wander past, noiselessly, or lie down under a portico to read aloud in singsong from the sacred manuscripts. On feast days, amid the broken, crawling *naga*s on the road, appear files of pilgrims — Annamite, Chinese, Siamese, Burmese, or Cambodian — laden with offerings and clad in fabrics of many colors.

It is in just such a setting and atmosphere that one should contemplate Angkor to get to know it. Every corner of the labyrinth becomes familiar. No haste or nervousness troubles the mind. Each stone is a lesson. Everything — nature, matter, decoration — seems to pray. Sometimes, emerging from my torpor, I have had to admit, with no possible retort:

"Well, well! You were praying, too!"

---

[17] Plural of tympanum; a semi-circular or triangular decorative wall surface framed by an arch (above) and lintel (below).

XIX

Saturday, November 1, 1913

Suppose you had an object that accomplished its every assigned task. It would doubtless be proper to ornament and embellish it, rather than fiddle around with modifications and further tasks, which would only generate still others.

Objects that we refine gradually lose their beauty. We gradually come to neglect the pleasures of the eye and the wonderful delights to the mind that they provide, and devote our bodies to a gradual well-being. Having stumbled upon the Cambodian cart, and having seen experience demonstrate its perfection, the Khmer modified it no further, for the needs that it met were definitive. The Khmer thus left their cart to the artists.

The draft shaft, once made of any old wood, was thenceforth fashioned of precious woods. The upturned front, intended not to catch on weeds, became a pretext for elegance. It was turned up in a volute, in a seashell, and then in superb *naga* hood-spreading. Here and there, rings of engraved gold or silver encircled the posts. The Khmer worked the sides, cut decorative holes in them, encrusted them. The axle and even its sheath emerged from the mouth of the legendary monster Rahut.

In this way it all follows an intellectual process: all crafts of a guild working to multiply an object's aspects, varying their decorative processes and their materials, raising their quality, perfecting their work to a supreme degree. It was the same for everything the Khmer people found useful. I have distinguished on the bas-reliefs more than ten kinds of elephant packsaddle, each as graceful and beautiful as the last, and, indeed, all adhering to the same principle. How many saddle forms do we have? One. But it is apparently the last word in comfort. Placed on a horse's back it awakens no artistic notion, but it provides an easy seat.

Children would grow up this way, immersed in legend, their minds filled from adolescence with the familiar images and forms of mythic heroes, their hands set atremble with a sacred restlessness.

Compare this condition with that of an automobile crossing villages, understood by no one, and not an object of admiration but, rather, of fear. Compare our children, aspiring to the use of machines, with Khmer children, aspiring to make the gods smile.

For intellectual culture goes hand in hand with artistic culture. The first, in sum, nourishes the second. The thousands of temple sculptures, regardless of the quality of their execution, represent legendary scenes. If at present we were to ask our country workers to depict on our monuments fragments of our mythology or history, would they not be a bit hard put to do it? The refinement and culture of the European masses are just about nil, and the milieus where they exist are as deprived of art as the ancient Khmer milieus were brimming with it.

Khmer knowledge of astronomy was advanced, Khmer sense of direction impeccable. There were more than three hundred hospitals in a country with one-fifth the area of France. Through the place accorded to child and wife, the bas-reliefs show the depth of family spirit. Nothing is more peaceful, prosperous, or happy than the public scenes, the games, the markets depicted on the stones of the Bayon.

The Khmer knew a great many alloys, bronze for statues and sonorous bronze for bells. They knew brazing, riveting, lost-wax casting. They were marvelous goldsmiths, deft with a hammer, expert embossers and gem-setters. They used the lathe to fashion the stone colonnettes of the temples. They knew how to assemble planks and how to warp wood by fire on templates. They used enamel and various glazes on their pottery, gilding on their monuments. The Chinese had taught them every craft.

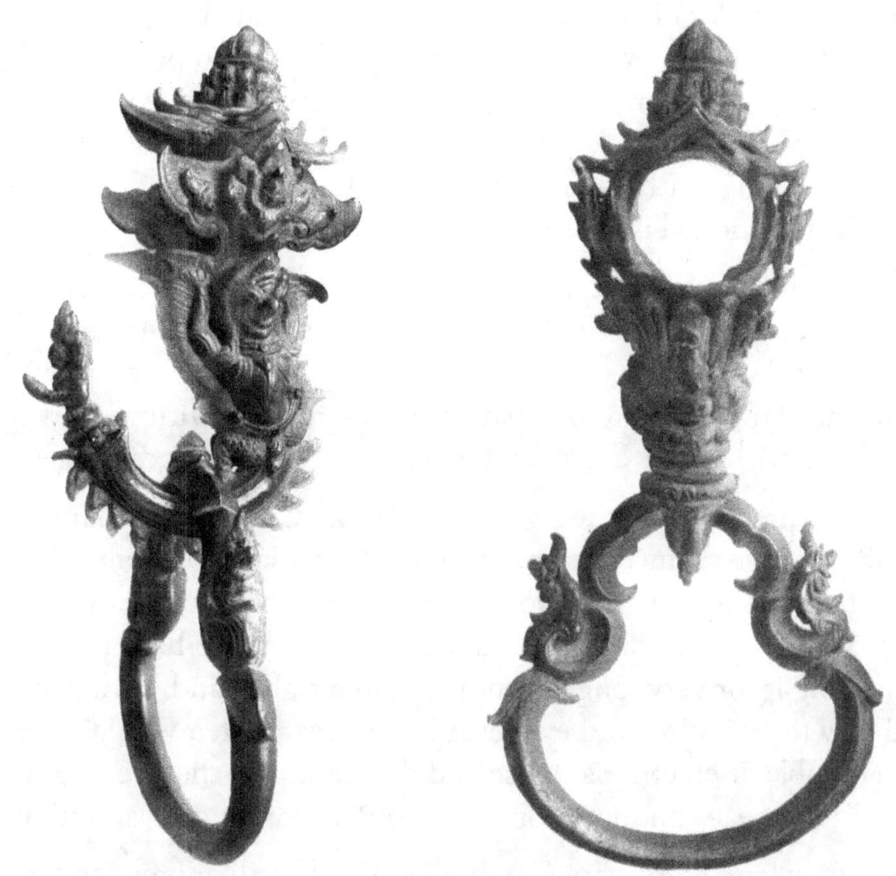

"…all crafts of a guild working to multiply an object's aspects…."
Bronze palanquin hooks in the shape of twin Garudas and a woman in prayer.

A cart or packsaddle passing through the villages was, from an aesthetic point of view, a lesson, a model of grace, beauty, and refinement. The side of an urn, on which the head of the venerated elephant served as handle; a musical instrument, wrapped in the coils of a serpent; the prow of a junk, upturned with a *garuda* head; a humble spoon, emerging from a supple dragon; the hook of a litter and its Hamsa[18] of molded bronze; the beam of a scale, adorned by the *naga* — and on and on, everywhere, from sacred object to everyday utensil, the gaze finds an excuse, a way to educate itself, clear, precise, and often wonderful.

---

[18] Author's Note: Sacred bird, usually a swan or goose, the mount of Brahma.

In their parades of warriors one sees javelin-launching machines mounted on wheels, protected battle tanks. They had powder for their festive rockets and mercury for embalming their cadavers. To ornament their utensils and litters they used ivory, scales, leather, the shimmering feathers of peacocks and kingfishers, and precious-metal leaf fashioned into sheaths or plating.

In the intellectual sphere, the Khmer inherited from the vast literature of the Hindus. All of this, in addition to the intense artistic development that I have sketched out, takes on a stupefying significance if we stop to compare our present state with what was already flourishing in Cambodia when Saint Louis ruled France.[19]

Eating directly with the right hand, in the Cambodian manner, would not have seemed barbarous to us. It would have seemed correct, necessary, the only possible gesture quickly to satisfy a need. We would not have had the fork — indeed, we have not been using it for very long — but that same right hand, veritable auxiliary to our mind and eye, purified in clear water, would have been capable of erecting a house and decorating it, that we might live a life of peace and harmony in accordance with our aspirations.

Not very long ago, every Cambodian would still apprentice for a few years at the monastery. There, in retreat and meditation, reading the *satras*[20] and learning the wonders of mythology, he would reach the end of his youth. Then, trading the yellow robe for marriage and the cultivation of a rice paddy, he would benefit daily for the rest of his life from the intellectual and moral lessons of his apprenticeship. No other country exhibits such mastery of its stories and songs. To understand, one must listen to an old man tell the epic at dusk, by the shadowy flicker of torchlight. Women depart. Boys sit near girls. Infants, rocked by the past, fall asleep. A girl of ten can sing all of Cambodia's songs. Try eliciting an equivalent performance from one of our children back home.

---

[19] King Louis IX (25 April 1214–25 August 1270) ruled France from 1226 until his death. He was the only king of France to be canonized.

[20] Author's Note: Tales, prayers, etc., as well as the Latan palm leaves on which they are recorded.

While preserving their condition as men bound to the soil, subject to the skies, drawing on nature for their lives' slightest necessity, the Khmer have managed to raise themselves to a level not easily gauged. Their material needs were insignificant, their artistic needs considerable. From disparate elements they forged a unique art. Though simple savages, they proved worthy, by their intelligence and the labor of their hands, of the civilization with which they were brusquely infused.

XX

Tuesday, November 18, 1913

Today is the Cambodian feast of the dead. For several days already there has been an unusual coming and going at the ruins. Groups of men and women come from great distances have been adorning the Buddha pedestals with fragrant sticks, fabric ex-votos,[21] and flowers. Yesterday evening began the ceremony, at the two large monasteries within the Brahmanic enclosure.

All the little bonze huts had been invaded. Torches burned at the gates. The air was heavy with resin, smoke, the odor of betel and food. Over the crowd the lights played in spots and flickers.

At a gate stood a matron, her heavy breasts bulging beneath a green scarf, a torch raised in one fist, and a basket of fruit propped, in the manner of a Kanephoros,[22] on her hip. Firecrackers snapped. Men lay smoking in dark corners. The sky was starless.

Around the great red Buddha, whose golden head was lit by an encirclement of candles and shrouded in smoke, and before the bones of the dead, preserved in little cups, all the bonzes chanted

---

[21] An offering made to a saint or divinity in gratitude for a prayer or wish answered.

[22] In ancient Greece the Kanephoros (or basket bearer) was an maiden (an unmarried woman) — indeed, a virgin possessed of purity and youth, qualities deemed essential for an efficacious sacrifice — on whom had been conferred the honor of leading sacrificial processions at festivals. For the most important rituals they were selected from aristocratic families.

the psalms interminably, fans in hand, shaven pates bowed. These places spread forth a warm light, in which the pale trunks of palms waded.

The orchestra had set up in the *sala*,[23] in great disorder. A hundred bare torsos gleamed. Along the bamboo partitions women listened and tried to protect their children's festive attire. The air was acrid, and the voices hummed like a beehive. Beyond the huts was the murmuring, swarming crowd. The five dark towers of Angkor, we knew, were out there holding up the night.

Shrill or deep, the haunting, slightly tremulous voices rose in prolonged calls of supplication. The Cambodians were calling to their dead. "Mother!" cried a man. "Daughter!" cried a woman. The moaning clamors rose up with prayers from every point of the horizon. They said:

"Mother, daughter, wife, husband, come! Hear our prayers! Come eat the food that we have brought you. Do you hear us? Be not unhappy. Mother! Wife! Eh!… eh!… eh!…"

A mother had brought her daughter guavas, which she had loved, and green mangos, which had used to eat with salt. A man had grilled some little fish for his late wife. A widow had come laden with palm-fruit cakes. And the lights, the smoke, the music — and the prayers and calls — filled the night.

A torrential rain fell afterwards, to the crowd's great joy. The spirits were favorable and sending the water to the earth to reward the Khmer's fervor, to wash away stains, to stimulate the rice in the paddies. And the sun rose triumphant at dawn.

By first light groups and lines were already streaming in from all directions on the great road, which still shone blue with nocturnal air and gleamed with puddles. Framing the procession were the monumental gate, the hood-spread *naga*s, the great trees, the temple — all under the flame of the sky.

---

23 A shelter open on the sides and used for festivities or by travelers.

Old women clad in white habits marched at the head of the groups. On shoulder poles men carried heavy, double loads of bananas, guavas, oranges, areca and betel, tobacco, grilled fish, cakes of coconut and eggs, or sticky rice, beans, and lard rolled in banana leaves. There were also palm sugar in bronze bowls, white flowers and lotus roses, packets of fragrant incense sticks.

The women wore their most beautiful *sampot*s, which rustled and still held the folds of trunk storage. The children's attire was ridiculous, but the young girls wore brilliant scarves. There were men in pink *sampot*s! I can do no better than compare these multicolored groups to clusters of flowers and fruits cast amid stones.

It is through the intercession of the bonzes and their prayers that the dead can taste the food brought them by their families on this feast day. Priests chanted their psalmody in unison, while crouching women filled great pots and arranged them around the priests. Rice flowed everywhere in white streams, like snow, spilling over, starching up the floor. The orchestra continued to play. The sun drowned all. New groups arrived ceaselessly. Scintillation, an indescribable hum. And beyond, always in view in every direction: old stones serene and impassible.

Thus this greatest of Cambodian feasts ran its course. They prepare for it long in advance. The poorest of the Khmer take part, asking for small loans never refused. The belief in one's dead is profound and alive in the Cambodian soul. A cadaver burned, the ashes and bones are collected in an urn by the rich, in a simple cup wrapped in white cloth by the poor. The precious relic is carried to the pagoda, where it remains. If rich, posterity shall erect in the pagoda's shadow a pointed *aedicula*,[24] with diminishing stages, to serve as a tomb. Otherwise, the poor remains languish in a dark corner, under the altar, hanging from the walls.

---

[24] Latin for "small shrine" or "temple."

But it is without melancholy, useless philosophy, or undue emphasis that the Cambodian looks upon what he shall one day become while awaiting a new reincarnation. And he arrives in gaiety with his offerings, his best clothes, and his little children to care for his dead — and for his future beyond the grave.

XXI

Thursday, November 20, 1913

A kilometer and a half separate Angkor Wat from Angkor Thom, the great royal city. A pretty road once ran from the lakes, twenty kilometers to the south, to the south gate of the city, passing the great temple on the way.

Back then it did not border on a silent forest but, apparently, on a multitude of huts, boutiques, and wooden palaces, and parading between them were, in one direction, all populations coming from Cambodia and, in the other, those headed to Angkor Wat from the capital.

Indeed, for more than five centuries the kings of Cambodia reigned from this spot. The ramparts enclosed all Khmer powers and genius, which in radiating out doubtless left no corner of the kingdom in the dark. Temples still to be found in the area dominated the outskirts. To the east, the vast Ta Prohm and Takeo on the hill; Mebon, at the center of its lake. To the north, Preah Khan, perhaps the oldest of all.[25] To the south, Phnom Bakeng, from whose summit one commands the entire region.

The surrounding forests were devastated. Not a centuries-old tree or rare species is to be found within a twenty-kilometer radius. All the temples had thick coffered ceilings of wood and were shuttered

------

[25] As previously noted, early archaeologists had the temple dates confused, because of the advanced decay of what were, in fact, the most recent temples. Mebon and Ta Keo date from the tenth century. Ta Prohm's foundation stone was set in 1186 AD. Preah Khan, dedicated in 1191 AD to commemorate King Jayavarman VII's victory over the Chams, is the most recent of those mentioned above.

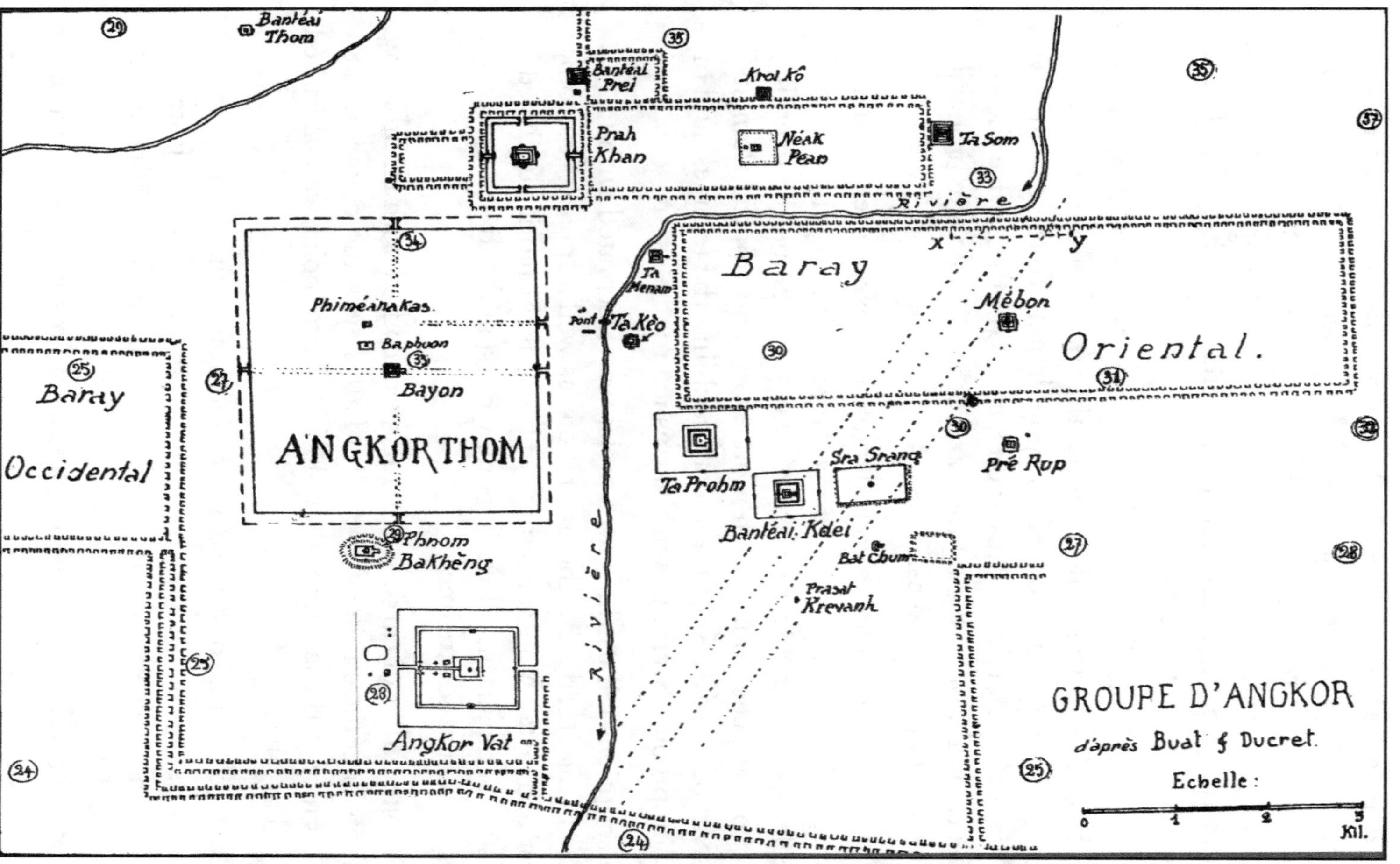

Groslier's Angkor Map: "Indeed, for more than five centuries the kings of Cambodia reigned from this spot."

with double-leaf wooden doors. Moreover, their construction had required multiple, complicated scaffolds. There had also been the palace and the dwellings to build in wood, and sampans to dig out of beautiful tree trunks tall and straight. And though bamboo and thatch were the chief materials for the erection of huts, hut frames were made of nice, big joists.

If we would like to form some notion of the regional landscape in ancient times, we should imagine the spread of the great rice-paddy plains necessary to feed the population. To the east and west of Angkor Thom two vast reservoirs, each covering twice the area of the capital's, were dug by the hand of man, and were probably connected to the big lakes.

There must have been a considerable number of arecas, sugar palms, and coconut palms everywhere, dominating the plains. The temples were visible from afar. It is easy to imagine the overall effect of the vegetation, much more exotic and tropical than at present; of the basins; of the moats doubling the temples; and of the sumptuous dwellings with varnished roof tiles.

Inscriptions tell us that the temples were decorated with tall masts flying standards. The bas-reliefs, as well as present custom, attest to a taste among ancient Cambodians for fabrics unfurled in the sun. Sampans and dwellings flew flags, and corteges advanced under a thousand streamers.

I spoke earlier of carts. Elephants were coiffed with embroidered bonnets or conical miters. Parasols of all shapes and colors marked the dignity of those whom they shaded. Litter poles were sheathed in gold or silver.

Corteges marched to the noise of sonorous music: trumpets, buccinas, sea conchs, cymbals, gongs, drums, and flutes. Jesters worked themselves into a thousand contortions. The Chinese and Siamese delegations had their designated places. Warriors wore helmets shaped into frightening heads and marched in smart order, spear points to the ground. Mysterious princesses, swaying in litters, passed in grace, surrounded by their female attendants.

There were also funerary corteges, transporting a golden urn; processions with sacred fire accompanied by a crowd of bell-ringing holy men; and the king, calm and superb, mounted on an elephant or on a shield, a cone of gold studded with trembling diamonds atop his head, his naked torso barred with a scintillating double baldric,[26] and the sumptuous flow of his belt held in place with scales of gold.

The precious fabrics were from China and India, and were but luxurious offerings for divinities. And the humble people who had crafted the marvels — Chinese merchants, and foreigners and travelers agog, some of whose vague accounts have reached us — were but the tumultuous sea that floated all this gold.

What I can convey here with phrases and controlled effects is nothing to what the simple, dry account of the bas-reliefs and documents reveals. I have, incidentally, devoted myself to drawing up that account. Though it seem monotonous, the work turns out to be a journey into the fabulous. My admiration for Khmer civilization is torn between its art and its life.

XXII

Saturday, November 22, 1913

L et us return to the city, now but a forest within walls. Much work has gone into uncovering the central temple and the marvelous Elephant Terrace. The other surviving structures are lost in the trees.

There is a profound tranquility, a green darkness. The ground is thick and muddy with humus. A monkey flees. And suddenly, before he can prepare himself, the traveler discovers a door, a *naga* spreading its hood, and then towers, basins, galleries. They are like

---

[26] A belt or sash worn over the shoulder, used to carry a weapon or to designate rank.

lightning bolts in the night, lanterns in a tempest, and there is no longer anything to distinguish these once-formidable places from their surroundings.

It is the same with the present-day people, who can be likened to the forest, full of mystery. In their gestures, their body types, their customs, their implements, one sometimes discovers a vestige of ancient times commingled with modern custom. One stumbles upon it suddenly, as if in the depths of the forest. It might be a jewel, a humble bit of pottery, the shape of a statue's lip, a corrupted word of Sanskrit.

The whole country holds vigil over the definitive slumber of a past from which it derives no profit, and from which it cannot walk away.

And still until now travelers have sung the praises only of Angkor, but there are other temples. Everything so far in this book, and everything yet to come, should serve to convince the reader. In the shadows of the Acropolis, of Egypt's pyramids, of all ancient capitals once masters of the world, and far more famous than this one, one would search in vain for a set of monuments comparable with those that stand in the shadow of Angkor, on a few square kilometers of land.

Suppose, of course, we took no more account of cities and palaces than we do here — for they have vanished — and review only religious structures. Where could we find, within a ten-kilometer radius of a central monument like the Bayon, an Angkor Wat, within whose perimeter the Roman forum would scarcely be noticeable; a Ta Prohm, with its city-like size and complication, and the five brick towers of Pre Rup; the delicious fortress of Banteay Samre; Banteay Kdei, its lake and wharf covering as much ground as Angkor Wat; the superb Mebon, rising like an island at the center of an artificial basin five kilometers long by two wide, with stone elephants adorning the foundations; ancient Preah Khan, almost as big as Angkor Wat; Prasat[27] Ta Mean Thom, near the river; Ta Keo and its unfinished towers; Neak Pean, on its circular foundation; Phimeanakas, with its outer walls and basins; the pyramid of Baphuon, as vast as the Bayon; Phnom Bakheng and Prasat Changkrang, with its beautiful lintels?

Beyond, in a country one-fifth the size of France, lie Beng Mealea; devastated Preah Khan, in Kampong Svay; Koh Ker, comprising more than ten groups; as well as Sambor — all these temples being as big as Angkor Wat. To the north lie Preah Vihear, Wat Phu, and Prasat Neak Buos. To the northwest, Banteay Chhmar, which we shall visit. To the south, Phnom Chisor and the vestiges of Angkor Borei, the ancient capital until Angkor Thom succeeded it.

Between these many giants, posted at every point of the Khmer horizon, are four hundred chapels, monumental bridges, endless roads. Ships deployed at sea as the monuments of ancient Cambodia are on land, at distances equal to those separating the groups, would all be within view of one another. The first in the south could signal to the last in the north.[28]

XXIII

Sunday, November 23, 1913

If each Khmer temple has its own particular character and we want to extrapolate a meaning... Preah Vihear is fierce; Wat Phu, perched on its mountainside amid bonze-planted trees, expresses a happy peace; solitary Preah Khan combines the sadness of death with the exuberant joy of leaves and flowers; Ta Prohm

---

[27] Khmer for "tower."

[28] Groslier's dramatic conclusion conveys how many significant structures the Khmer built in this relatively small area. His analogy of the temples as "ships deployed at sea" that "could signal" each other from south to north may hold true for the Angkor group but does not for the distant temples of Koh Ker, Preah Vihear, Banteay Chhmar, Wat Phu, and many others. Even from the top of Angkor Wat, more than 200 feet high, the line of sight to the horizon is only 19 miles.

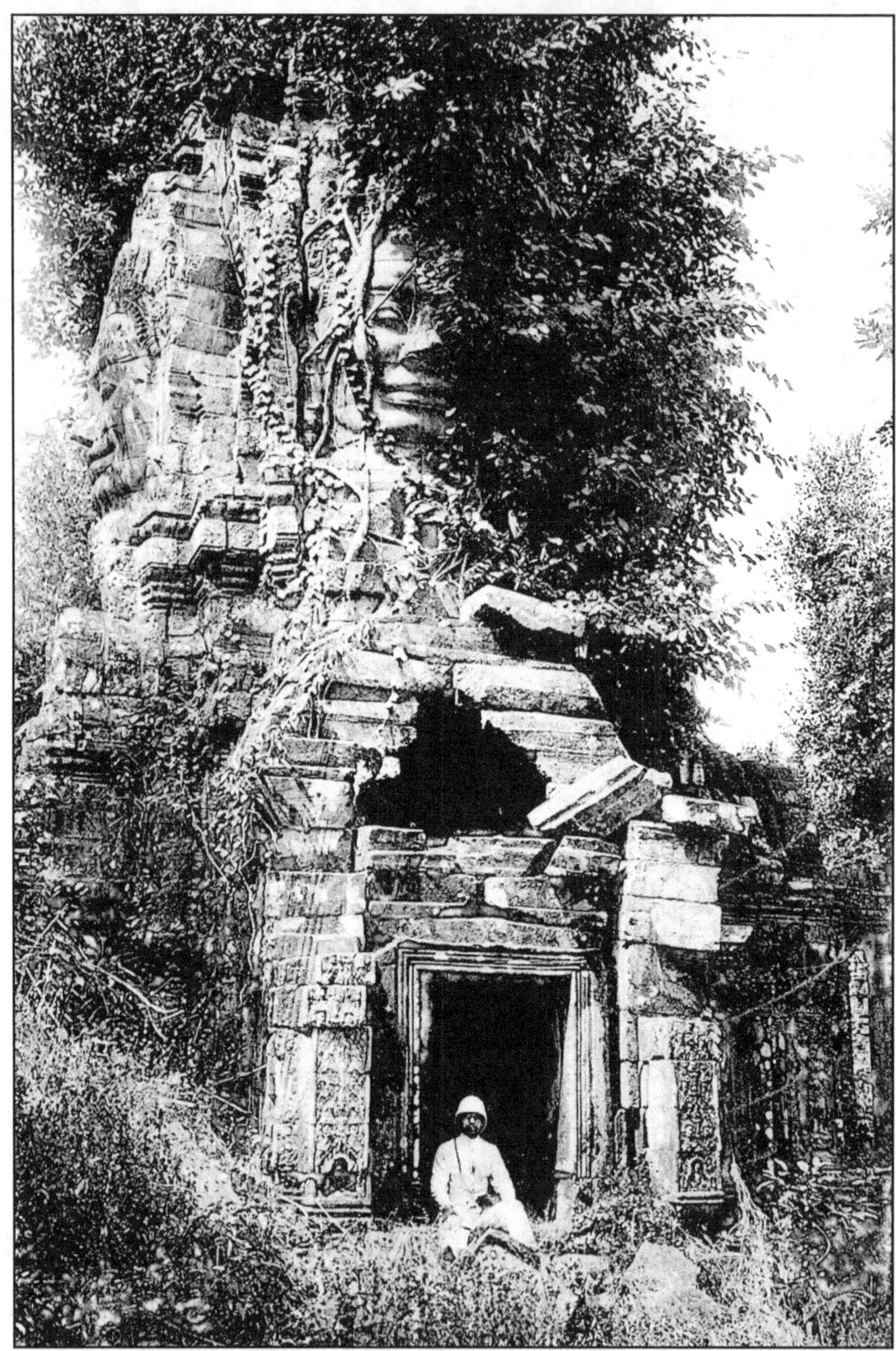

"...the Bayon, stranger, more arresting, is the temple of charm and serenity."

exudes a singular solemnity; and dominating them all is brilliant Angkor Wat, sumptuous symbol of glory.

But the Bayon, stranger, more arresting, is the temple of charm and serenity. If Khmer monuments generally do not command attention in and of themselves, the Bayon, with the peaceful smile of its towers, takes you prisoner, penetrates you with its charm. It is afterwards impossible to free yourself from its grip.

At the exact center of Angkor Thom, the Bayon sports thirty-seven harmonious towers around a large central one, the sanctuary. They are parabolic in profile, square at the base. To each of the four cardinal directions they show the gentle lines and rounded forms of a smiling face. The smile seems hesitant, animated, or precise in accordance with the hour and the light. The four faces are those of the god Brahma or Shiva.[29] They are as high as a man is tall.

Their headband crown, blending imperceptibly into the architecture, is topped with a low pediment, which dwindles to a triple lotus blossom. The faces meet ear to ear and rest on a necklace of rosettes. Great pendants dangle from the ears. A jewel, then, serves as intermediary between life and stone, and a flower crowns the whole. Is it possible to imbue an architectural conception with more poetry and life, so as to subjugate the mind not solely to the beauty and harmony of the forms but also to a gravely smiling sentimentality?

With tree trunks shining like candles, the forest spreads from the outskirts off into the distance. The towers are so arranged that on the temple's terrace, where young trees form green vaults, one is always in the shade.[30]

Whichever way one turns, that serene face smiles back, always the same, always enigmatic and charming, whether in joyous

---

[29] A century after Groslier wrote these words the debate continues as to whom those faces actually represent. For the latest theories consult *Bayon: New Perspectives*, edited by Joyce Clark, River Books (Bangkok, 2007).

[30] Today all the trees have been removed from the Bayon, to prevent further damage to the structure. As the book cover and left photo show, the temple was still overgrown in 1912.

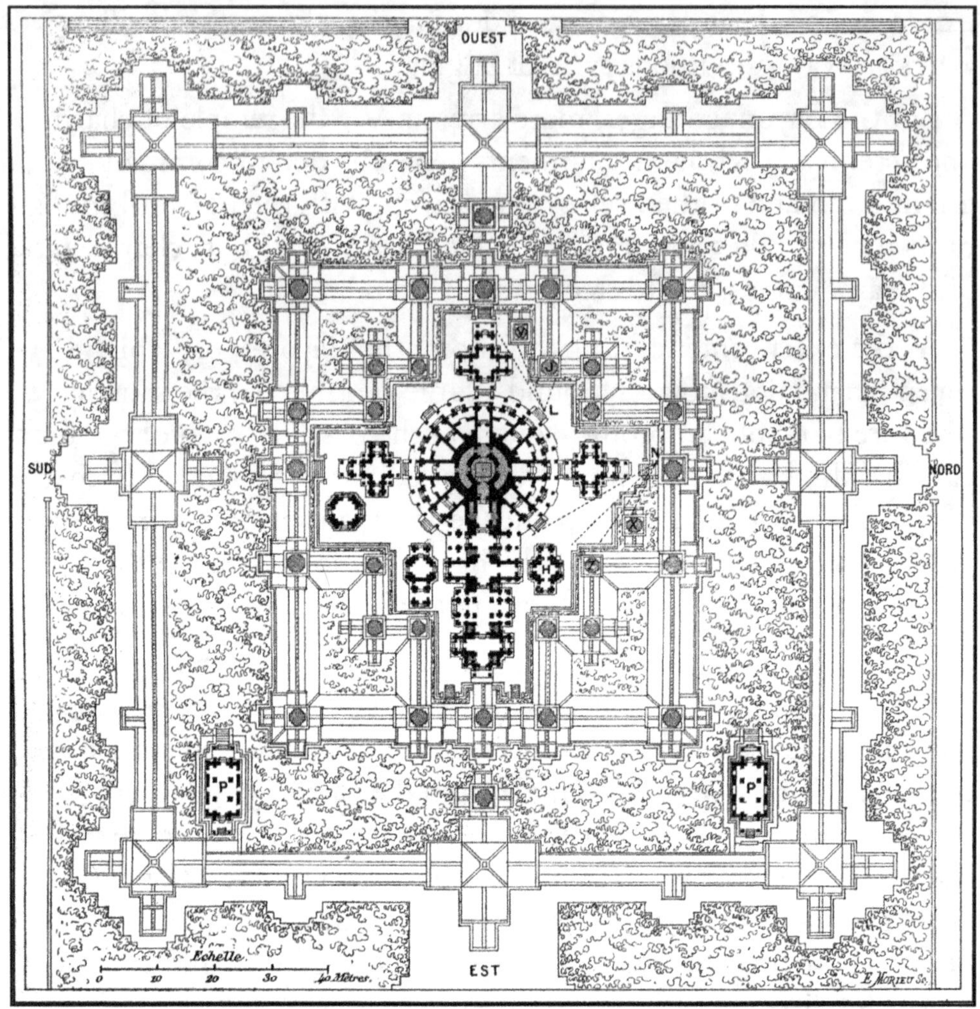

Bayon temple site plan engraving by E. Morieu, 1896.

sunlight or violet shade. It is everywhere, reflected, as it were, in the nearby land, whether that land gleam like a mirror or lie in darkness. The face is stained red with lichen and streaked with mauve in tear-like courses. The lips are meaty. Over its forehead garlands of foliage hang like hair, or branches thick with leaves stand out like plumes.

Old temples of competent but undistinguished art might succeed in combining the mysteries of the past with the mysteries of nature, and they might display all the beauties that architecture can express, but they cannot bear comparison with what radiates from the Bayon, for at the Bayon it is all somehow tangible, directly stated by stone become man, stone become God. It requires no interpretation. It is not light that is smiling but a mouth. What penetrate us are not the uncertain meanings discerned by our imagination but gazes, true gazes, cast on us by eyes of rain-softened contour. Their nobility and calm are human, not cold like the nobility and calm of line and mass. Everything is latent, eternal life. God is there, truly present. He smiles. And all that is no more lives on in his smile.

It is stupefying how figures like these can emanate such charm, for in addition to being huge they are exceedingly stylized. The lips are quite prominent, and the mouth nearly touches the nose. The neck fuses into the chin. The eyes are exaggeratedly oblique and unnatural, but in many cases the rains have erased surface details, making the eyes seem closed.

Because of the present state of the eyes, the gaze is imprecise: not focused at a pupil but dwelling in the entire orbital, to peculiar effect. In absolute solitude the faces express their age-old thoughts to the four corners of the earth, but as soon as a man appears they seem to smile only for him. The man, below them, watches their gaze settle on his fragility, and a deep intimacy is swiftly established.

Ah! If our heart aches sharply, if our soul is tossed by some human tempest, I do not think there is any place on earth more attuned to confidences than this. Nowhere else will our raised eyes find a gentler attentiveness to share in our dreams and all the while engage us with a smile.

The Bayon is not a temple in ruins. It allows no evocation of the human suffering or pride at its origin. It has neither vanity nor splendor. It seems to have risen from the earth of its own accord. It is like a dream. After a while it exalts one's joys, and assuages one's pain.

XXIV

Tuesday, November 25, 1913

In all the old structures that have come down to us, no two are so different in conception — so opposed, I would even say — than the Bayon and, coming two centuries later, Angkor Wat.[31]

So deeply do the two diverge in the very essence of the inspiration behind their respective construction that it is hard to unravel the effects and causes that drove the architects and so rapidly developed their concepts.

Angkor Wat is a prodigy of craft. It is handiwork carried to perfection, the reign of resolve, the domain of leafy flourishes, petals, lapidary embroidery. Line is its tyrannical queen. The layout is glacial. Stone, rigid stone, is a goddess. The zeal for decoration, the will to dazzle, bursts forth from every block.

Nothing of the sort at the Bayon. There material is unpolished, ill used. The design is vague, picturesque, so clumsy that galleries run along foundations at a gap of eighty centimeters. The decoration is sober, broad, colored in execution. The bas-reliefs display almost no legendary scenes — but scenes of life, of men, of household episodes. No petty concerns come through. Unlike those of Angkor Wat, the artists of the Bayon did not leave the praying to the stones. They did their own praying. Only one thing seems to have hurried them along: getting the heavy work over with, so as to sculpt the two hundred faces of their god, for through that face they would express their fervor, the mysticism and serenity of their religion.

At opposite ends of a little Cambodian road stand the triumph of intelligence and the triumph of the soul, one to the south and at the other, three kilometers away, to the north.

Do these two temples not rather belong at opposite poles of the earth?

---

[31] While Groslier has reversed the chronological sequence of these two monuments, his stylistic contrasts remain intriguing.

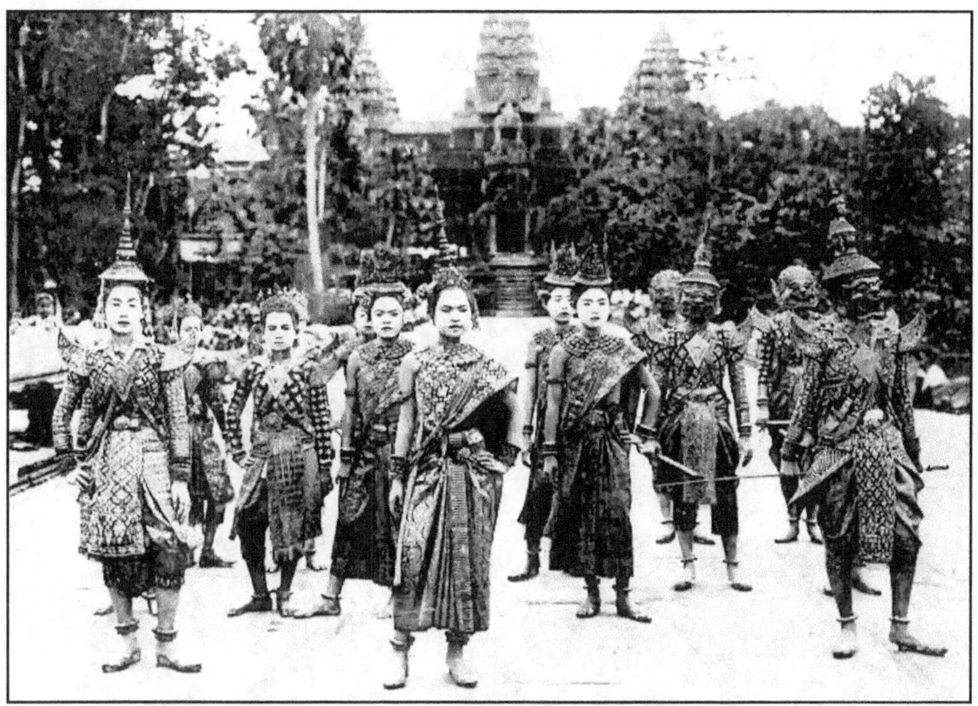

Cambodian dancers at Angkor Wat. Date unknown.

XXV

Thursday, November 27, 1913

There was dancing yesterday evening, and five small actresses, aged eight to thirteen years, came to perform their strange gestures before a group of tourists. This popular troupe, organized by one of Norodom's former dancers, who retired from the Palace to marry near Angkor, is, to my knowledge, the only one in Cambodia outside the royal dancers of Phnom Penh.[32]

I thus watched the popular show with some emotion. Though the naive movements of these girls lacked the impeccable rhythm and slow, flexible mastery of the royal priestesses, I was at least able to witness the healthy joy of the people and confirm that the old beliefs still had some life in them.

---

[32] See *Cambodian Dancers, Ancient and Modern* by George Groslier. DatAsia Press, 2010.

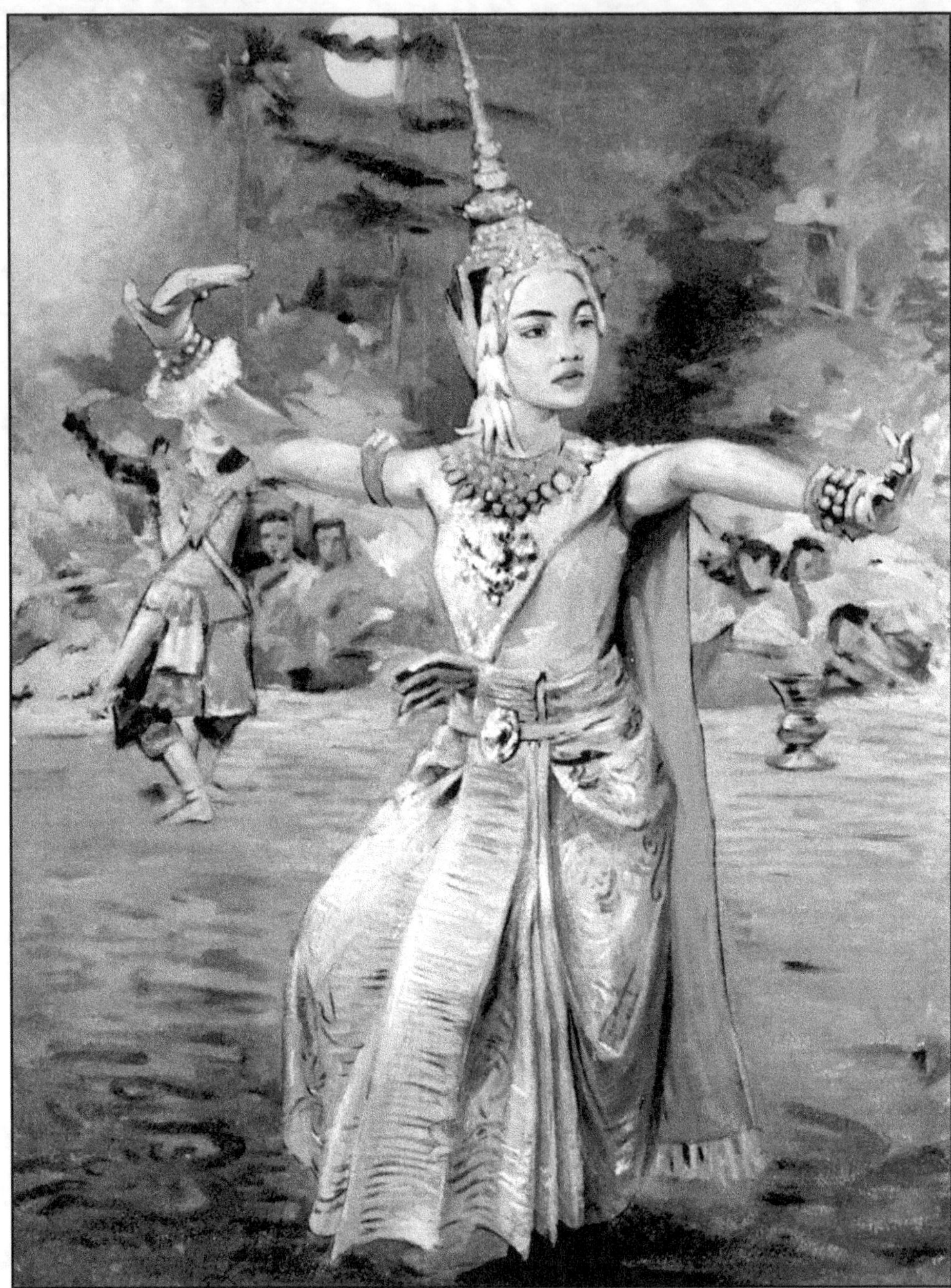

"Danseuse dorée (Rôle religieux)" – "Golden Dancer (Religious Role)"

George Groslier's 1912 painting shows royal dancer Ratt Poss performing under a full moon in natural surroundings like those at Angkor Wat. See *Cambodian Dancers – Ancient & Modern*, DatAsia Press, 2010, for details.

The girls were charming, in the shadow of the great temple, on the banks of the moats. They were no doubt poorly dressed and humble of condition, but the needs of civilization had neither fancied up their appearance nor compromised their convictions.

More than thirty torches burned around a rectangle covered with mats. Children kept the flames alight. The inhabitants of all the surrounding villages had come for this rare event. The cries, the laughter, the discussions, and all movement came to stop as soon as the actresses made their appearance.

Ahead of them came their mistresses, clad in white, dignified and collected, their heads freshly shaven. Other women followed, carrying dance accessories on platters covered with a vast cornet of red fabric. The choirs, followed by the orchestra, settled in properly, and the show began.

Darling in their illusory luxury, a bit self-conscious in the anachronistic clothes, but under scintillating peaked tiaras, the girls assumed the ritual poses. In the French provinces we see dancers in pink skirts, yet there is always something of a melancholic air about them. But when we are little children our inexpert minds cannot detect it. We are in ecstasies over circus games, and the horseback rider seems to us a princess.

If ever there was a people who could disregard age and vicissitudes and retain the eyes and soul of a child for its festivals and legends, it is the Cambodian people. The tinsel and the outmoded velvet and the few sequins still gleaming seem full of magnificence. For the forest inhabitant, scanning day in and day out the mud of rice paddies, a piece of tin on a rare, festive night has all the glitter of a diamond — a gem, incidentally, unknown in these parts and mentioned only in fabulous stories.

Well, traditional dance, that age-old institution figuring among the old bas-reliefs, this purest manifestation of Cambodian art, this theater that brings the myths and poems to life, before which the Khmer feels his greatest enthusiasms, this thing that would require of him neither trouble nor work nor money to maintain — that dance is dying. What is needed is a former actress, settled in the country and counting on no one but passing tourists for support, to train, educate, and costume five little girls at her own expense. Then the whole region — which happens to be the heroic region — would thus incidentally witness a return to its past. This is revelatory of Cambodia as a whole.[33]

Let us take a deeper look. No Cambodian has ever cut out a root that was burrowing its way into one of his temples. Busy with his own affairs, he has let his institutions crumble. The sole focus of his efforts is the rice paddy, and the sole goods he manipulates are his pot and his fishing net.

He is practically unaware of his own king. The monasteries, following in the same ineluctable disintegration, are crumbling in turn. How many doors are now shut to monks begging their daily bread?

Students grow rare in certain parts. Never have there been more illiterates than at present in a country where formerly, without exception, every male subject knew his alphabet.

What happens to a people like this when its monarchy, a once-formidable autocracy of the sort that has left traces in very few countries of the world, shrivels to near-irrelevance? What happens when an institution like the monkhood, the former ferment, heart, ideal, and refuge of an adoring population, an institution that had outlived the past and even stone — for the bonze has remained standing at the threshold of his toppled temples — declines? What happens when customs, dreams, art, the rhythm of life, and all other things irredeemably crumble one after another, bit by bit, in

---

[33] To preserve and perpetuate the sacred art of Cambodian dance, the Nginn Karet Foundation founded the Conservatoire Buppha Devi—named for its royal patron, Princess Buppha Devi—near the temple of Banteay Srei in 2009. At the Conservatoire, expert teachers of traditional dance and music present a rigorous arts curriculum to children from rural farming families, sharing the refined disciplines of classical dance, folk dance, music, and shadow theater, enabling them to discover their country's ancient culture and traditional values. [www.NKFC.org]

such a sparsely populated land? What can the people hold on to?
And what might we call such a helpless, drifting ship, afloat on
its destiny, without beauty, without captain, without purpose, and
soon without memory? What might we call it if not a wreck?

In a few years nothing will remain. Only after considerable
rummaging in huts scattered at random amid rice paddies do
I find the rare vestiges of old industries: pieces of bronze, broken
pottery unearthed by scavengers of tubers. Have I not learned that
the gold jewelry found by certain natives has been hammered and
melted down? And so the treasures of Angkor have ended up in
Chinese hands.

The dancers, meanwhile, sweetly mimed the story of Prince
Souvannaphon and Princess Ket-Souyon. From time to time a
clown added a note of the grotesque to the idyll. Since the tourists,
beaux-arts lovers all, for whom the show was being put on fell
asleep, and since the torches had burned through, the dancers
departed, weary, with children and old women in tow.

A few moments later, there was nothing but trodden grass, the
slumbering waters of Angkor's moats, and a little smoke in the
night. Ah! Symbols!

XXVI

Friday, November 28, 1913

Noon. The sun blazes over Angkor Wat. Burning,
astonishingly limpid air. All along the moats the bamboo
tufts, so slight as to bend beneath the dew, stand as if
petrified. Not the slightest breeze.

The heat tumbles from the sky and rises from the earth. It seems
tangible, like the light dazzling all eyes and making every shape
tremble. Not a bird or insect. The very oxen have ceased ruminating
and gathered under the trees, their big eyes half-closed. Men sleep.

All lies crushed and stifled. There is lukewarm water in the distance, so still it seems oil. The green of the trees is discolored in the crazy light. And Angkor, on which this flame weighs, lies in shadow, for the light falling from the zenith does not touch its façades; Angkor starkly etched, and so hot that no dog can walk on its stone avenue; Angkor, with no beauty but the beauty of its line, is squashed grey, like a great pile of ashes left behind in all the burning.

XXVII

And now the sun is fading fast. Evening splendors draped upon the temple's own. And the arboreal curtains, the arrangement of entrances, the layout of the sanctuary, the breadth of the panorama daily make a fairyland of this ever-shifting hour.

First the moats and the floating weeds enter the shadows. Meanwhile, on the far bank, isolated by the shadowy foreground, the whole temple blazes. Then, as in a phantasmagoria, the shadows creep up and gradually extinguish the temple, plane by plane.

At this season the evening sky is always heavy with dark, rigid clouds and their strange reverberations. Storks wheel around, and it is just about time for another cloud, an opaque, black, sibilant cloud — the bats — to take flight from the towers.

From dislodged stone slabs the natives contemplate the apotheosis. Their scarves gleam. Here night has fallen, and its coolness and dreams have begun; yet over yonder the red streaming continues.

Ox bells tinkle, and the enormous, fearsome-looking beasts congregate peacefully at the command of a naked child. Women bathe on the bank. Wet fabrics cling to their full bodies. A tall, black man has just drunk, head cast back, from a copper vase, and the water gleamed in such a way that in his savage humility the man seemed to be drinking down azure.

With the air turning green, the five lonely towers gleam on, resplendent as gems. We come to the final verse of the poem, enduring but an instant. A last, fleeting sunbeam clings to life. And then it is night.

O Poet, come sit, at this lyric hour, on stones still warm and draw forth, from the air as from a well, the quietude of great things.

Come scan these seconds, each in turn, with proper words, in cadence divine.

Merely let your genius take flight: this slumbering water and the things it reflects, these stones, this sky, all will render it immortal.

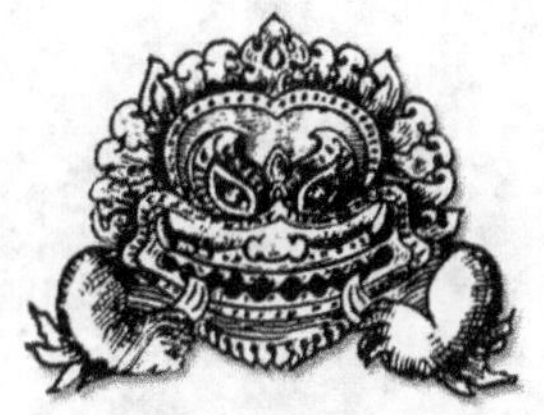

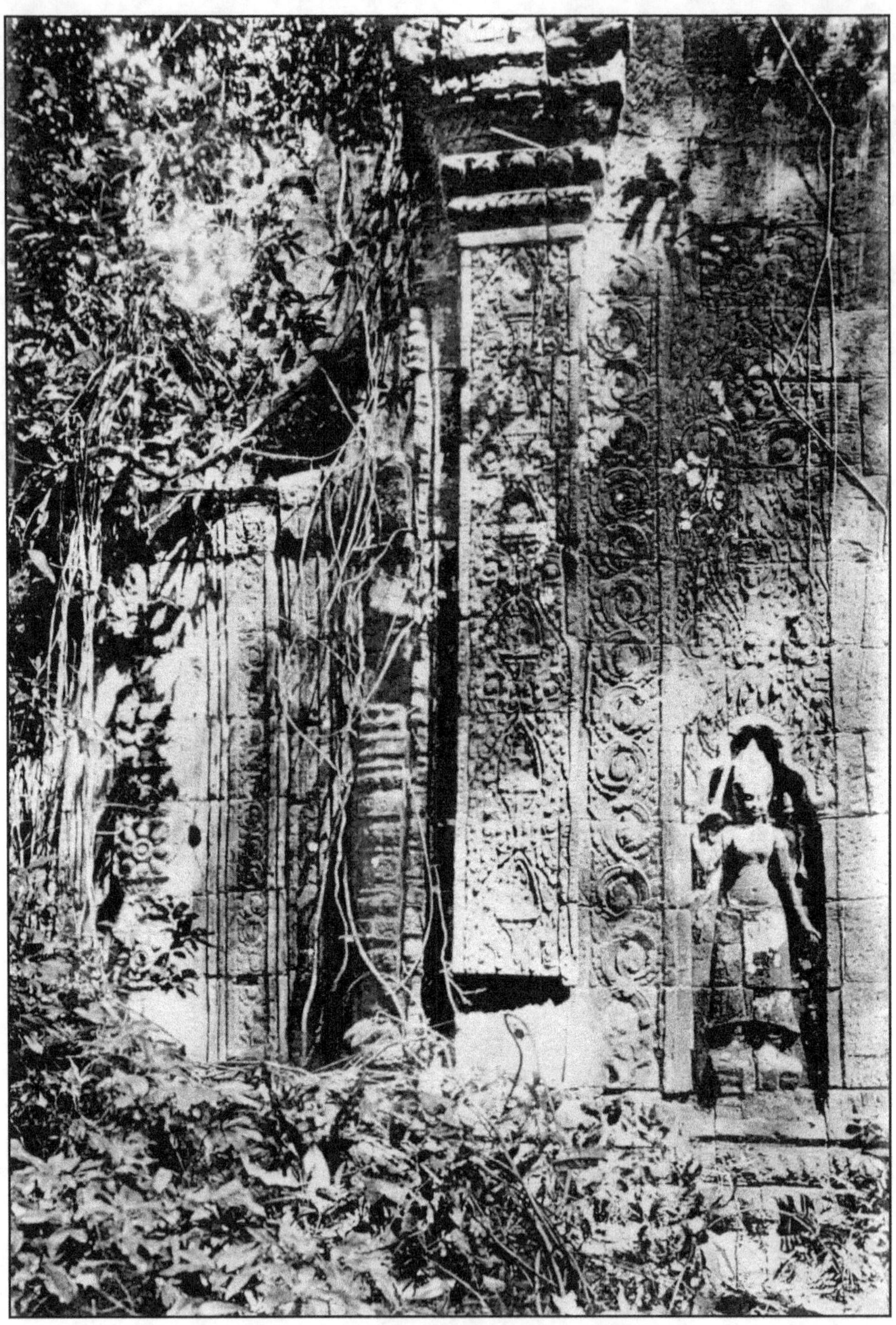

Ta Prohm. Pilaster sculptures, post, and devata.

6
Meditation at Ta Prohm

Editor's Note:

Just over a century ago, the then twenty-six-year-old George Groslier penned the shortest—and perhaps most vivid—temple description to appear in his second book, *A l'Ombre d'Angkor.* Three years later, Parisian editor Augustin Challamel typeset his words in a single paragraph, sans images.

Those fortunate enough to have visited jungle-shrouded Khmer temples (yes, there are still many to see) will immediately resonate to the veracity of his words, even as they feel nostalgia for this humbling shared experience. For those who dream of following George's path into the Cambodian wilderness his piquant words offer a taste of things to come.

The more I meditated on his words, the clearer it became that they were too evocative to rush. I took the liberty of organizing them into four-line, free verse stanzas and presented them to George's daughter Nicole. Hearing her read her father's words in perfect French, and gaining her approval, reinforced my confidence to present George's words—in English and French—as a poem; albeit formatted differently from the original 1916 publication.

As in other sections of this book, George's original photographs are supplemented with engravings by Albert Tissandier's work, *Cambodge et Java - Ruines Khmères et Javanais 1893-1894.*

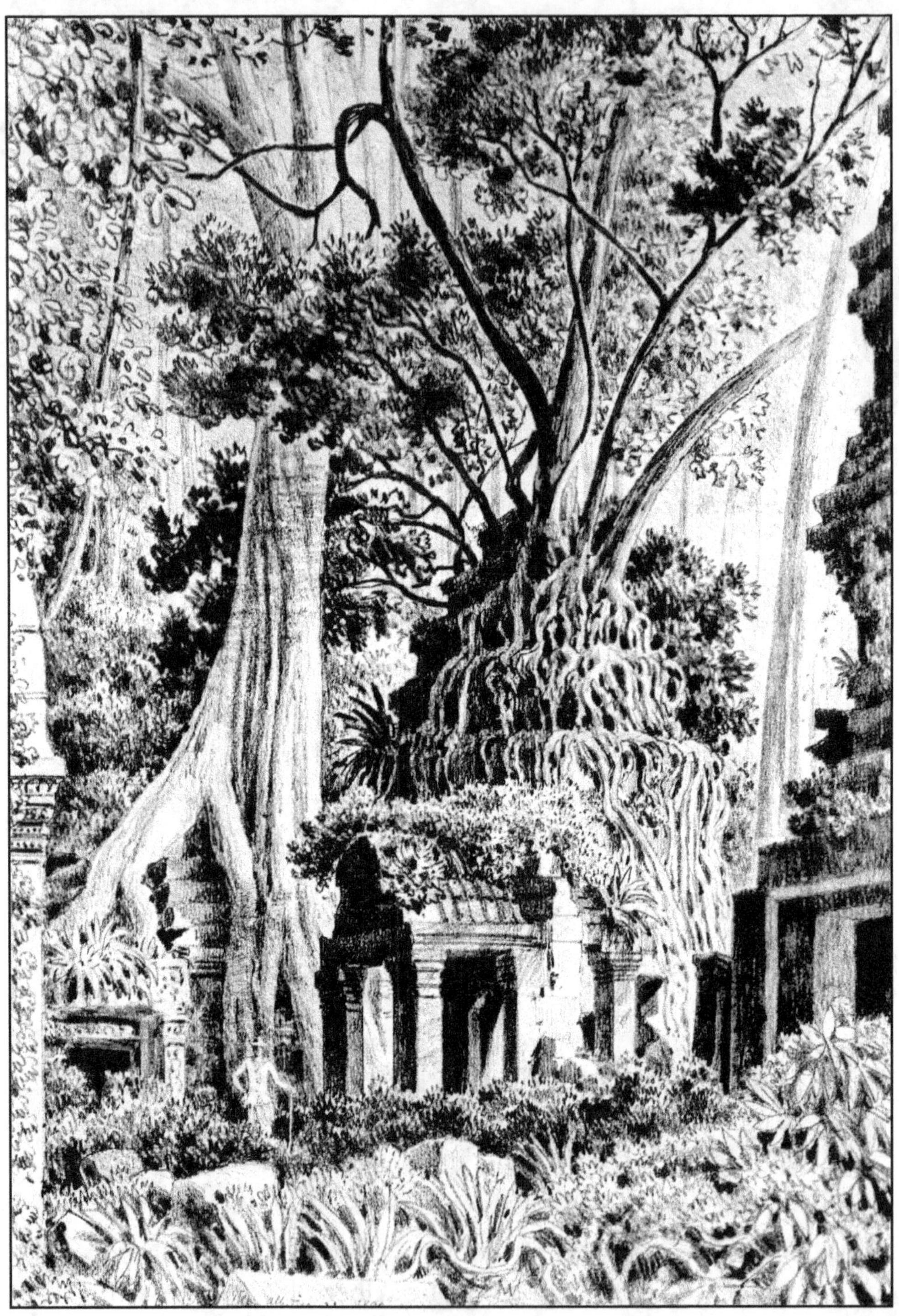

Ta Prohm engraving by Albert Tissandier, 1893.

Ta Prohm

XXVIII

Friday, November 28, 1913

George Groslier

Silence.

    Grey trees and green stones.
Shafts of light slipping through beyond somber vaults.
The poly-chromatic trails of rain
on walls still erect.

A monstrous tree,
its trunk running along the side of a gallery,
righting itself, cracking the gallery,
and rising to mingle with the canopy of leaves.

In a black hole, a small leaf gleams
like the wink of an eye.
Stone slabs heaped,
like cresting waves in profile.

The great corpse of a kapok
leaning against a tower,
creepers dangling.
Here and there, rare flowers peppered about.

An endless file of red ants.
The squeak of bats one has startled,
and on one's skin,
the brush of their limp wings.

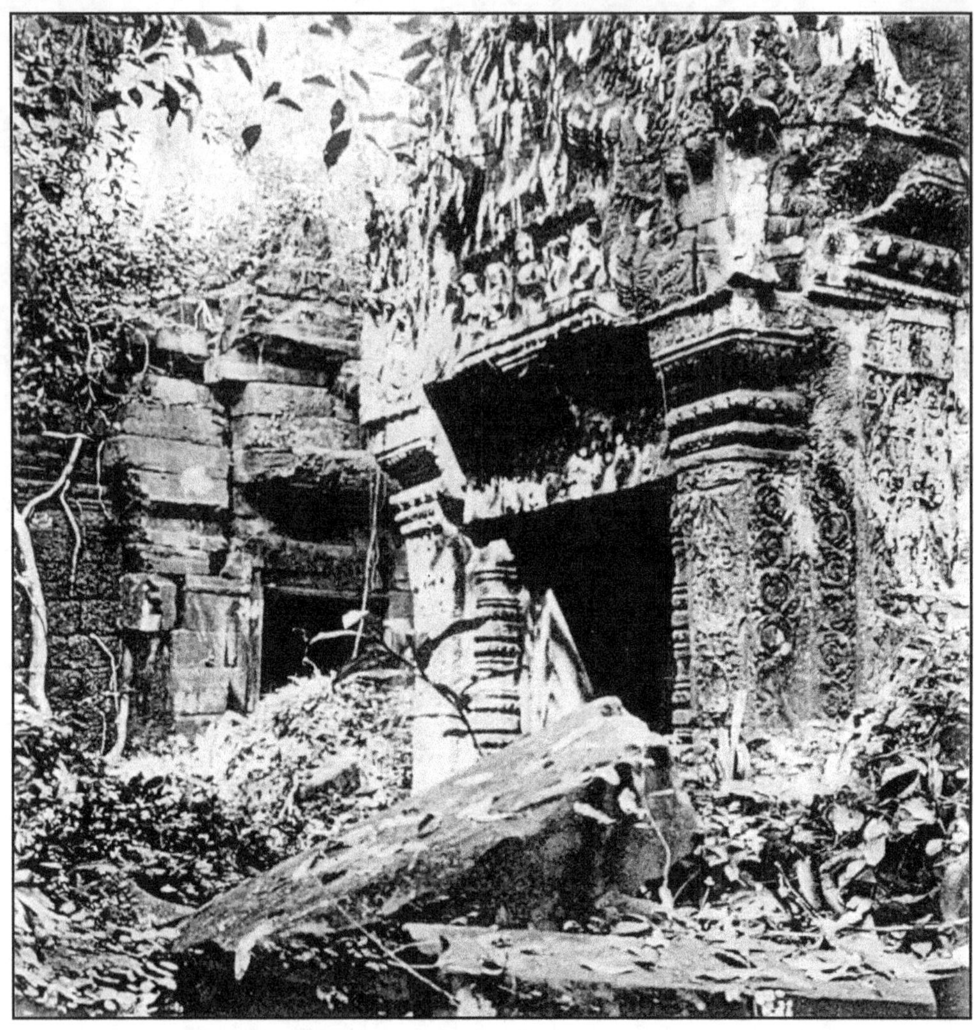

A court at Ta Prohm photographed by George Groslier, 1913.

Pedestals toppled, idols in chunks,
fallen flowers of stone.
White, meaty corollas of saffron,
shrubs, brambles, ferns, palms.

The red blur
of a squirrel in flight.
The fall of a branch,
sunlight sparkling on a lintel.

The crumbling of vaults underfoot;
columns dislodged,
formless chunks,
a pilaster that might have been sculpted yesterday.

Austerity, sumptuous grandeur,
or just intimate little spots;
gay, sun-drenched courtyards
breached through a gap by the foliage.

Beyond, the striking dark, yawning hole of a gallery.
The motionless assault of brambles.
The binding of blocks by tree root,
or their toppling.

Red stone pocked like a sponge;
sandstone of blue, pink, pale grey.
Dead trunks of rusty hue.
Stagnating water, lush moss, beds of dead leaves.

A lovely insect, still and jewel-like.
Still more columns,
fortified walls,
sculpted legends.

Still more towers, toppled or intact,
tall or tiny, bare or verdant.
Great stretches of teetering vaults.
Chambers.

Everywhere bushes,
fronds, bowers, garlands.
Vast ficus trees
with roots spread like octopi.

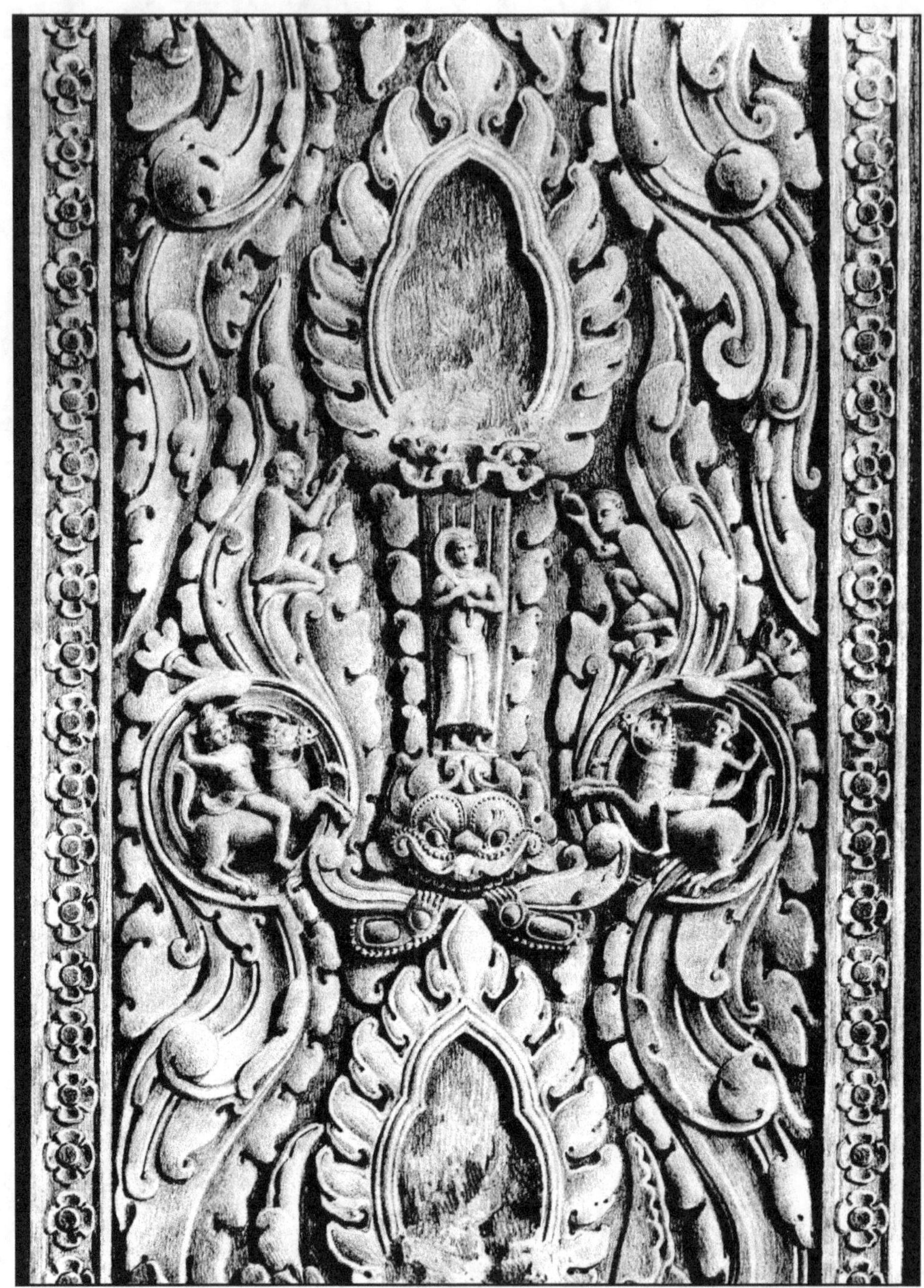

"Calm, terrible gods; symbols;
the smiles of women."

Ta Prohm pilaster engraving by Albert Tissandier, 1893.

Here, the remains of an inscription.
There, the mortise of a door.
Calm, terrible gods; symbols;
the smiles of women.

Not death,
but immobility.
Not sadness,
but contemplation.

Wind hardly known,
shifting light,
oppressive cool,
ineffable odors.

Voila, to the east of Angkor Thom,
the temple of Ta Prohm;
one of the largest in Cambodia,
one of the most devastated.

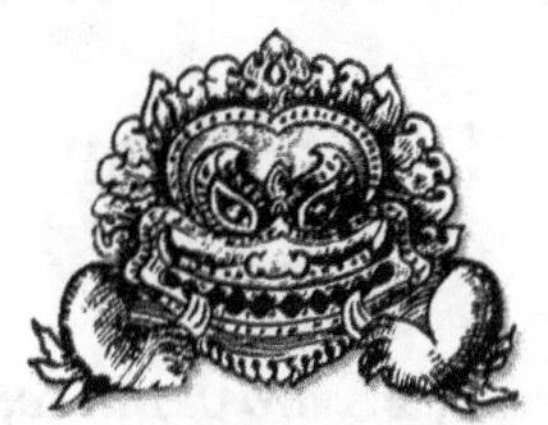

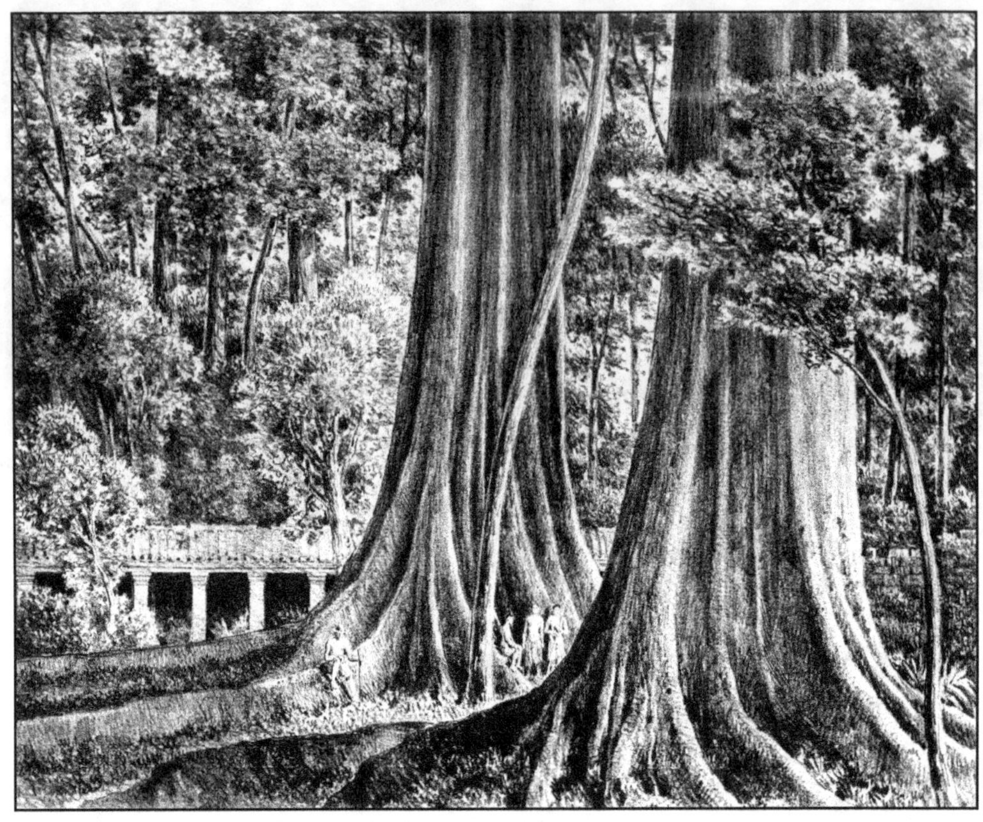

Ta Prohm engraving by Albert Tissandier, 1893.

Ta Prohm

XXVIII

Vendredi, 28 Novembre, 1913

George Groslier

Le silence.

Des arbres gris et des pierres vertes,
des échappées de lumière au delà de voûtes sombres.
Les traînées polychromes des pluies
sur des murailles encore debout.

Un arbre monstrueux,
dont le tronc longe une galerie,
se redresse, la fait éclater
et s'élance se mêler à la voûte végétale.

Dans un trou noir une petite feuille miroite
comme un clignotement d'œil.
Des dalles sont accumulées
avec des profils de vagues qui déferlent.

Un grand cadavre de fromager
penche et s'appuie sur une tour,
des lianes pendent.
De-ci, de-là on voit des fleurs rares.

Une file de fourmis rouges interminable.
Cris de chauves-souris que l'on effraie
et qui vous effleurent
de leurs ailes molles.

Socles bouleversés, tronçons d'idoles,
fleurs de pierre tombées.
Corolles blanches et grasses des safrans,
arbrisseaux, ronces, fougères, palmes.

Fuite rousse
d'un écureuil.
Chute d'une branche,
éclat de soleil sur un linteau.

Écroulement des voûtes sur lequel on marche,
colonnes déplacées,
tronçons informes;
pilastre semblant sculpté de la veille.

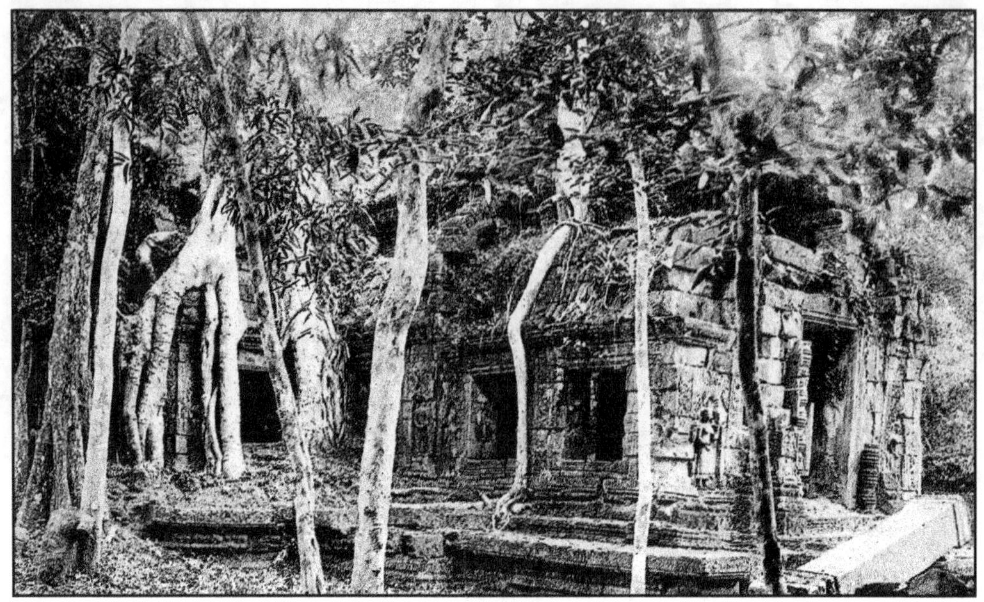

Ta Prohm, early undated photo.

De l'austérité, de la grandeur somptueuse,
ou bien des coins intimes,
des cours gaies pleines de soleil
que laisse passer un trouée de feuillage.

Au delà le trou béant, obscur, impressionnant d'une galerie.
L'assaut immobile des ronces.
La ligature des blocs par des racines,
ou leur renversement.

De la pierre rouge et trouée comme de l'éponge,
des grès bleus, roses, gris clair.
Des troncs morts aux tons de rouille,
de l'eau qui croupit, de la mousse grasse, des lits de feuilles mortes.

Un bel insecte immobile, tel un bijou.
Encore des colonnes,
des murailles,
des légendes sculptées.

Toujours des tours, intactes ou renversées,
hautes ou minuscules, nues ou verdoyantes.
Des pans de voûte en équilibre.
Des cellules.

Partout des arbustes,
des frondaisons, des berceaux, des guirlandes.
Des ficus immenses
aux racines étalées comme des pieuvres.

Là, un reste d'inscription,
ici, la mortaise d'une porte.
Des dieux calmes, terribles, des symboles,
des sourires de femmes.

Pas de mort,
de l'immobilité.
Pas de tristesse,
du recueillement.

Vent rare,
lumière mouvante,
fraîcheur lourde,
parfums indéfinissables.

Voilà à l'Est d'Angkor Thom
le temple de Ta Phrom;
l'un des plus grands du Cambodge,
l'un des plus bouleversés.

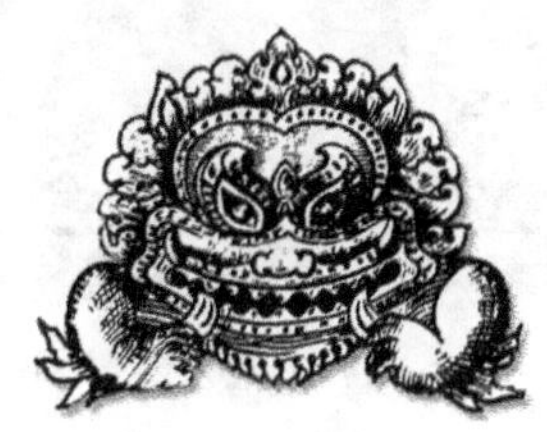

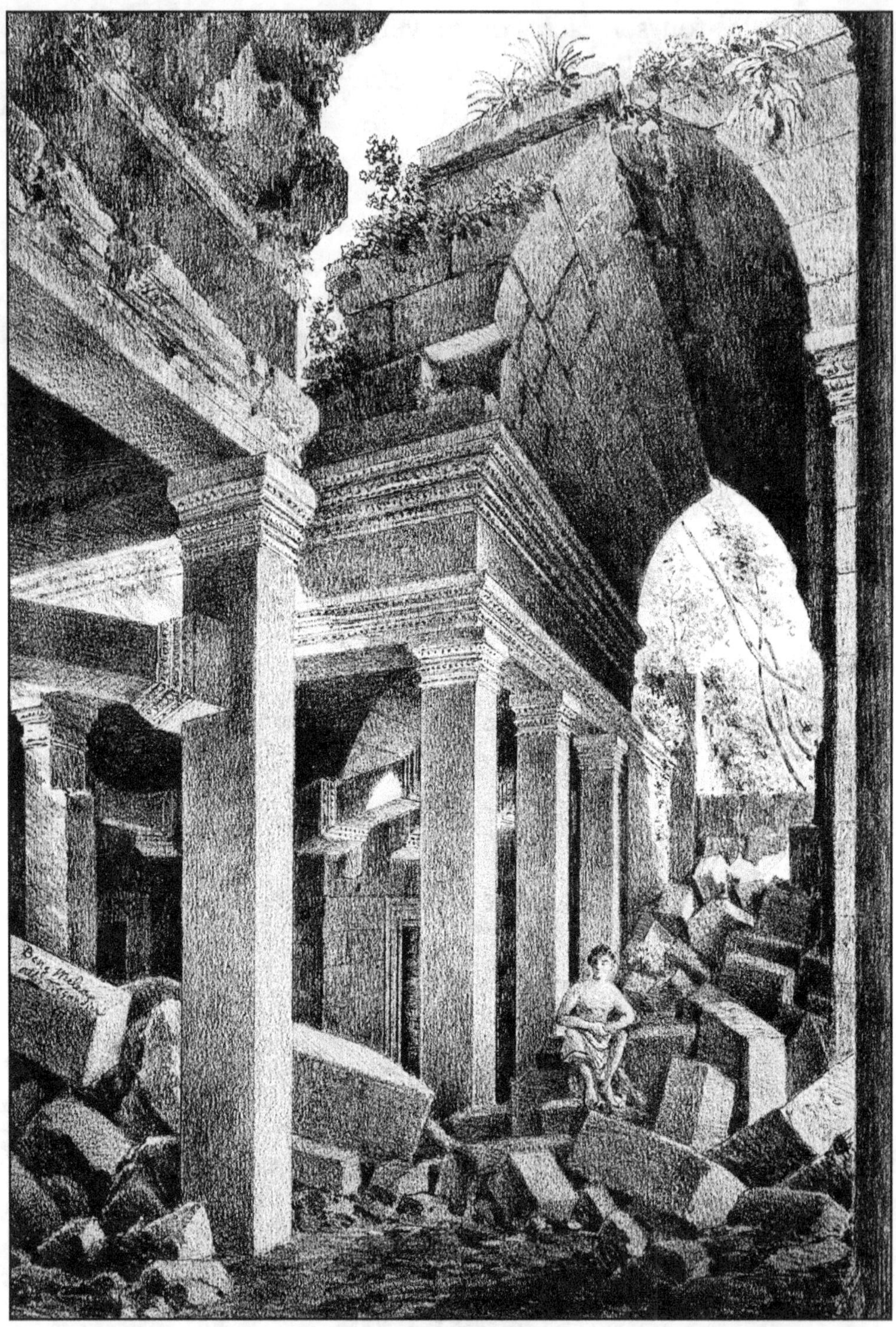

Engraving of a hall at Beng Mealea by Albert Tissandier, 1893.

7
Beng Mealea

XXIX

Tuesday, December 2, 1913

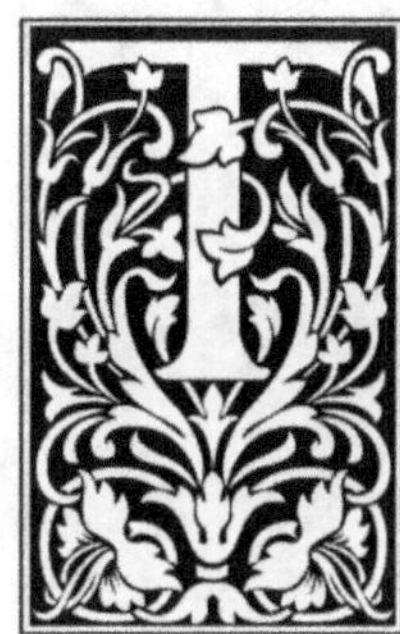he temple of Beng Mealea — fifteen hours east of Angkor by ox-cart — is located on the road linking the capital with the great Preah Khan and with Koh Ker, one hundred fifty kilometers to the northeast.

It is painful to see the ornamental flourishes of the old temples pitilessly destroyed and entombed by the supple, vibrant flourishes of the earth. An incalculable number of exemplars of this unparalleled art lie broken and buried, as formless blocks.

The builders here worked a bluish-grey sandstone as fine as marble with a skill and mastery that have never been surpassed. Nearly as vast as Angkor Wat, the temple is to Khmer art what the Sainte-Chapelle is to the Gothic.[34] Wherever intact it displays nothing but masterpieces of finesse and variety. And four-fifths of it is nothing but debris.

Yet if dark, victorious warriors, drunk on conquest or liberation, had not wrought a first destruction upon these monuments, the

---

[34] King Louis IX commissioned this church around 1240 AD to house his collection of Passion relics. Considered one of the highest examples of Gothic architecture, it was heavily damaged during the French Revolution. Today it still stands on the Île de la Cité, in the heart of Paris, the only surviving building of the Capetian dynasty's royal palace.

79

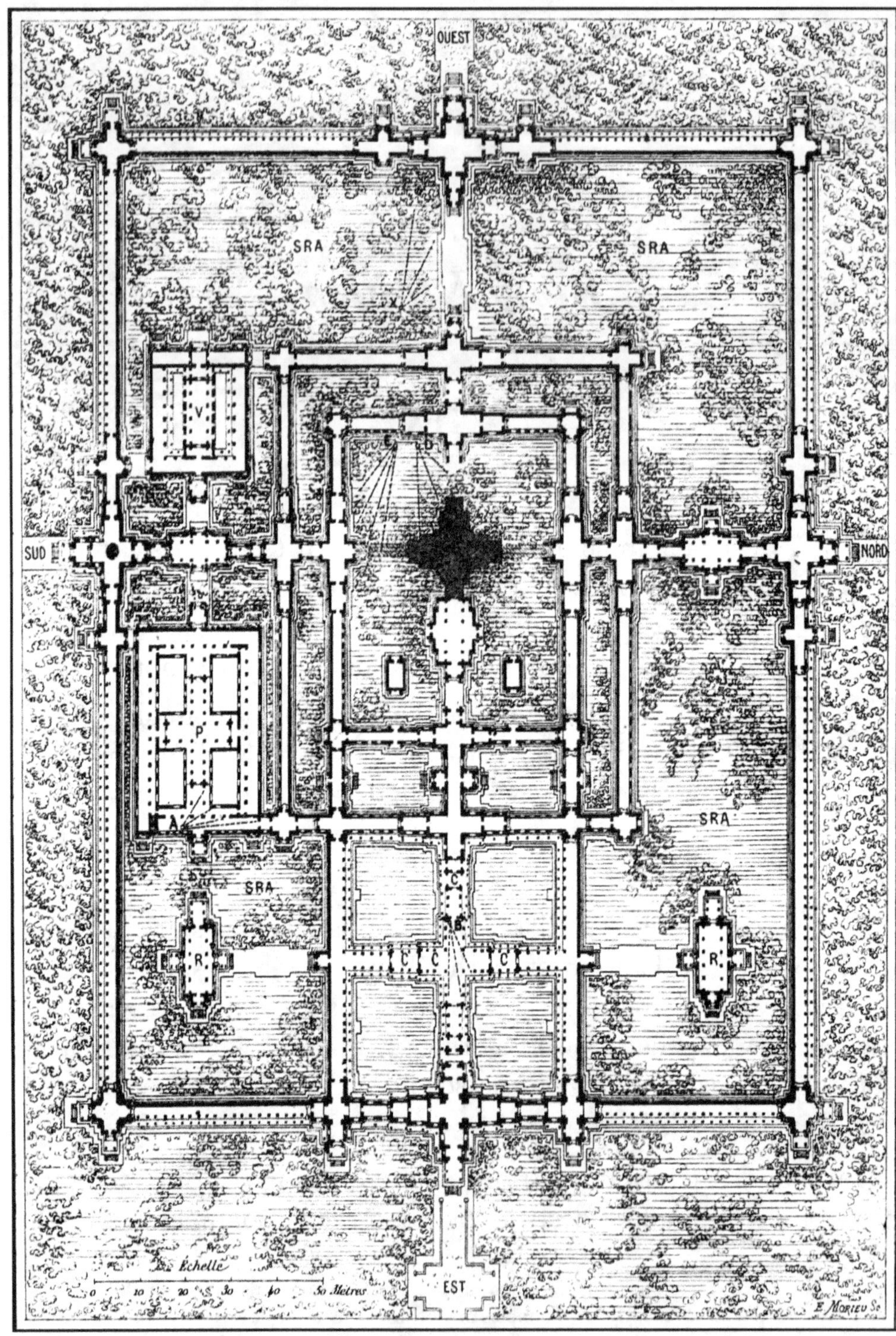

Beng Mealea site plan drawn by Albert Tissandier in 1893.

vegetation would never have been able to spread with such utter liberty. Especially here, the still-standing towers of the perfectly built sanctuaries would never have allowed roots to penetrate and swell between stones so excellently joined.

Galleries neglected by vandals have remained exactly as they were, between massive walls of seamlessly jointed stones. Beneath the shelter of these vaults neither moss nor the finest creeper has secured a purchase on life. Only humidity splits the stone a little towards the bottom, and even the big cats dare not penetrate the mysteries of age-old shadow.

The sanctuaries, meanwhile, are almost always devastated top to bottom, for it was at them above all that war and revolt directed their wrath. And it was in devastation's wake that the vines crept into these corpses, now exposed to the sky, and supplied the humus necessary for trees to sprout and roots to complete the ruin.

If you searched carefully, and dug them out from under the crushing heaps, you could exhume a great many masterpieces. More than intact, they would be in much better condition than the works we now observe at our leisure. In fact, since destruction followed so closely on the heels of construction, the collapsed blocks protect one another. If you slip through a hole in the rubble at the sanctuary of Beng Mealea (one of the ruins where it is possible to do so), you find a smiling *devata* and a small, polygonal column ringed with lotus flowers.[35] Protected as they have been from centuries of rain by the colossal superstructure, the sculptures have retained their shine, their polish, and the vigor of their execution. Meanwhile, out in the open, tilting lintels have exposed their graceful surface — a god's gesture, a lotus blossom — to the rains and falling branches, and all has been erased.

It is a gross error to believe that having twenty of the group's lintels makes having sixty superfluous. To consider just one little

---

35 The appendix article "Death of an Angel" may offer a rare glimpse of the *devata* George saw, as well as her sad fate.

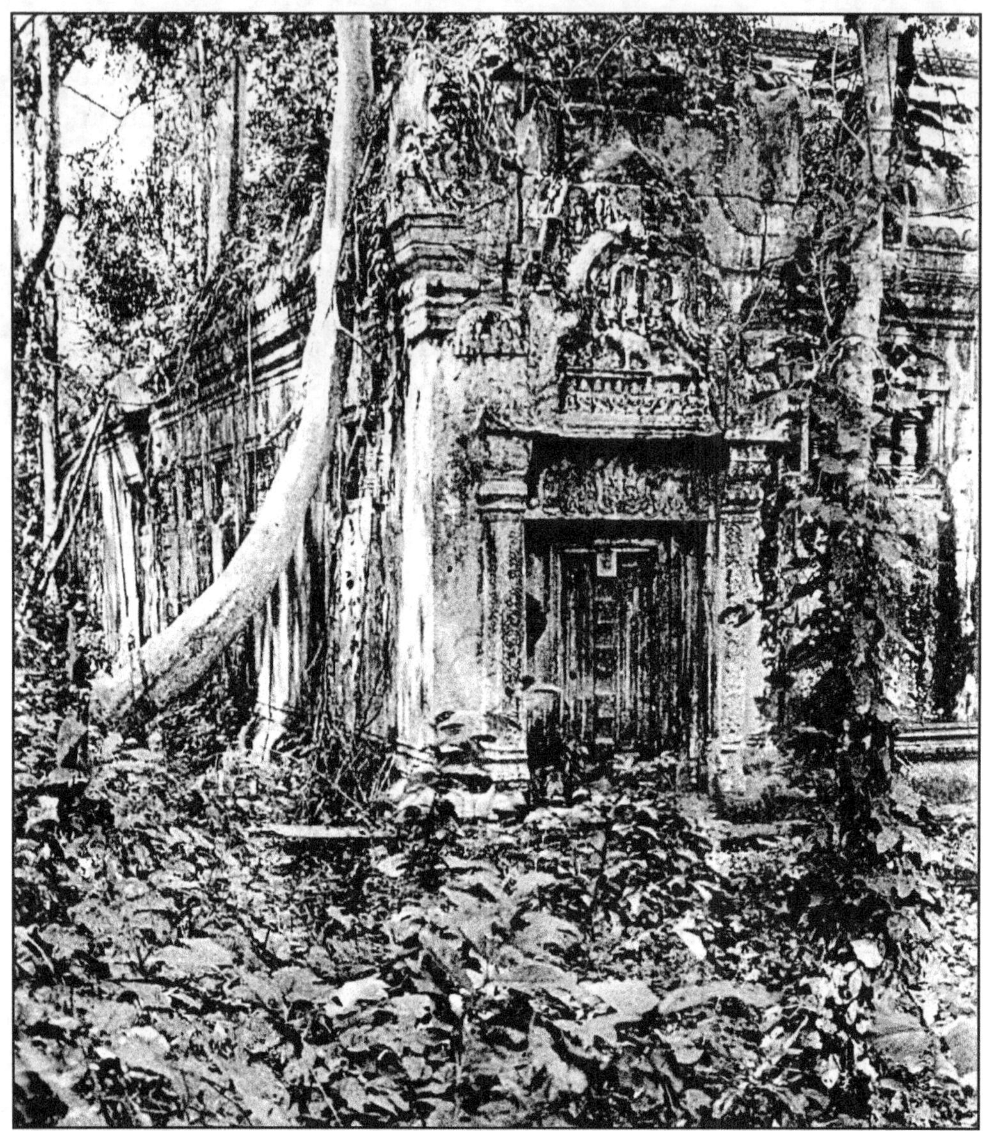

**Beng Mealea. Southwest corner of the southern structure
and sculpted pediment.**

motif, let us take the frieze that runs like a garland under the
entablature of every structure at Beng Mealea. This motif varies not
only on every structure but even on every face of a given structure.

From a general principle, the alternation of hearts and pendants,
it flourishes in twenty ways. At the sanctuary it consists of *rinceaux*

and *culots*,[36] lotus and small volutes. On the southwest structure
a Hamsa head appears at the center of each heart. On the same
structure's base, the Hamsa, now appearing in the band molding,
is replaced by the torso of a figure in prayer. Elsewhere that figure
alternates with the Hamsa. On the third perimeter wall a bird
alternates with curls, and not one of the leafy curls resembles the
next. At the cruciform colonnade the praying figure is replaced by
dancers, by male archers, by men carrying burdens or wrestling,
and the pendants form pearly pompoms.

It is not easy to say which of these varieties is the loveliest, for
all are charming and deliciously executed. Rather than suppose
them the same, it is doubtless accurate to imagine the lost motifs
as being different from those visible at present. Like nature, which
in a single form has carried beauty to infinite variety, the Khmer
decorators carried to infinite variety the forms they possessed.

In no way do we stray from the narrows of truth in saying that
a single temple contains more forms of lotus, obtained through
stylization, faithful copying, or varying methods of manufacture,
than do the great surrounding moats.

If the Cambodian decorators elsewhere resorted to their
prodigious powers of multiplication, often running to excess — at
Angkor Wat, for example — and always with a certain ostentation,
here they achieved an admirable moderation of their genius. Thus,
with everything rigorously scaled to its importance, Beng Mealea
emanates a powerful, sober harmony, making it a temple of the first
rank. We may consider it the prototype, the spare, classic exemplar
of Khmer art.

The gallery walls, taller here than anywhere else, and made of
select materials, are uniform, their blocks matched with extreme
and unique care. They are set back from their broad, sharply
relieved foundations, giving the whole its power, and anchoring

---

36 *Rinceaux* are ornamental foliate or floral motifs. *Culots* are architectural ornaments, such as
the starting points of volutes, which are spiral curves or whorls.

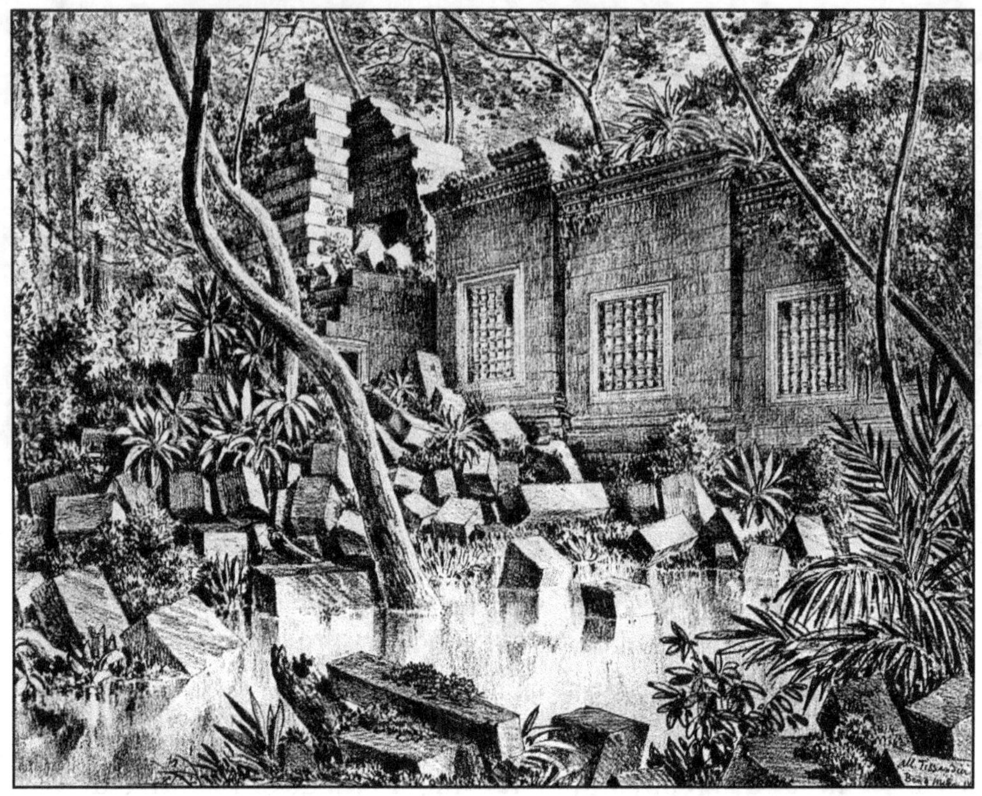

A façade at Beng Mealea. Engraving by Albert Tissandier, 1893.

it to the ground. Only high up, skyward, above the beautiful, polished, naked walls, broken here and there by nothing but lofty, horizontal windows, does the aforementioned frieze underscore the energetic form of a molding, pearled with lotus.

But the riches of the decorative and chiseled arts are concentrated entirely on the doors. Indeed, the layout of Beng Mealea has increased their number incalculably. And the lintels, the posts covered with flowers and legends take on an even more sumptuous and rare character because surrounded by vast, austere, simple surfaces.

What could I add to this little sketch that would not be overly particular or technical? I seek to omit such matters. These are impressions jotted down, notes for painting.

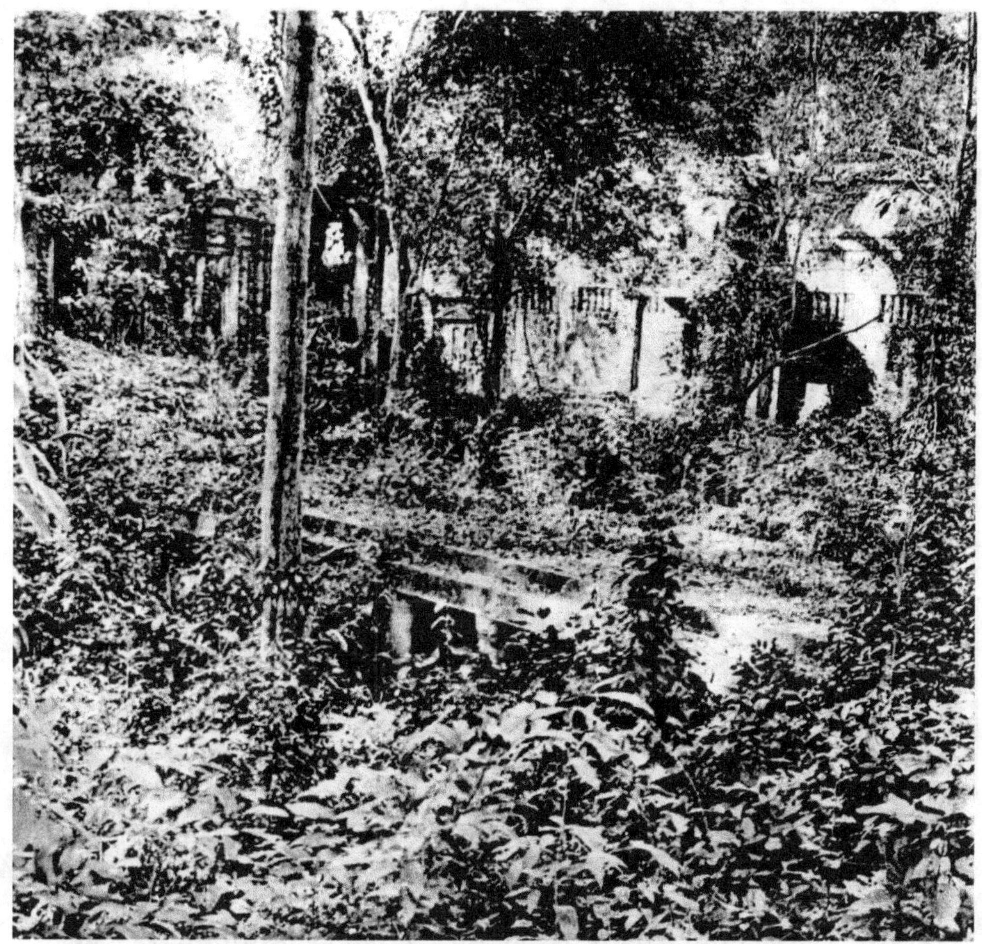

**Beng Mealea cruciform platform on colonnettes.
In the background, annex structure to the southwest.**

XXX

Thursday, December 4, 1913

The sylvan charm of Beng Mealea is that of all temples lost in the forest.

Set aside intellectual and philosophical matters, resist whatever sense of desperation you might carry around inside you, and they shall lack the sadness that you might expect. Instead they shall offer up a calm gaiety, a happy serenity. They brandish the smile of old men.

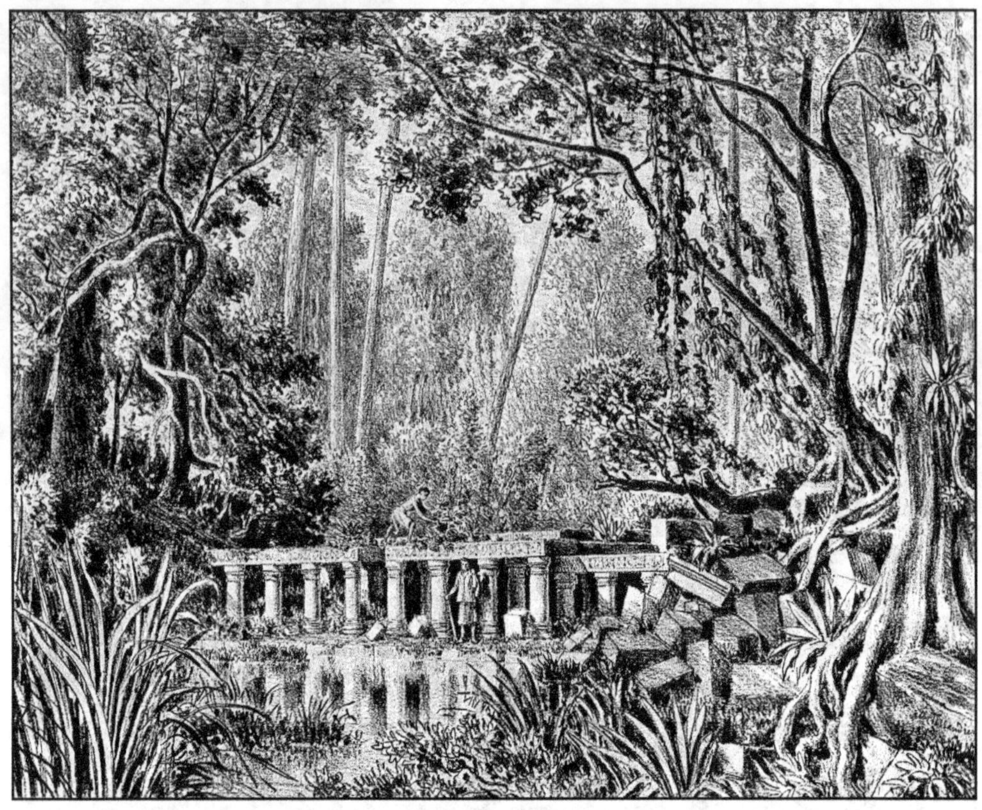

**Beng Mealea's east access road on round columns crossing the moat.
Drawn by Albert Tissandier in 1893.**

Sunlight falls upon them in patches. Troupes of monkeys leap
from treetop to treetop, launched like projectiles by the give in
the branches. The marks of honey bears show on the smooth tree
bark. In the galleries and the corners of walls stand termite nests,
furrowed like the circumvolutions of monstrous brains. Every step
is muffled by a thick layer of humus and debris pulverized by time.

Not a fissure or crevasse goes unfilled. Foliage hangs there like
immobile finery. The heat and the wind, here always attenuated, let
a little water stand in the sacred basins long after the rains. Mosses
lend them ever-changing hues. Daylight filtering through the leafy
vault takes on its color. It brushes past the relief of the decorations
or gleams on the broad leaves of orchids, which bloom like splayed
hands. The pale tree trunks are mauve.

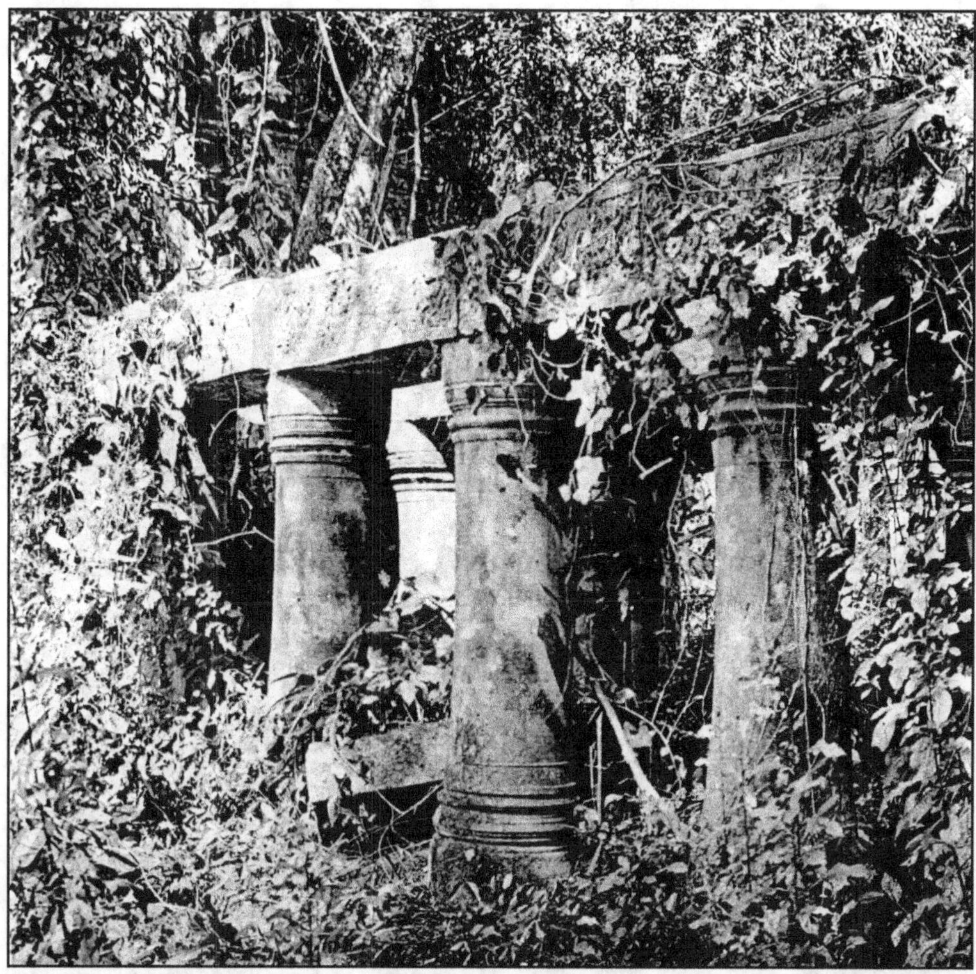

The Beng Mealea moat crossing photographed by Groslier twenty years later.

The magic of the reflections, the patient fingers of wear, the mosses and garlands all imbue the stones with a sort of vegetal life. One conflates the sculptor's *rinceau* with the living stem. If a wind rose up one wouldn't know which would tremble. The underside of the entablatures are unfathomable, haloed as they are by sunny fragments. At the corner of a wall a divine dancer smiles in sudden light, and a great tuft of blooming orchids above her casts flower shadows on her womanly gesture. Elsewhere, on the convex foreheads of a tricephalous elephant, broad, varnished leaves shudder as if set in motion by the fabulous animal's passage.

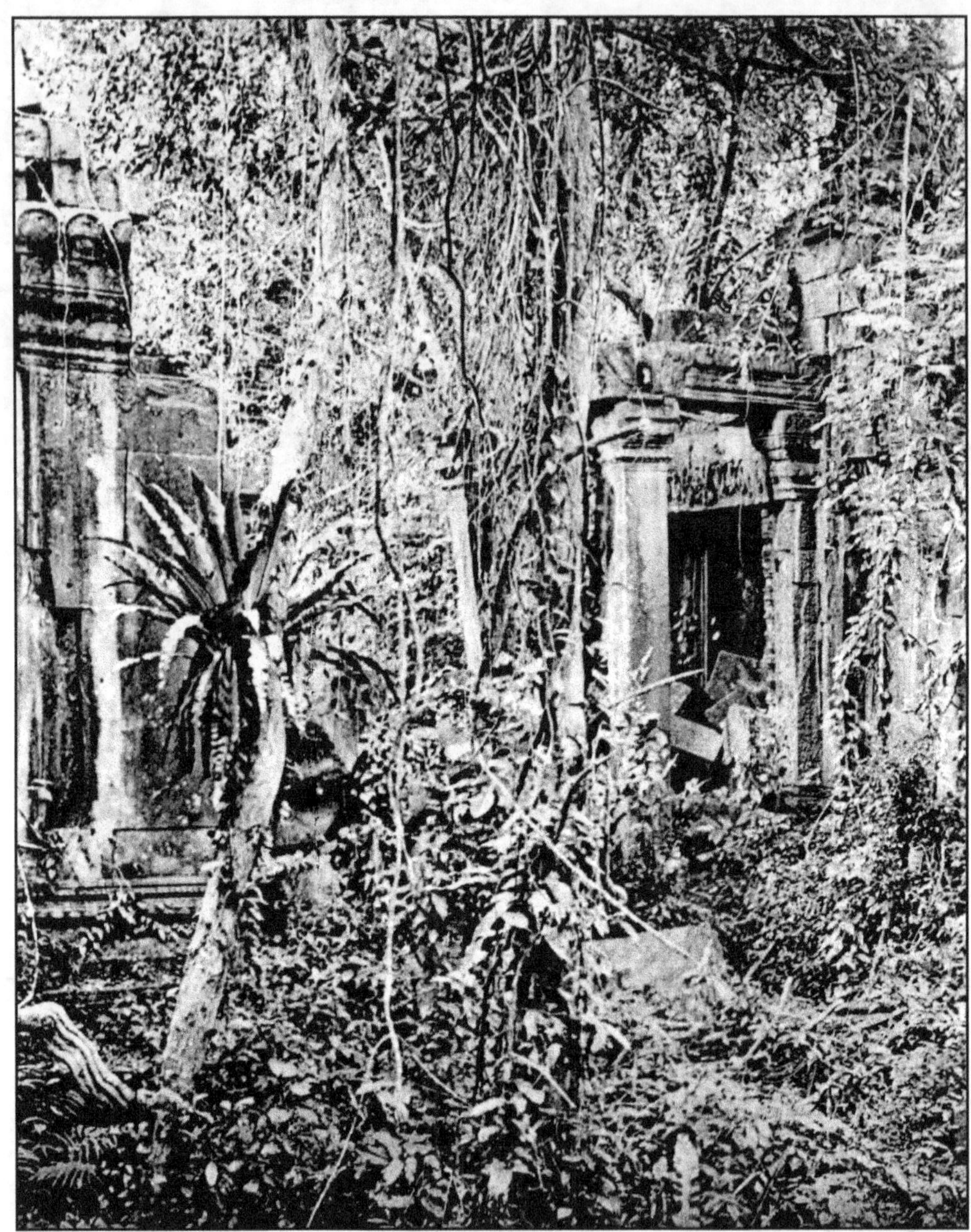

A courtyard of Beng Mealea.

Trunks mingle with columns. A natural jasmine clings to a stone leaf. On the tympanum, a head of hair; on the wall, a mantel. The slab is covered in moss, the fissure full of slumbering water. The ancient battle between nature and stone has been fixed in intimate union. Too closely joined, the elements have come to resemble one another, each losing its particular significance.

From atop the superstructures, beneath the treetops, the structures emerge isolated, lost, sun scorched, storm beaten. They seem gloomy and laid bare, like rocks in the sea.

Each portion of the extraordinary whole seems thus to live for itself. Each has its well-defined purpose. One sees not a gate and its ornamentation but a wonderland. Twenty stanzas does the poem comprise. One is sung in the sun, another in shadow, another in the night. An emerald vapor envelops the whole.

In the loud silence, a sweet peace is your companion, its soft hand rewarding each thing with a caress.

XXXI

Friday, December 5, 1913

At times my body succumbs to fits of great fatigue. I have been on the road for eight months. Camps in the open air, a folding table, and a cot: these have been my home. If a man wishes to bear it in impunity, solitude demands ever-vigilant will and intense industry in work.

For the past fourteen days I have wandered devastated Beng Mealea. I am perpetually scampering up toppled structures, leaping gymnastically from stone to stone to reach interesting spots, standing erect to sketch and scribble accounts, pushing apart the brush, whose thorns catch on my clothes, the laces binding and trip up my feet. I am a broken man. Every evening I must pluck off the ticks, which swarm in the moss and rotten wood.

The nights are full of strange sounds. A panther made off with a cage of chickens yesterday under my *sala*. It is no use trying to convince yourself that there is no danger, that panthers never climb into huts, that they flee at the least sound. You still never quite sleep soundly with such cruel beasts on the prowl nearby. All these circumstances amount to a state of excessive excitement, enhanced by fatigue and fed by solitude.

Then I am overcome with sadness. Like a veil it settles over everything and is ruffled by the slightest movement. With that veil in hand, one is helpless, inactive — like wretched fishermen standing on the bank with empty nets in their arms.

I reach a point where I wonder whether my efforts will succeed; whether they and my conviction will advance by a single step the science to which I have devoted myself. An insomniac forced to inaction, I ruminate over the sad hours of my exile, and my youth thus spent reveals to me the bitter fate that awaits it.

Letters from friends, which become increasingly rare, and reach me at irregular intervals, are full of everything that I miss. Their authors are surrounded by affection and gaiety. If by unfortunate chance I receive them while I happen to be discouraged I find such letters as painful as unsalvable wounds, apt to finish me off. They introduce into camp, where I struggle with fatigue, doubt, and despondency, a fatal nostalgia for my loved ones.

Though I draw straight from the brimming poetry of nature, from tropical beauties, and in them find rare joys and new sensations, am I not perhaps neglecting equivalent things that might exist in France, things to which I might at least be better suited?

I prefer to believe not. I prefer to believe that the steady force that has brought me here to the very heart of the country where I was born and that urges me on to study its history was an obscure force of destiny. I prefer to believe that it makes sense to pay for these satisfactions with the fatigue and privation that they entail, that make one worthy, but that are in turn the source of passing bitterness.

I would like to paint but do not have the time. I have been sent here. Whatever is expected of me, I must make my harvest as rich as possible. It is a matter of trust.

The strictly archaeological study of a given site no doubt requires faculties of observation, synthesis, and I would even say method analogous to those required for the painterly study of the same site. In both cases the eyes are the first intermediaries, and in both one makes use of the forms, particularities, and characteristics of the thing studied. We needn't discuss whether both endeavors produce the same satisfactions, but I must admit that I am not engaged in the work that I was supposed to do, the work that I was trained for. The result is a vague discomfort, due to my inability to do both.

Though after much time spent in a given structure I come away with a copious harvest of documents, observations, and even findings, my joy is tinged with the vague regret that I have left behind some other thing that I might also have carried off. Every time there is a little failure, a betrayal, perhaps an instance of negligence. The charming effects, the soft light, the harmonious groups that I have glimpsed, and that have gladdened my soul and eyes — those fleeting impressions that I have been unable to try to capture on canvas — linger in memory like so many regrets.

So what's my hurry? Everything. My increasingly frequent states of exhaustion. Time's flying past. The unknown that lies ahead. My inexperience, hampering me, frightening me, but waning as they days go by. The seasons, changing the look of things, opening or closing communications. Fevers I might catch. The impatience to compare and verify elsewhere what I have found here, the irresistible impatience to see and get to know something else and to have reached, at long last, every mysterious corner of this land.

The Khmer past is such an enigma, a world so unknown in the current state of knowledge, that any progress is as yet but a scratching of the surface. When the lives of many initiators and pioneers have passed in the sifting of these rich spoils; when many specialists from every branch of human knowledge have found in them something to exhaust their industry; when at last we are convinced that Egypt and Greece were not as rich in comparison with distant Cambodia as we have hitherto believed, then the enthusiasm and fervor of those early believers shall come to be understood. Everything that they will have brought from that land of fire and solitude shall assume its true value.

In moments of disenchantment it is from these thoughts that I draw courage and hope. These at least never forsake me.

XXXII

Sunday, December 7, 1913

The more I study different groups, the more convinced I become that the destruction wrought by vegetation is slight before the ravages of men.

A great many Brahmanic divinities have been slashed by chisel blow, but this should not take on undue importance, for in these same temples the same divinities appear two meters away, in plain sight, and have remained intact. Other temples — Angkor Wat, Preah Vihear, Beng Mealea — show no systematic mutilation of the ancient gods.

Revolutionary frenzy, in a horde of assailants, blows through like a whirlwind, topples the idols, burns, sacks, and pillages the temple, but one cannot imagine its operating meticulously, its stopping a long while to scratch out the head of some particular divinity on bas-reliefs left otherwise intact.

Always within arm's reach, these localized mutilations seem to be the work of new temple occupants. Their cult differed from that of their predecessors. The idols and sects differed. As devotees of, say, Vishnu, they would have spent their time effacing the depictions of one of Shiva's manifestations. This very specific scratching could not have been carried out simultaneously with the complete destruction of a temple, but only earlier. Indeed, I have often found examples of it mixed in amid ruins.

In none of the devastated groups do we find very old trees. All are at most aged one or two centuries or members of fast-growing species: ficuses and kapoks, adding a meter to their height every year. Also, a great number of tipped decorative motifs, mixed into the completely toppled ruins of part of a structure and exposed to the sky and elements, show, with very few exceptions, scarcely any more wear than motifs that have remained upright and protected. Here, then, we have a few corroborating facts to argue in favor of a relatively recent collapse of the temples.

Inscriptions and documents inform us of their incalculable riches. What do we find? Nothing. In all the sanctuaries the pedestals have been toppled and great holes dug in their place by treasure hunters. Meticulous excavations at the Bayon and Angkor Wat have managed to unearth not even a pea-size bit of silver. Every corner of the temples was pillaged, and pillaged early, either by conquerors or by insurgents.

However, the incidents of collapse that we know are recent do not date from that time. We are thus justifiably surprised to infer that a new destruction, not limited to the toppling of roofs and columns, must have taken place. Beng Mealea in particular shall provide an explanation.

The Khmer assembled their sandstone blocks without any cement to bind them. The perfection of the joints and the weight of the blocks sufficed to keep them balanced. But wherever they judged that oblique or horizontal forces could come into play the builders bound their materials with double Ts in iron, which they then fixed with lead seals or by mortise.

At Beng Mealea a vast, cruciform colonnade delimits four courtyards, the whole being circumscribed in a rectangle of galleries. The architraves are made of monoliths, each pair meeting at a column. To keep them from splitting apart, the builders united the architraves by double Ts in iron, of which the mortises survive.

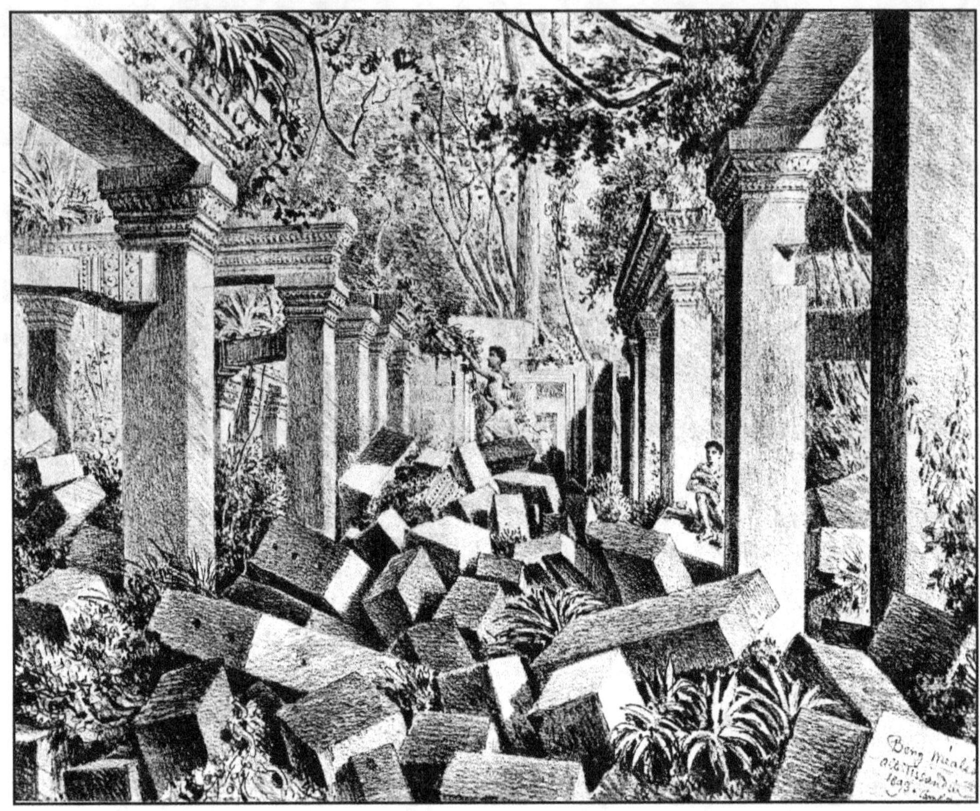

Toppled galleries at Beng Mealea, drawn by Albert Tissandier in 1893.

Without exception — and I insist on this point — all the roofs have been sapped, toppled to the architraves, and their irons exposed, only where the topplers expected the irons to be. Entire blocks have been left intact on architraves between columns: i.e., where there are no joints.

The lintels were affixed to their walls, lest they fall forward, by the same crampons, and all the lintels of Beng Mealea have been rudely pierced at the extremities, two holes destroying the sculptures, for the obvious purpose of disengaging the iron anchors, of which only the mortises remain.

We find the same everywhere else. At Angkor Wat, preserved in relatively perfect condition, the iron seekers did not topple the vaults. But again, without exception, there are gaping holes dug into the gutter funnel, above each architrave joint: i.e., above each column. All that remains at the bottom of each hole is a trace of the crampon. The same depredations are in evidence on every staircase landing in the temple. The tenons attain impressive dimensions: thirty-five centimeters in length, twelve in width, four in thickness. Their weight must have exceeded ten kilograms.

This, then, was one of the motives behind the recent devastation of old temples. We can easily put a value on the spoils. Judging by the mortises of Beng Mealea, we are dealing with crampons of two or three kilos. The seal required about the same weight in lead. A colonnade comprises two hundred twelve columns. That makes six hundred thirty-six kilos of pure, hammered iron and as much lead. The whole temple contained three times as much. That was the prize for ruining this wonderful group, and it was a veritable fortune for the vandals. All the temples were thus mines of iron, and sometimes of lead, all of it already worked and saleable.

These brief explications shed new light on the role of oft-maligned vegetation, which appeared only because the path for it had been cleared. The galleries that men respected, and thus which did not have metal crampons, are still intact in almost all the temples, despite the vegetation. In fact, small groups located near villages, sometimes surrounded by monasteries, and where vegetation has never penetrated with any vigor, have likewise been sacked. Moreover, brick monuments, for which iron is useless, are in relatively good condition and have only in rare cases (Mebon, Pre Rup) completely collapsed.

XXXIII

Whereas the great temples of Cambodia have been pillaged by treasure hunters and destroyed by iron thieves, others have been and are still being pillaged by present-day bonzes. These degenerate builders construct their bad pagodas on the very sites of the old structures, and make use of the old materials. They take materials from the ruins, with no consideration for or knowledge of the principal pieces, and so thoroughly modify their look that all archeological research in such places has become impossible. At Lolei, for example, they have used wonderful lintels as stair steps and paved inner grounds with sculptures. One treads on these incomparable vestiges.

To set up their monastery, they have upset an entire central gutter system that began at the center of the four towers and ended at beautiful gargoyles, at the open mouths of monsters. The gargoyles have vanished. Indeed, to the north one has been replaced by a perron.

At Wat Nokor, they have painted the sculptures, walled up the sanctuary, and erected a modern pagoda between the outer wall and the ancient sanctuary. At Hanchey the steps of ancient staircases mingle with the materials of the terrace.

I wish to draw the attention of government administrators and of the École Française d'Extrême-Orient to this matter. Even if we allow the yellow priests to remain on the sites, we might still at least forbid them to touch a single one of those stones. It seems to me that we could even demand that they devote some of their idleness to basic maintenance. Few necessities could be more pressing — especially when so cheaply met — than that of delaying as long as possible the complete ruin of ancient Cambodia.

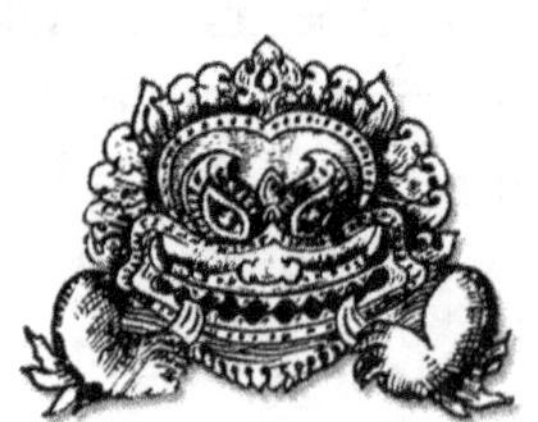

8
Lolei & Bakong

XXXIV

Thursday, December 11, 1913

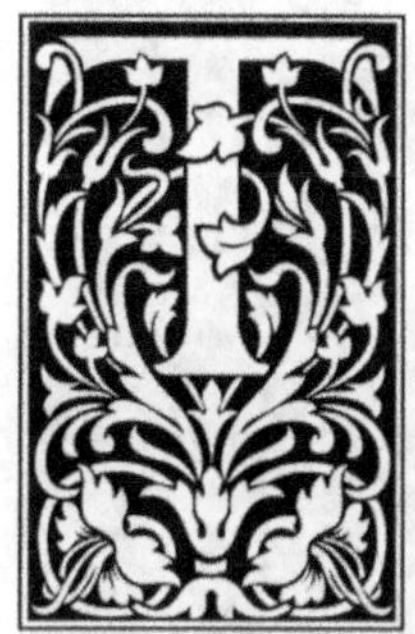he view from the uppermost foundation of the temple of Bakong is not of vast, ever-sullen horizons, as at Wat Phu and Preah Vihear, but of the country's most fertile plains.

Roads more than twenty meters wide stretch forth in a fine sand from which carts raise clouds of dust. Now, in December, the rice paddies stretch to the horizon. One sees women with small, gold chains on their arms and men in silk *sampot*s headed back from their bundling at the rice paddies.

It is palm-wine season. At sundown strong, agile men climb to the tops of the palm trees, bamboo cups in their belts, red torsos aglow amid the fanned-out green leaves. They cut the trees' shoots, hang the bamboo cups beneath the wounds, and return the following day to collect them. In this way, for two months, is collected the sweet, smoky-tasting sap, which flows like a fountain.

At the foot of the temple, beneath lemons and grapefruit, reigns the happy peace of monasteries. There we find the ancient sacred basins, spread with the pink-porcelain cups of lotus blooms. Beyond stand great trees, in which the cormorants have established their city. They look after their little ones and soar past, necks swelled with fish. When the heat is at its peak they linger

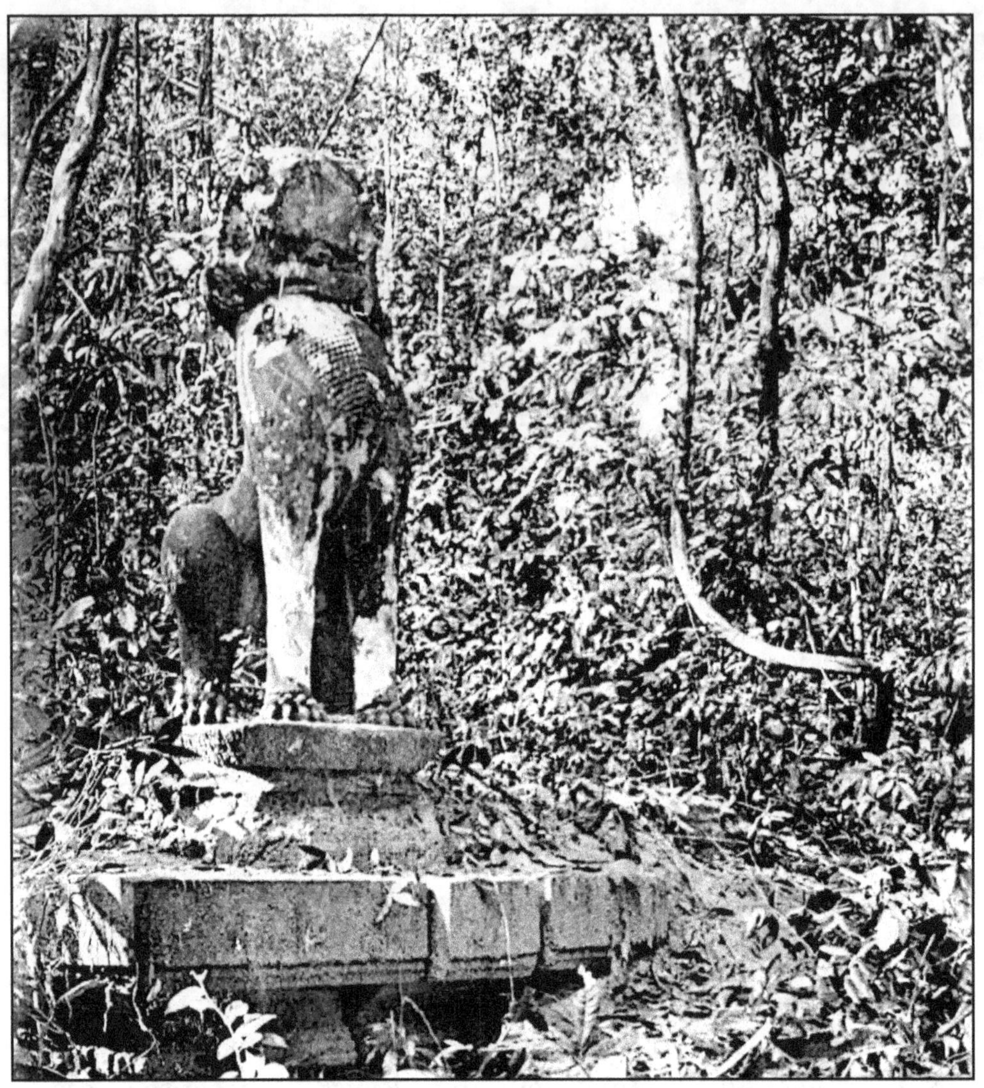

**Ruins in the forest. Khong Pluk, 6 km east of Beng Mealea
(height of lion: 2 m 30)**

immobile on the treetops, spreading their wings in the sun, like so many crucified birds.

Never in Cambodia had I felt so strong a sense of life and prosperity as when I left the banks of the Mekong to penetrate into these lands. The area around Angkor is but a desert. None of its villages could compare with the villages here.

At sundown, on my way out of Beng Mealea, I arrived at the village of Damrong, which lies at the foot of an ancient tower. For two hours I walked through rice paddies as tall as my horse's rump. They stretched out to the horizon, where began the glade — the desert — that I had been crossing since dawn. Red clouds like spindly splotches of jabbing brushwork fled across the sunset. At the zenith, having already conquered its domain with pearly softness: the full moon.

Processions of women, traveling along a path lined with high cacti, arrived at the same time as I. It was their voices that I had heard singing from afar. Their torsos were wrapped in scarves, and flat baskets rode their hips. Men followed behind.

The path ran under an arch of vegetation. Up there the beautiful coconut palms were copper red, but down here, in the shade of a hundred different shrubs, thick and tangled, the ground was scarcely visible. The ever-present bells of the beasts tinkled. Then came the village, with naked, big-bellied children, wolf-faced dogs, huts behind sapodillas, kitchen fires, the sound of pestles beating a paddy, a few calls, a few monotone chants, dusty carts gathered at the fringe of the paddies, a frugal meal — and night.

Ah! What drives me to continue on past such oases? Need I have loved ones waiting for me? Need I have habits, vanities, and ambitions? Here I see the happiness and serenity that nature freely offers up to all, but I partake of them for no longer than the fleeting moments of dusk. Why?

XXXV

Friday, December 12, 1913

The temples of Bakong and Lolei comprise two brick groups. They stand near the large center of Roluos, twelve hours by cart from Beng Mealea. Bakong rises from seven stone

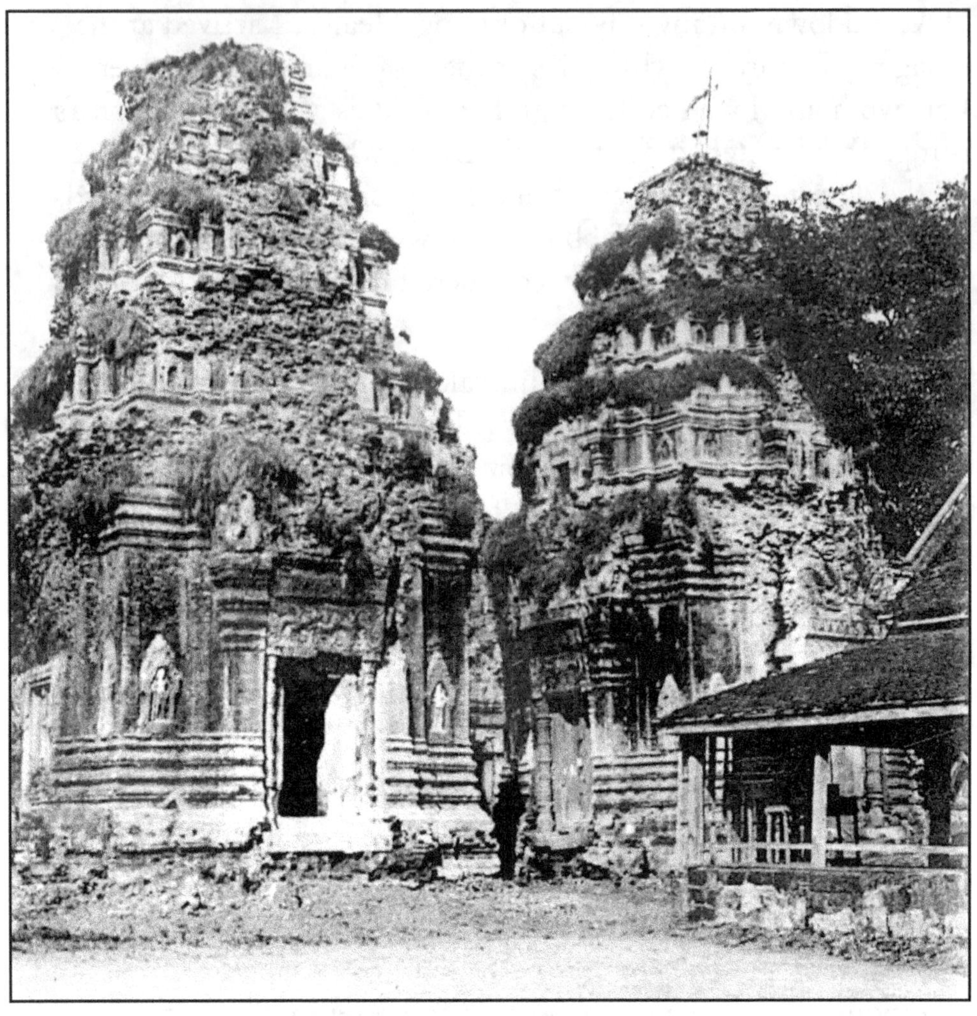

Lolei. Brick towers (height: 10 m).

courses of decreasing size, Lolei from three. They loom over one of Cambodia's most fertile plains.

The ancient Cambodians built a great many towers in brick, for reasons unknown to us, but they still used sandstone for the joints and decoration of doors. In certain places, moreover, the walls, now red, reveal thick coats of plaster-mortar, sculpted and modeled to excess.

What we find here, then, are construction methods very different from the ones we know. They are no more characteristic of a period than of a region, for we find instances scattered throughout the centuries, dating back to the temple of Hanchey, which lies north of Kompong Cham and bears on one of its pilasters one of the oldest known inscriptions (sixth century). We have already seen the towers of Angkor Thom, Pre Rup, and Mebon, as well as these here, erected sometime around the tenth century. We have also studied the sanctuary of Wat Phu, located to the north and built with the same materials.

These monuments are not exemplary for these reasons alone. I have often remarked the somewhat excessive decoration of certain groups. At Beng Mealea we found balance, a harmonious distribution. However, the decoration at Lolei and Bakong, as at brick monuments in general, smacks of the prodigious and the neurotic. They represent the rococo in Khmer art.

If the brick walls had been left bare around the lintels, the false doors, and the sandstone pilasters, the details might have taken on a different character. They would have somewhat resembled a wonderful lace neckline on a woman's pleated dress. But the overlaid plaster was nothing but festoons, garlands, finials, and valences. Those towers must have looked like the lard castles that one sees in butcher shops on feast days.

Forgive the vulgar comparison, but it is accurate, and nobody will mistake me for a detractor. From the perspective of science, architecture, or craftsmanship, Lolei and Bakong are still truly prodigious and deserve the same recognition as Angkor. In fact, I shall give an example:

The Khmer lintel is a monolithic block of sandstone about one meter sixty long and fifty centimeters tall. At the Angkor group it generally has a central motif: a monster head. From the mouth issue two garlands, which form a lowered hoop all around the stone. The hoop rests on two broad volutes on the capitals of the two posts. Above and below the garland, in their respective directions, new *rinceaux* fill up the free space. Everything is boldly

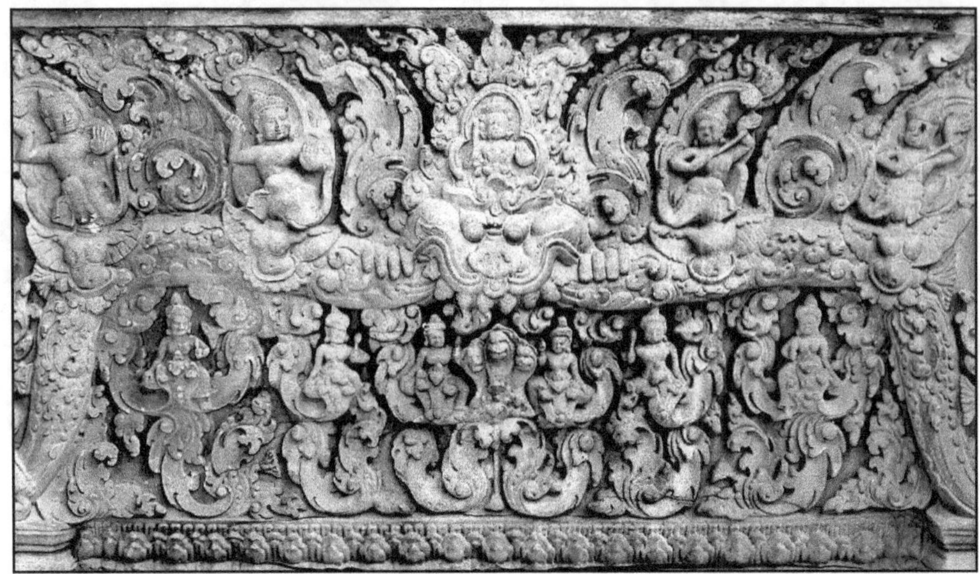

Modern photos (2009) of two Bakong carved lintels. Following Groslier's comment "as if things weren't complicated enough..." note that the lintel above features four large-breasted flying winged *elephants* in frilly skirts!

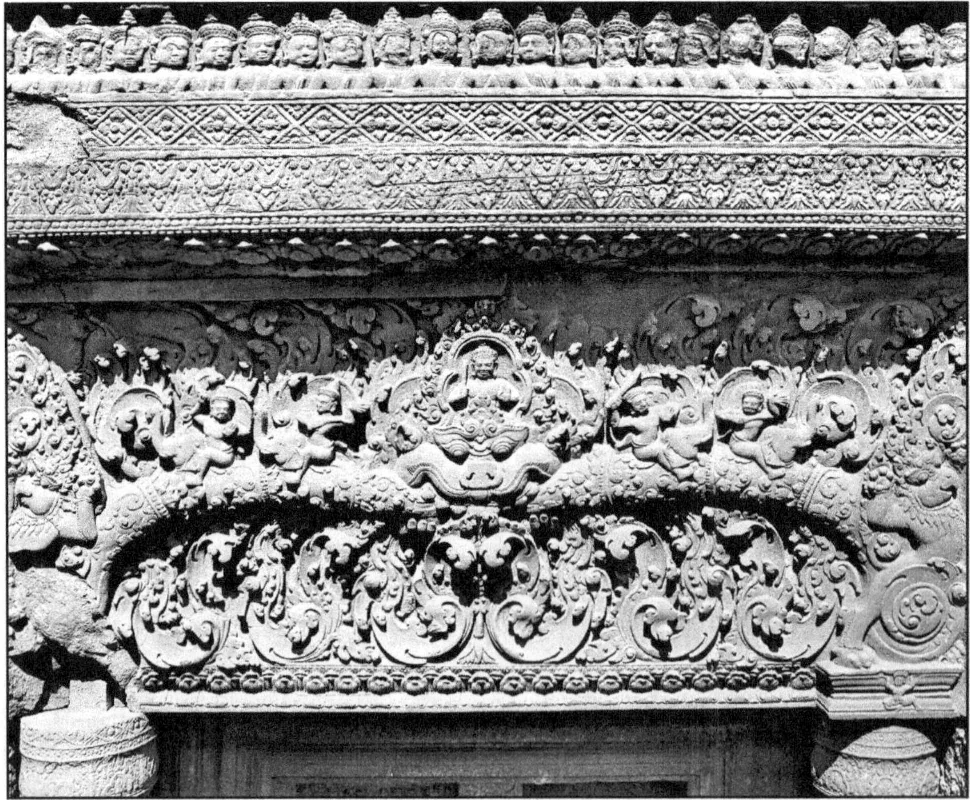

brought forth from the material and admirably handled, with exemplary art and purity. Now note the principle's transformation at Bakong.

The garlands? These are now but *makaras*[37] issuing from one another's mouths. As many mouths as coiled trunks. The body of each *makara*, meanwhile, is replaced by small *rinceaux* and complex vines. Astride each head is a figure holding in his hands a club, a saber, a lotus. From the last *makara* of each extremity issues a *naga*, with its seven hoods spread. The *naga* too is not alone, with another figure riding its neck.

The central motif is a world unto itself. We recognize the monster as the same, but its hands now hold two lions by the hind legs. The lions mingle with the *rinceaux*, and at the center of each *rinceau* is a figure in prayer. Meanwhile, the lower *rinceaux* metamorphose into three-headed *naga*s — a concession to simplicity, for they might have been heptacephalous! However, each head is crowned with a panache of volutes.

Between the *rinceaux-naga*s, though they nearly touch, dangle lotus flowers. And — I nearly forgot — between the lions, under the monster head, a five-headed, central *naga* rears up. The upper space, between the lintel border and the garland of *makara* heads, is filled with lacy, curled leaves that alternate with the *makara* trunks.

As if things were still not complicated enough, the lintels of Bakong are crowned with a small frieze of lotuses and two band moldings, one adorned with lozenge-shaped motifs, the other with a succession of twenty-three torsos with joined hands. The whole covers a little more than a square meter.

If one believes that a snake-man dressed in tinsel, perched atop a pile of bottles, passing his head through his legs, and playing a melody on his violin constitutes plastic beauty, then the art of Bakong is a great art.

---

[37] Author's note: Monster with an elephant's trunk and, in general, a fish's body.

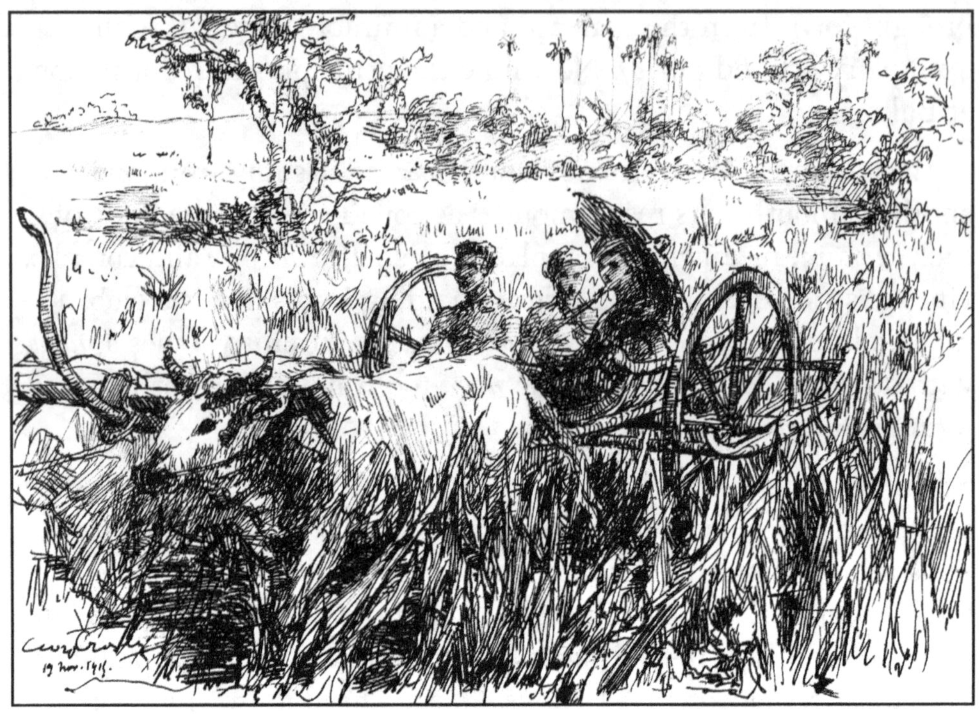

Groslier's charming sketch of an ox cart on Nov. 19, 1911 remains accurate, as seen in the modern 2009 photo below.

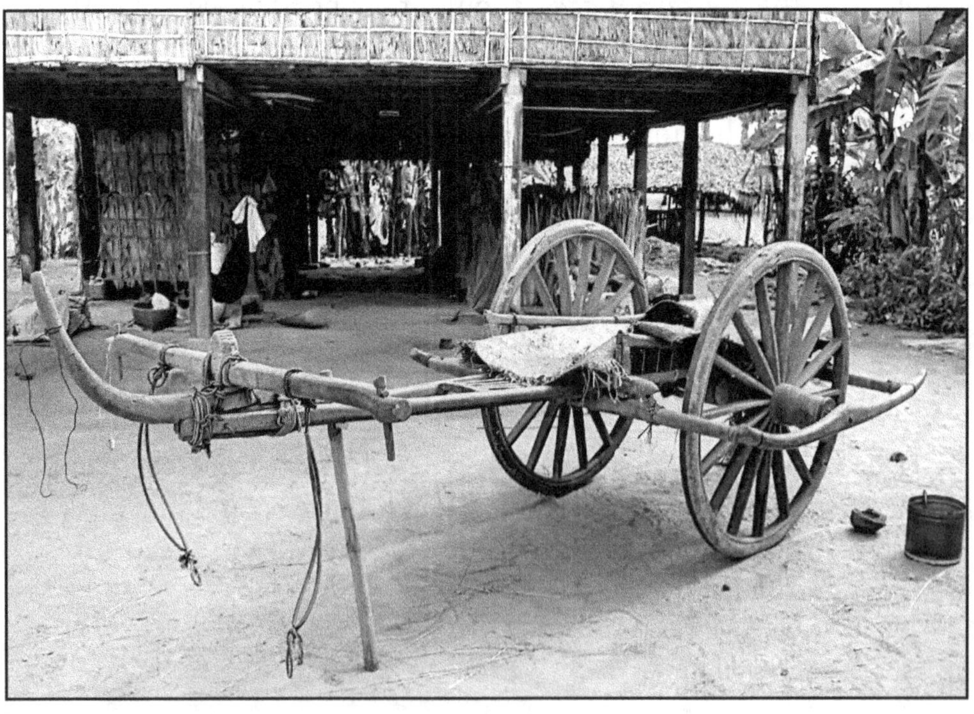

XXXVI

Thursday, December 25, 1913

Christmas night. I have stopped my caravan at some harvested rice paddies. Alone there amid the straw, on a soft threshing floor, stands a light shelter put up by the natives to defend their goods against the birds. A few palms rise up in the distance. A moonless night, resplendent with stars, has fallen suddenly.

My coolies and cart oxen are asleep around the dead fire. An owl has cried out plaintively in search of crabs. And certainly I too, weary, forehead skyward, might find sleep amid such calm and isolation if my mind, prompted by the date, hadn't noted a certain strange character in the ill-defined particulars of this otherwise featureless place.

At another time, in Judea, on a sweet night with a starry sky, at this hour and in a similar landscape, a child was born into this world, and his mother wrapped him in swaddling clothes under a shelter much like this one. Here are the straw and the oxen, the palm trees in the distance. Soon, perhaps, tardy shepherds will arrive. Are we not camped on a well-traveled road, not far from a village? Those near-naked shepherds, expecting no mystery, will pass by with the supreme indifference of their race. But how could their ghostly passage, and the noise of the bells, not bore right into me?! And will my eyes not search ahead of them to pick out the luminous guide?

What has actually happened is much more beautiful. Truly, if the most fortuitous and natural of circumstances can — by succession, chance, coincidence, and the state of one's mind — take on such colors and meaning, then I have come to understand the causes of inspiration and why poets see legend in place of reality.

The light of torches suddenly appeared at the spot where the cart road emerges from the trees. And from the shadows where

I watched I soon made out three — three! — bonzes. The great yellow fabrics draped over them blurred in the flickering light and seemed flecked with gold. They were carrying objects that I could not make out, as Balthazar, Melchior, and Caspar had carried gold, frankincense, and myrrh. They passed and vanished.

Ah! Chase down the magi who have just passed! They cannot have got far. Bring them back. Go to the nearest village and seek out a young mother whose breast is heavy. Let her come with her newborn baby. She will not have the long veils of legend or a head ringed with light, but what does it matter?! You, fix torches to those stilts and prepare the crèche. Gather round in a circle, that the light may play on your faces and shoulders.

Here is the child. Woman, put the child there. The ox has warmed the straw with its breath. Set your gold on the ground, old Melchior. Balthazar, burn a little frankincense. And you, Caspar, pour the myrrh over the child's little feet. And while a hundred countries in solemn feast adore the divine child and sing his praises, let we who are lost in the wilderness, the silence, and the night contemplate this humble reality, which needs such few illusions to seem for us a dream.

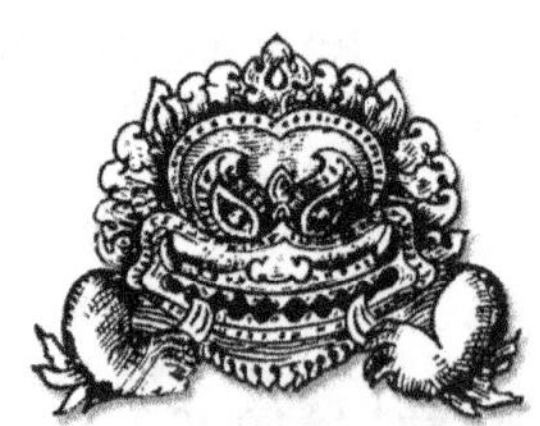

9
Banteay Chhmar

XXXVII

Thursday, January 1, 1914

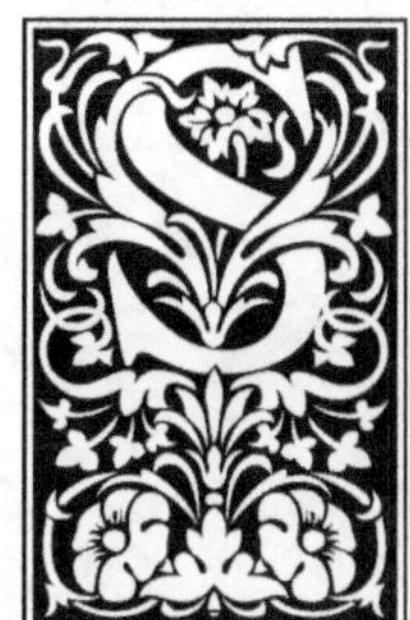

uddenly, as if mechanically triggered, the annual aeolian[38] regimen has established itself. Kites begin to rise from every corner of the kingdom. Rattan straps taut in their frames vibrate in the air like the buzzing of hornets. These light toys shall gently rock the nights, each with its windy, monotone murmur.

For the past three days I have been following the road to Banteay Chhmar, once again heading for the north of the country, toward the Dangrek mountains, where Preah Vihear has already drawn me. But whereas that temple, at the very north of the country, stands atop the great rocky barrier, Banteay Chhmar, in the northwest, has at its foot an endless carpet of glades. Wind and walking oxen raise clouds of sandy dust, which covers us like ash and grinds in our teeth. The broad, sun-dried leaves of the trees fall with a metallic sound.

The roads we travel bear the footprints of the sole living beings that wander these solitudes. We recognize the double crescent of the ox, the ring of the horse, the incisive marks of the deer's nervous hoof. Elsewhere, in spots where the last of the slumbering water has evaporated, the hardened mud shows the slender stars

---

[38] Relating to, caused by, or carried by the wind. From Aeolus, Greek god of the winds.

of wading birds or the broad plowings of wild elephants. And then, atop the rest, near the cart ruts, come the prints of men, children, loyal dogs.

These tracks, erased every morning by the wind and then laid down again, are the whole life of the forest momentarily petrified: the great and fearsome mysteries of night, the earth stirred up by big cats in battle, grasses trod upon as they sleep, and the terrible convergence of tracks at water holes — the age-old tragedy of guile and instinct.

After several hours' march, fixated on and frustrated by that same horizon ceaselessly unfurling ahead, we come suddenly to a crossroads. There are cut trees and a multitude of human footprints: a nearby village, a way station, a little smoke and humanity. A dog barks, and at last, beneath the banana trees, the thatch roofs appear.

XXXVIII

Saturday, January 3, 1914

Angkor was once linked to Banteay Chhmar by a road that the current cart road parallels, cuts, and crisscrosses. These ancient roads that one stumbles upon radiate out from the ancient capital to all the great structures.

Invading trees aside, they have retained their old look. The carts are the same as the carts of old. One rides them along broad earthen levees that dominate the plains from a height of two, three, or sometimes five meters. Traveling thus, one can travel back eight centuries, especially if, like me, one is on a pilgrimage to the temple that stands at the road's end.

The plains undulate to the horizon. The great holes dug to the left and right of these dikes, to supply the earth for them, have become ponds shaded by clumps of trees. From these ponds issue bands of mandarin ducks, egrets, and red-headed cranes. Lotuses and beautiful mauve flowers with pointy petals bloom.

For centuries caravans have drawn water and a little fresh air from these artificial basins. In the forest the road takes on another character. The verdure is more intense, more tangled, alongside the road than in the surrounding area.

At river crossings the old bridges, or their remains, still stand. Almost all are in good condition. Yesterday I crossed the Spean Top, which spans the Stung Sreng. This remarkable bridge is more than 150 meters long and has 27 arches. At low water it clears the river by more than ten meters. The river flows in a torrent between the close-packed piles and falls in a cascade off a step erected downstream by the builders. The banks are steep and the whole superb.

In this region the road crosses a series of small bridges. For the four great ancient roads known to us, we may estimate the number of such artful and refined works at a hundred, all of them adorned with a parapet of *naga*s with spread hoods.

Indeed, the Khmer were not content to erect temples at random. They linked them, for each temple marked an agglomeration. They built vast, decorated reservoirs, with steps, perrons, or piers. They reworked slopes and esplanades, as at Wat Phu, Preah Vihear, and many other places, so as to erect their monuments. They had sewers, like the complicated system of conduits at Angkor Thom. They raised dikes around their cities — or ramparts ringed with moats.

These many displays of industry and ingenuity are never restricted to half-measures but instead always achieve a moving grandeur. Nothing could stand in the way of the Khmer. It is as if they had never even hesitated.

From atop pedestals moist with lustral waters, with the calm smile given them by sculptors, the divinities that inspired these efforts were no doubt satisfied. Land and rock had been stirred up from there to the distant horizon, as delimited by their protective gaze.

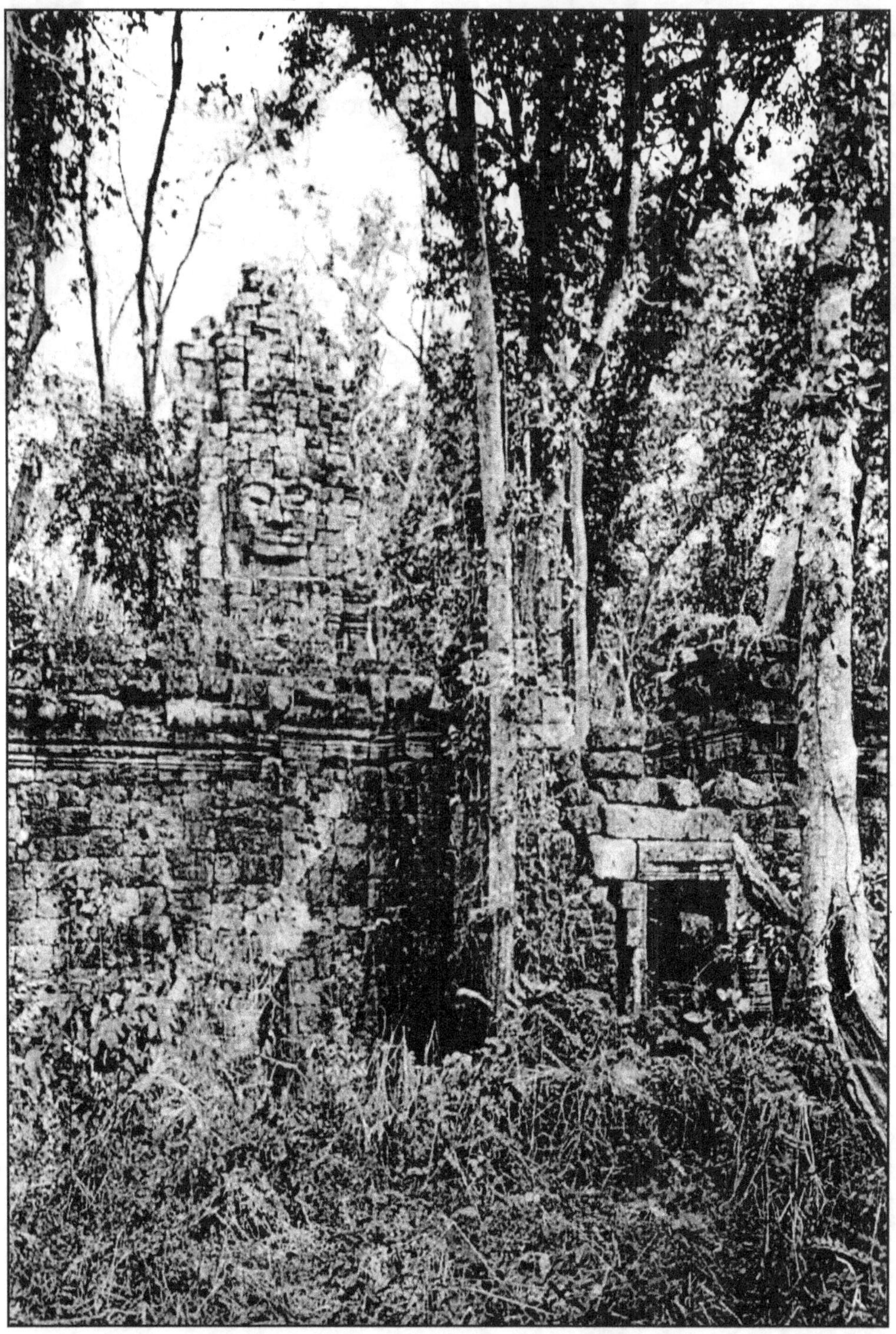

Banteay Chhmar. West wall and four-faced tower (height: 8 m).

XXXIX

Friday, January 9, 1914

It took me ten days of uninterrupted work, from dawn to dusk, to survey Banteay Chhmar. No other temple in Cambodia is so vast or lies in such ruin, and nowhere else have I found so many thorns and brambles. But nowhere else have I felt such deep emotion while studying stones on site and re-erecting them one by one on paper.[39]

This group is one of the oldest in Cambodia, dating back to about the end of the eighth century.[40] It is also, I think, the world's largest temple in area, and the one farthest from Europe. I am now convinced that the original plans were too hastily drawn and are almost entirely erroneous. I shall provide some figures, for only they can carry sufficient eloquence and authority.

A first wall of limonite blocks 4 m high and 60 cm thick forms a rectangle of 830 m east-west by 600 m north-south. It is surrounded by a stepped pit 65 m wide. Outside, 200 m from the four central gates of the outer wall, arranged on extended axes, stand four temples, averaging 25 m by 38 m, and each in turn surrounded by walls and a pit. The temple at the south gate is double. A sixth temple stands some hundred meters from the southeast corner of the huge perimeter wall. All the exterior temples were topped with four-faced towers. Such was the imposing belt of buildings, well worthy of the building we shall now explore.

Roadway-levees 13 m wide, composed of slabs, cross the pits and lead to each axial gate. Giants 2 m tall formerly carried the *naga* parapet. The four gates were once four 8 m towers. *Garuda*s reared up at the corners.

---

[39] For more historical information, additional photos and a site plan see the appendix articles: "Banteay Chhmar: First Automobile Visit by Groslier in 1924" by Darryl Collins; and Groslier's detailed 1937 article "A Khmer Marvel: 'Banteay Chhmar' Ancient Cambodian City."

[40] As with the other temples of King Jayavarman VII, Banteay Chhmar was actually built in the late twelfth or early thirteenth century.

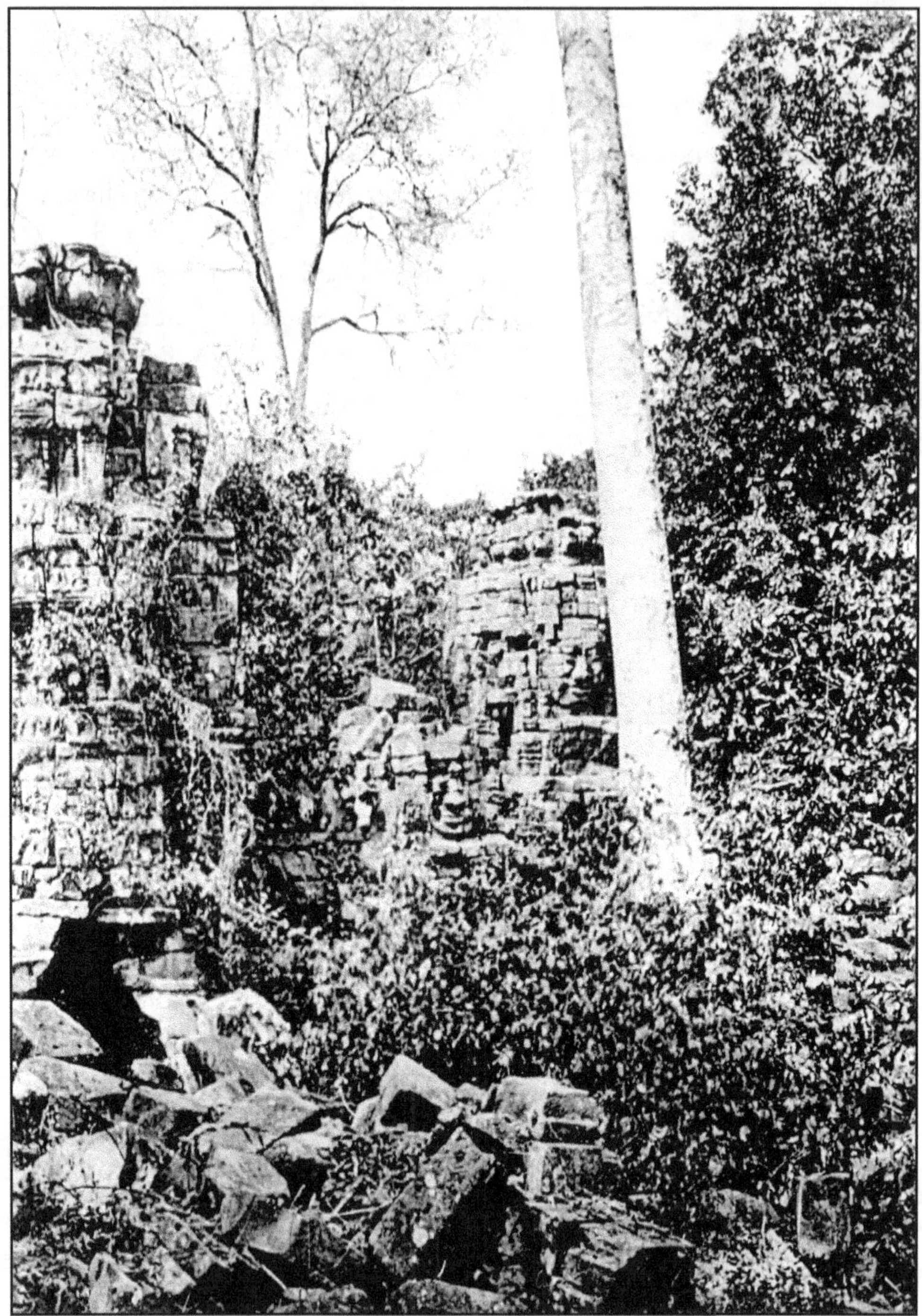

Banteay Chhmar. Set of towers, photographed from the roofs of the central passage (height of tower on left: 12 m).

Entering from the east, we see first, to the right, a vast basin of 60 m, lined with fourteen steps; a new monument; and then a vast, lovely, grass-covered low terrace, its floor strewn with *nagas*. It measured 28.70 m by 25.30 m.

A new wall, comprising a colonnade and its sloped roof. The interior wall is covered, as at Angkor Wat, with a strip of bas-reliefs and 2.60 m high. It measures 249 m east-west and 181 m north-south. Each façade, 56 m long, has a monumental gate comprising three porches and topped with three towers. This living enclosure, swarming with warriors by the thousand and depicting scenes from the lives of the ancient Khmer, has partly collapsed. At each of the four corners, a toppled tower.

And now we penetrate the temple proper. A superb colonnade, with a double sloped roof, traces out the ever-present cross within yet another perimeter wall, of 25 m by 30 m. The frieze, 1.5 m tall and running from column to column, is decorated with an uninterrupted stream of dancers, arms raised, separated from one another by flowers or by *nagas* with spread hoods. The high windows of the outer wall are barred with colonnettes of turned stone.

A new vaulted gallery, squat and dark, 135 m east-west by 55 m north-south, delimits an area of intercut galleries, courtyards colonnaded or cramped, and secondary structures in a complicated arrangement. The vast surface area of all these walls is profusely decorated.

Outside this fantastical, monumental center, but still within the area set out by the colonnade of bas-reliefs, on the north, south, and west axes, arise new towers, ringed by their own galleries and flanked with new structures in alternation with vast, decorated basins.

In the empty spaces — there still are some — walls 33 m long meet at right angles and outline courtyards. Need I say that there are new structures within those courtyards; that to the north and south of the first colonnade stand two aediculae on bases 3.60 m

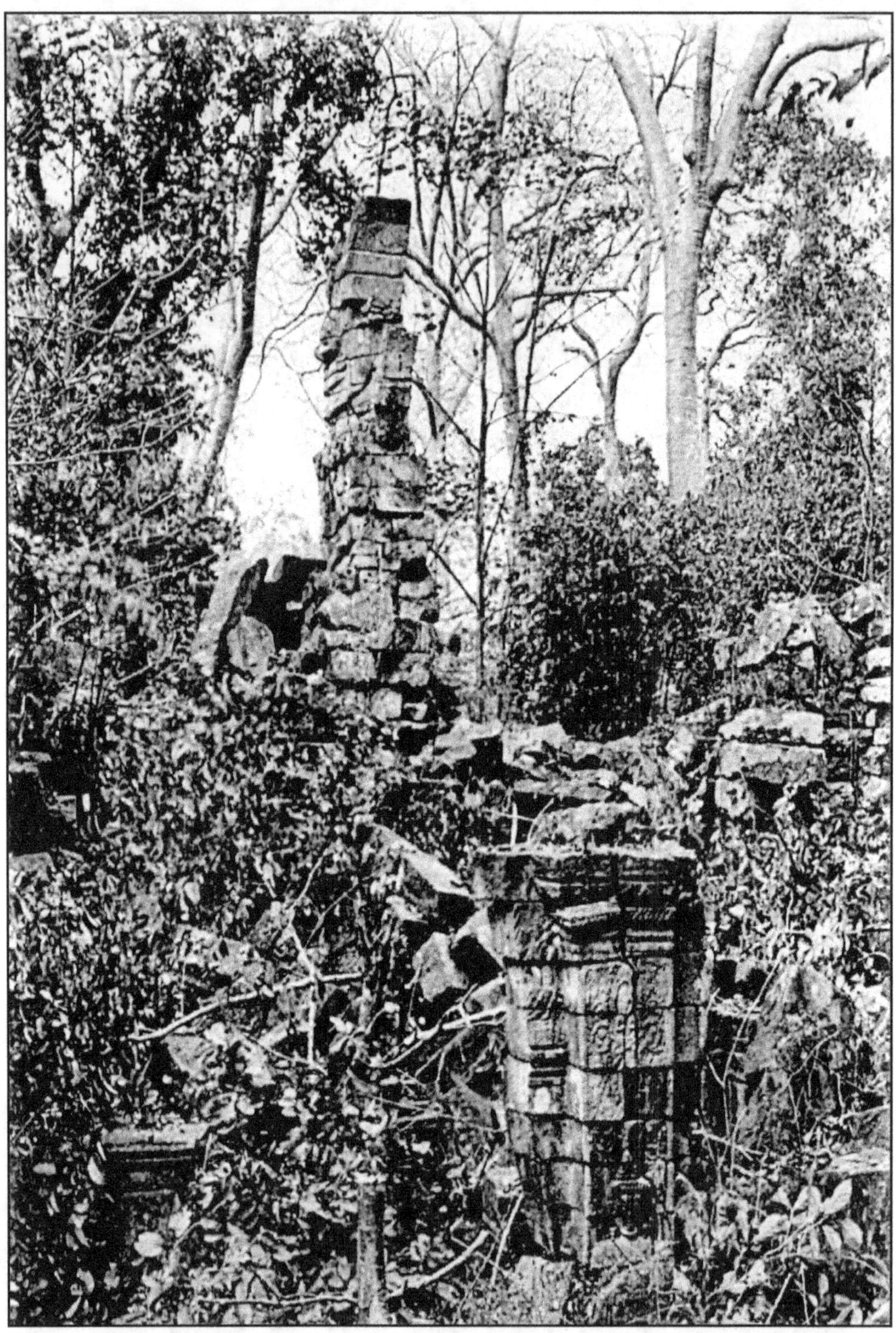

Banteay Chhmar. Remains of a four-faced tower (height: 8 m).

high, on each of which are sculpted forty-nine grimacing giants, their arms raised; that cruciform terraces precede the main gates?

From this whole, which already sets the mind reeling, rose fifty-five towers, half of which showed the same four faces seen at the Bayon. Only three of those towers are limited to 6 m in height. The others vary from 8 m to 14 m. To judge from a still-evident progression, I think that those of the sanctuary were taller still, and have collapsed.

The lowest of the vaulted galleries reached a height of 4.50 m from the slab floor. There are doors and false or walled doors, baluster windows, and false windows everywhere. The base of each tower takes up about 18 m2. This astonishing stone structure rests on a molded base. The whole thing was roofed. At the rickety summit of a tower is a lotus blossom, whence emerges a conical stone, which carries is turn the mortise of a terminal mast.

To the east of this ensemble, beyond the small exterior temple, was dug a reservoir of about 1.5 km by 1 km north-south. The extracted earth forms the outlining dike, walled with steep steps. Dominating its east side is a beautiful stepped terrace, extending 60 m along the east-west axis. On an island at the center of this lake, now but a swamp, stands yet another temple, with a wall of 27 m by 37 m and pits 17 m wide — and, in front, more basins!

To take stock of Banteay Chhmar, the surrounding area, and the preparations for its construction, we must consider it almost certain that five square kilometers of land were cleared and that in effect a rectangle of more than 600 m by 500 m was covered with sculpted stone. Yet the quarries lie more than 20 km away. At present the scrubland extends north all the way to Siam, and the inhabited regions of Cambodia lie at a brisk two-day march across it.

The temple has entirely collapsed. Only about a third of the towers are still standing, and these are but piles of material 8 m or 9 m tall. Whole structures have been sapped. No other temple

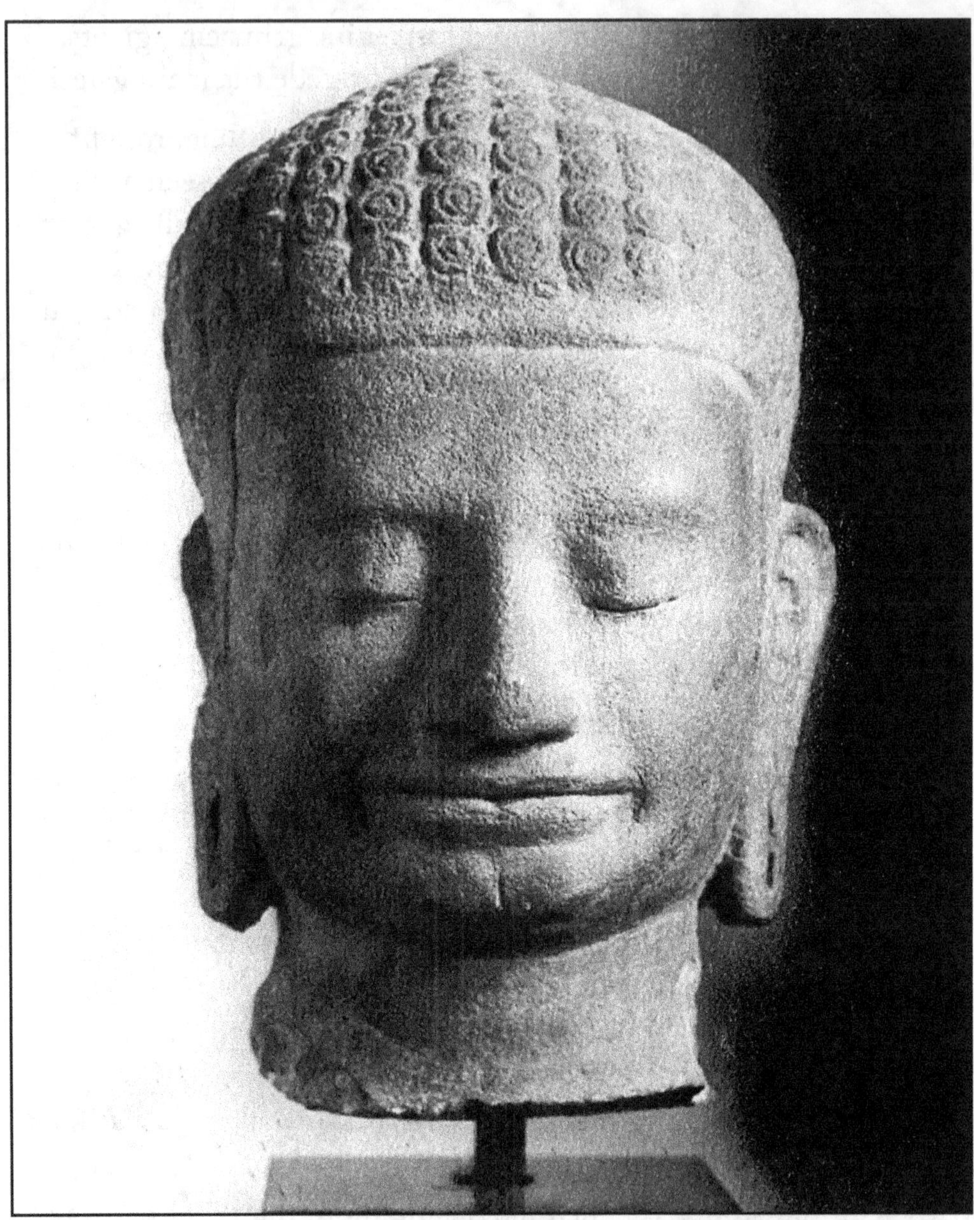

This non-stylized Buddha head found at Banteay Chhmar exhibits a barely noticeable *ushnisha*—the cranial bump at the top of the head symbolizing enlightenment—that is one of the Buddha's 32 attributes of perfection. The unusual cleft chin is also a trait shared by many *devata* (goddess) images at Angkor Wat. Groslier included this photo as Plate XIX in his 1925 work, *Arts et Archéologie Khmers. Revue des Recherches sur les Art, les Monuments et l'Ethnographie du Cambodge, depuis les Origines jusqu'à nos Jours. Vol. II, Parts 1 and 2.* Height: 0.32. Probably ninth century. Unknown origin.

in Cambodia has seen such devastation. Here, aside from the brambles, vegetation is all but absent and cannot have toppled the least part of it.

There has been much work done since initial construction. Connections between galleries have been changed. Here, new doors were opened. There, doors were hermetically walled up. From the plans we can see that certain inner areas could be reached only by complicated detours. Elsewhere doors lead onto doors, their sculpted pediments facing each other across a gap of sixty centimeters. Also, a great many depictions of Buddha mingle amid Brahmanic sculptures.

With the near absence of verdure, the chaos appears savage in the sun, like the aftermath of a storm of stones. The slabs are burning hot all day long. One must advance carefully, for the ruins still shift underfoot. Towers teeter at the critical point of their equilibrium, and it seems as if a noise would topple them. And smiling here and there, amid the devastation of columns lying on their sides and porticos ripped from their walls, are the great, calm faces of the *prasats*.

O formidable god, what is it makes you smile? This death and destruction, or perhaps the memories playing out behind your shut stony eyes?

XL

To this day the accepted idea is that Cambodia was a Hindu colony that owed its past glory and riches entirely to India. There is a general and exclusive focus on Hindu dogma and mythology.

Of course, in maintaining that the country would never have got as far as it did without India, one should not forget — as has too often been the case, in my view — that Cambodia was already fertile ground. With its economic civilization set and its material concerns taken care of, Cambodia was ready for the religious and intellectual speculations inculcated by the elite who made it their land of choice.

Before our time the Chinese would go to Cambodia for commerce and to market their goods, hoping to create a demand that only they could supply. As a result, various native populations were substantially elevated from their savage state. There was an awakening, if you will, to a whole other economic life. It is of singular importance, too, that Chinese — exclusively Chinese — commerce not only flourished throughout the Hindu period but also continues to flourish in the present day, and as a monopoly. In fact, Cambodian stores are virtually unknown in Cambodia.

The Chinese accounts in our possession date back all the way to 222 and continue down through the centuries to the famous account of Zhou Daguan in 1265, by which time the Khmer civilization had already reached its apogee.[41] They testify to this state of affairs and are confirmed by the country's current state.

There is no Cambodian system of weights, for example. The units used here and called by Cambodian names are Chinese in origin. On the bas-reliefs of the Bayon, which date back to the ninth century, I spotted a junk of unquestionably Chinese origin, similar in form, capacity, and rigging to the modern Chinese junks used to transport rice. Cambodia's few industries import most of their raw materials from China. As an example, I shall cite only the vitrified lead used to adorn all pagoda pediments and Buddha pedestals, and imported from the Middle Kingdom at 13 francs for 60 kilos.

In vain would one search a Cambodian hut for any Hindu object whatsoever, just as I have searched for them in vain on temple bas-reliefs. The bed, the water cup, the arms, the rare insignificant objects of hut or temple are those of any primitive people, the same as one would find in Moï country — in a

---

[41] There are two recent Chinese-to-English translations of this important text: In 2007 Silkworm Books released *A Record of Cambodia: the Land and Its People*, translated by Peter Harris. In 2010, Solang and Beling UK released *A Record of Cambodia's Land & Customs*, through Authors Online Ltd with translation refinements based on Khmer language, history and culture.

word, the objects that any man cast naked onto the earth would naturally and immediately hit upon. The huts, the pagodas, and the clothing of Cambodia have nothing Hindu about them. This fact has gone practically unrecognized, and justifies my assertions now.

The necessary arguments would take up too much space here. I shall provide them elsewhere. The thing to remember is that one can travel anywhere in the country without coming across any economic evidence of Hindu origin, but at every step one comes across industries, utensils, clothing parts, and food that are Chinese.

Once that has been established, we come face to face with the monuments. Are they Hindu? They are Hindu in purpose, and they once sheltered Hindu idols. But make no mistake. That is where the family resemblance ends and the wonderful, extraordinary personality of the Khmer people begins. The consequences of common religion and mythology are to be found, say, on pediments, in the appearance there of a *makara* on a tympanum or of a Krishna lifting a mountain to protect his shepherds. In truth, these depictions simply had to be there, for we know that the Khmer lacked religion and mythology.

But the monuments are laid out in a manner different from that of Hindu structures. They are even opposed in concept, for the chief principle of Hindu architecture demands a diminution in the height of towers as they approach a sanctuary. Khmer towers gradually get taller as they approach the holiest spot.

Such divergent views of overall and fundamental design are rather suggestive. From the standpoint of decoration and effect, the Khmer way does not fail to be preferable, for it shows the crowd not a gate and wall that hide the rest but, rather, a totality of progressively ordered structures.

These observations run counter to generally admitted ideas, because learned pens are accustomed to writing, all too often, of the Hindu temples of Cambodia.

What was there in India in the sixth century, when the first stone buildings were erected in Cambodia? The question is all the more upsetting because there was nothing to bear comparison. The Hindu temples that predate the Cambodian temples were but reworked caves, sculpted in the rock. They were doubtless superb, but not the slightest memory of them is to be found in Cambodia. Vast stupas, which also predate Cambodia's heroic age, have come down to us from Gandhara: hemispherical stupas crowned with five-story stone parasols, of which not a single faint echo exists in Khmer country.

If, then, the Hindu architect inculcated his science in the Khmer worker, why did he not transmit the architectural principles reigning in India for centuries? Moreover, how did he transmit building plans and techniques that he himself had never used, that he never would use, and that were no doubt unknown to him?

It therefore seems that the Cambodian builder was left to his own devices when he erected the monuments that would ensure his fame. How did he go about it? He went about it as all primitive peoples with limited means go about building in stone: that is, through the simple copying and enlargement of their wooden house.

We are already familiar with this wooden house. It figures in the bas-reliefs and has survived down to the present day. This, then, is the capital and definitive solution to the problem: from Banteay Chhmar to Angkor Wat, we find the same interlocking roofs, superposed gables, offset gates, frame windows placed at the correct height for a man sitting on the floor, and the gallery-colonnades — all features of the wooden house.

Beyond recognizing these particular forms, we see stones treated as if they were boards and joists! If not for an inability among Cambodians to conceive of anything else, why do we find, from the first century to the last, this lack of development in their architecture? If we admit this inability, then may we not reasonably claim that the Hindus found, in addition to a flourishing economy, an extant architecture in Cambodia, and that their chief contribution was the substitution of stone for wood?

Thanks to the Hindus, then, the Khmer genius was made immortal. They made extreme demands upon it. They imposed not new formulas but pretexts and new means of expression. All I can do here to conclude is repeat the sentence written earlier to open the discussion: Khmer temples are Hindu only in purpose. The claim that Hindu architects were behind their construction is mere word play, for we now know that those architects, whoever they were, did nothing but copy the local houses, respecting their arrangement and look. It was the French who erected the silver pagoda in Phnom Penh fifteen years ago. Need we call its architecture French?

I shall conclude these overall views — though at present regarded with mistrust, they are the summation of a hundred minute observations, a hundred concordant facts, which can give rise only to special or technical discussions — with some new inquiries, focused this time on the purely Hindu heritage of the Cambodian people.

Where ought we to find traces of this heritage? In religious and mythological matters, of course, and the traces are many. The Rāmāyana and Mahabharata are the national poems, to which the Cambodians have made only the slightest changes. The Hindu pantheon is evident under all the Khmer names. The language includes a great number of words from Sanskrit and Pali, intact or corrupted, and generally relating to religion, worship, philosophy, and the monarchy. The harp of the Khmer bas-reliefs is the same as that of the stupa balustrades of Gandhara. The jewelry of the sacred women of Angkor can be traced directly to India.

In sum, the Cambodia of the heroic age has a plainly primitive and native basis. That basis is obvious if we factor in, on the one hand, the state of the economy and everything Chinese that comes along with it and, on the other, the country's intellectual state and everything Hindu that comes along with that.

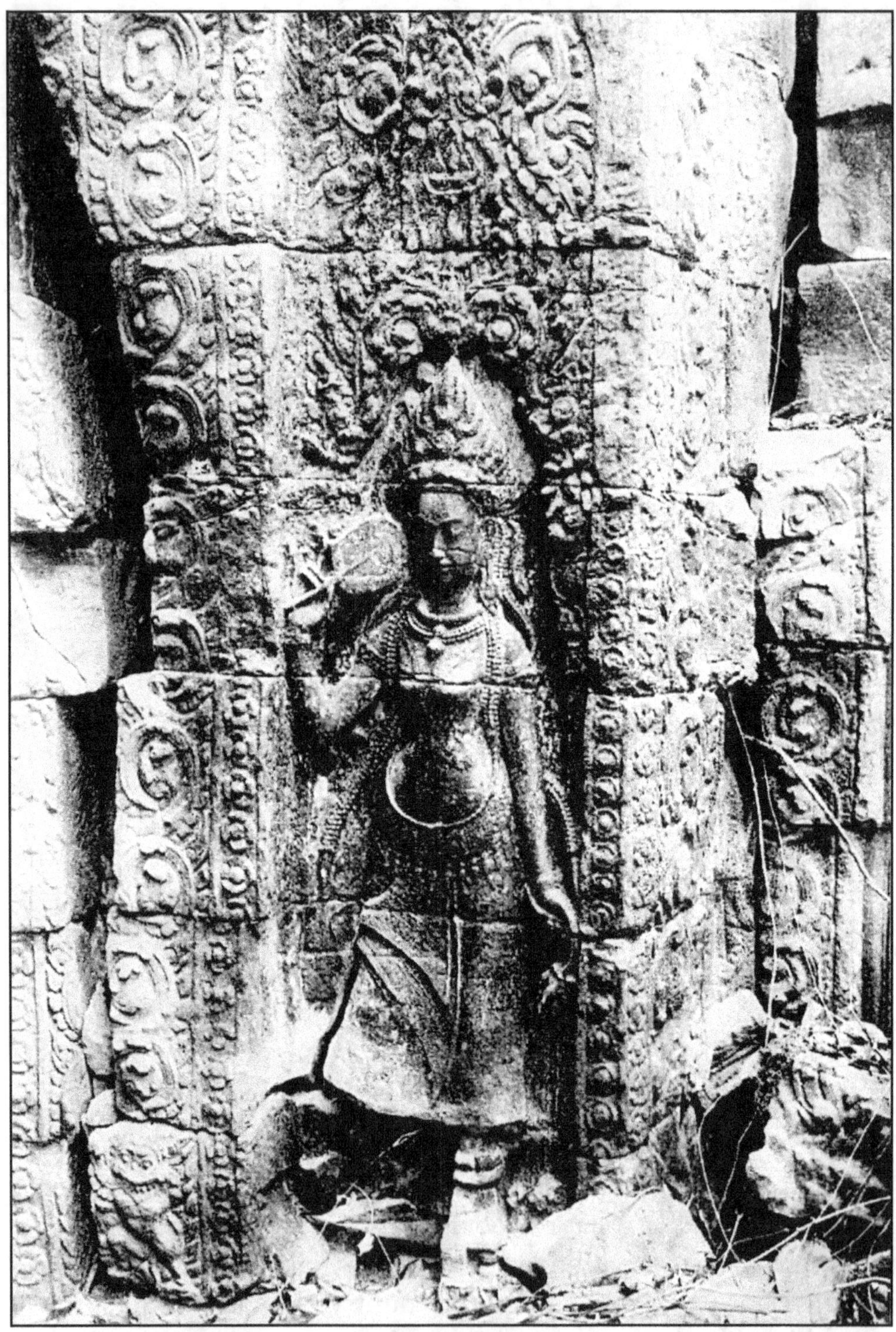

One of the numerous *devata* nymphs on the walls of Banteay Chhmar.

Made possible by the Chinese, inspired and exalted by the
Hindus, Khmer art emerges in all its originality. It invents that
unique being the *naga*, the four-faced tower, the *Garuda*-caryatid,
the terraces-on-columns of Beng Mealea, the roofs of Wat Phu —
a hundred elements that may be ranked among the most beautiful
creations of universal art.

XLI

It is no more possible to follow the chronological development
of Khmer art than it is to deduce inviolable rules for it.
Epigraphy has provided us with the construction date for many
temples, and I have often noted the disparity between these dates
and the dates required for any logical artistic progression.

If we begin with the near-certainty that the Khmers could not
and did not build with stone before their Hinduization, because
nothing remains of the pre-Hindu period, it seems possible
to follow in the succession of monuments a vague, gradual
refinement that could ground the development of a science that
began at square one.

From one end of the country to the other, the same errors
appear. There are no advances in construction. Moreover, many of
the most beautiful bits of sculpture are to be found in groups that
epigraphy has classed among the earliest, whereas at Angkor Wat,
the most recent temple, the corresponding bits — the *devatas*, for
example — are strikingly inferior.[42]

We are faced with a considerable number of monuments —
Preah Khan, Ta Prohm, Preah Vihear, Banteay Chhmar — all
of grand dimensions, that resist arrangement in any progressive

---

[42] Dating error aside, Groslier's opinion seems to contradict the evidence: the 1,800 *devata* at
Angkor Wat clearly represent the pinnacle of this spiritual and artistic Khmer concept. The *devata*
in all the other temples combined do not equal them in quantity, and only a small percentage of
those outside of Angkor Wat can compare in complexity, variety, and technical execution. Even
King Jayavarman VII, the most prolific Khmer builder who followed Suryavarman II, did not
enshrine as many *devata* in all his temples as those in Angkor Wat alone. Visit www.Devata.org
to examine images of the various types to draw your own conclusions.

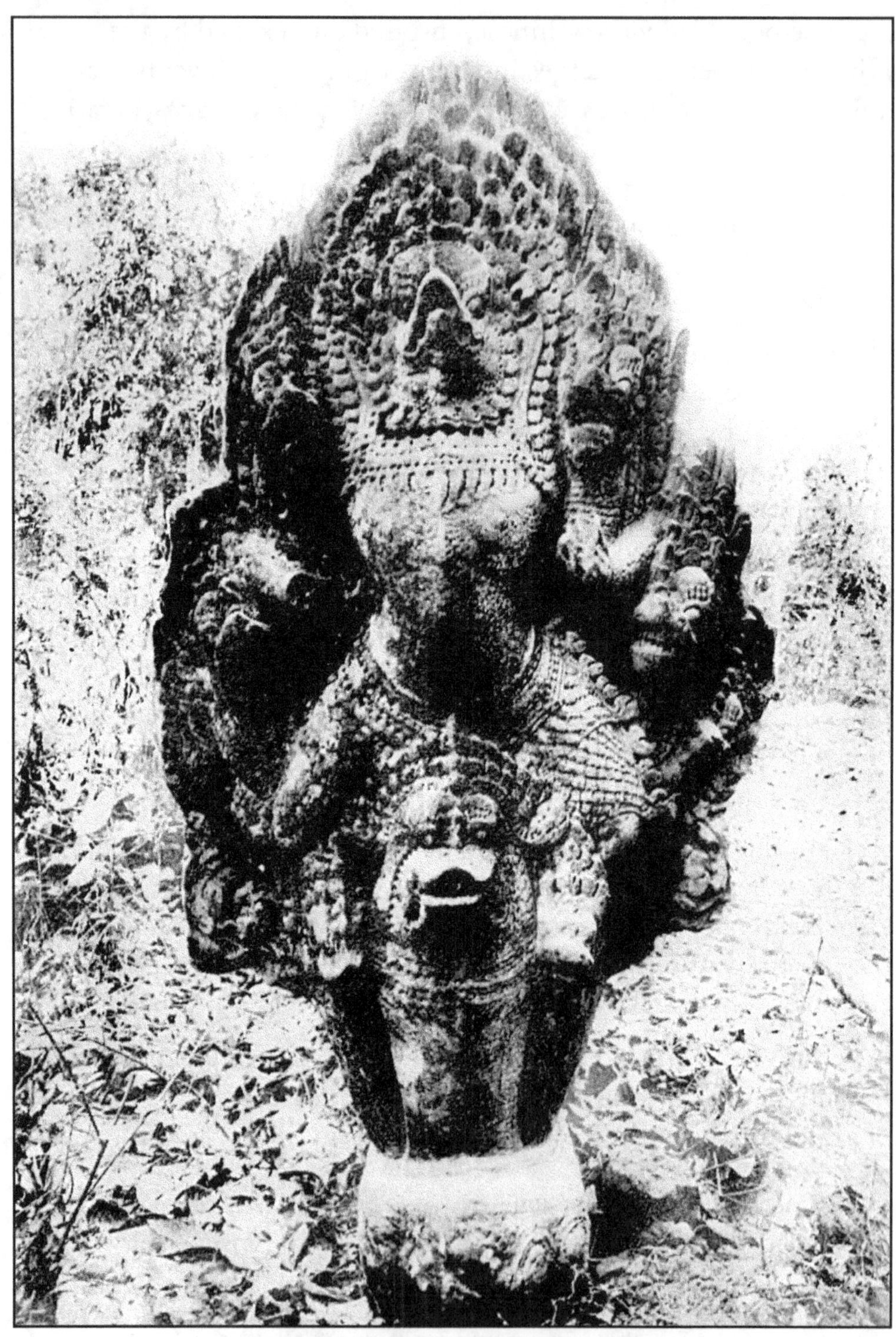

Garuda straddling *naga* at Banteay Chhmar.

scheme. They seem contemporaneous, their art identical in execution, inspiration, and composition, but their inscriptions assure us that four centuries elapsed during their construction.

We might try to find our way through this labyrinth and discover on these flowery walls some decorative element whose appearance in a certain temple will allow us to situate that temple in some logical scheme, as coming before or after some other. I have found nothing of the sort.

All the temples contain the same *rinceaux*, the same flattened leaves, the same rosettes, unevenly executed, and reliefs that vary within the same group. On the bas-reliefs of Banteay Chhmar figures the same scene of heaven and hell, depicted and laid out in the same way, as at Angkor Wat. We find the same four-face towers, as well as *Garuda*s at the corners of the wall gates, at Banteay Kedei and at the enormous temple that we have just visited.

Devata-caryatids support the bases of the great terrace of Angkor Thom. We have mentioned similar ones at Banteay Chhmar. Particular lintels formed of dancers occur both at Preah Khan and at Ta Prohm. Giants carrying a *naga* adorn the dikes of Angkor Thom and of Banteay Chhmar alike. Small structures with false half-vaults can be found just about everywhere. Equally prevalent, I have found, are sacred guardians, their hands resting on cudgels.[43] On the three enormous successions of bas-reliefs that went into adorning Banteay Chhmar, the Bayon, and Angkor Wat at intervals of two centuries, there is no particular object, ornament, costume, or jewel in one group that does not figure in all the others. I could list them for pages and pages. And if slight differences of interpretation or conception are nevertheless found, they are such as to defy any attempt to situate them in some chronology.

The Bayon and Angkor Wat are pyramidal. Suppose we therefore conclude that they represent an architectural and decorative

---

[43] At the Hindu and Buddhist temples of South and Southeast Asia these guardians are called *dvarapalas.*

advance over the flat monuments. Any system that we try to base on this supposition collapses immediately. Banteay Chhmar includes a pyramidal group of remarkable effect, whereas Beng Mealea, Angkor Wat's near contemporary, is entirely flat.

Shall we say that the laws of Khmer decoration, in keeping with the great universal principle of going from the simple to the complex, have complicated the decorative elements as these elements have aged? If so, we fall into error. I have already mentioned the fantastic lintels of Bakong and Lolei. Though earlier, they are ten times more complicated than those at Angkor Wat. We have noted the simplicity of Beng Mealea, though it is certainly later than all the other groups. From Banteay Chhmar onward, we find the *naga* straddled by *Garuda*, whereas the *naga* at Bakong is thick and coarse. It is quite obvious that the opposite system, from the complicated to the simple, is equally inapplicable.

I had momentarily thought that the monuments' decorative sculpture, in keeping with architectural demands, had become more and more superficial as the structures multiplied. I found too many counterexamples to persist with that idea. If archaeological conclusions are to carry their full value, they must follow from arguments that are beyond question. One hesitation, one challenge, a sole exception can topple everything.

And thus, after years of study, at the sites themselves, with almost two thousand photographs, methodical notes of the bas-reliefs, and surveys in hand, my tentative conclusion is that no conclusion is possible. In my view it is impossible, with the current state of knowledge, to set out the development of the Khmer arts. Stumble onto any clue whatsoever, and immediately, in the same place, another clue appears to call the first into question.

This remark has its importance and its causes. The causes are known, but they have hitherto been considered mere unempirical supposition. The imbroglio now raises them to the status of facts, for it was the empirical observation of the causes that provoked the imbroglio in the first place.

The inconsistency of decoration in single temples, and the way the remarkable rubs elbows with the clumsy, are, as we can easily imagine, due to the variety of artists necessary to erect a monument, and not to a succession of periods. A sculptor working in the year 900 could very well have been more skilful than another working a hundred years later. We lack a transformation in the art to guide us, but differences in craft provide no substitute.

Could we perhaps adopt the method of carefully comparing the best sculptures of all the temples? No more than any other. Imagine, for example, a temple lying in some remote part of the country. The capital, home of the court and important personages, attracts all the best artists, because it offers the best pay. As a result, the distant temple, though contemporary with some other erected near Angkor, turns out to be inferior, for lack of good artists.

What are the causes of Khmer art's singular fixity, its tendency to remain the same from the earliest to the latest period?

Rivalries, differences between the various parts of the kingdom, and even the different races that populated them might have hampered the logical development of a single school. Mixtures, influences, leaps ahead, and reversions lay behind the lack of unity and regular progress in art, despite the steady uniformity of religion, politics, and convictions. The number and grandeur of the monuments, their hasty and successive construction, speak only to the desire of a ruling class that would yield before nothing and was subject only to the fluctuations of a recently introduced theogony.

If we include what I said in the previous chapter, have we not now accounted for the disparity between the mediocrity of the actual construction and the splendor of the design? The construction was the work of an obscure, resistant, steadfast people of deep-seated impulses, and the design was drawn up by an aristocracy that knew how to instill passion in its artists, how to set them soaring. Have we not now accounted for the flight that redeems the architecture's poverty?

True, the intellectual and religious Hinduization of Cambodia did not occur overnight. From the remote past of its slow penetration no structures survive, no decorative motif whose distant apparition, certified by history and epigraphy, can provide us with a specific starting point.

How, concurrently with the literature that was definitely introduced in the sixth century, and from which they drew inspiration, did the originally Hindu elements of the Khmer decorative art become transformed in Cambodia?

How were they adapted to brains still nascent and primitive?

By what trials and errors did stone succeed wood?

These are great questions, whose solutions lie tangled in a transformation of the people. The results are such as one would search the world in vain to find an analog.

From a purely plastic standpoint, the problem seems to me perfectly clear. The phases during which stone replaced wood are easy to discern. In fact, I have pointed them out.[44] Here I shall limit myself to saying that, in plan, elevation, and section, a Khmer monument in stone can be executed in exactly the same way, and in every detail, in wood, and that the treatment of sandstone shows aspects of craft peculiar to the treatment of wood.

When they took to sculpting stone, Khmer artists had already been marvelous sculptors of wood since distant times unknown to us. They spontaneously used common age-old principles and all

---

[44] In the original edition Groslier cites *Recherches sur la vie des anciens Cambodgiens, d'après les bas-reliefs et les documents*, at the time a work in progress. In 1921 the Parisian publishing house Challamel issued the completed work: *Recherches sur les Cambodgiens d'après les textes et les monuments depuis les premiers siècles de notre ère*. The 432-page volume includes 200 photos and 1,153 original drawings by the author, all drawn from Groslier's work in Cambodia in 1909–14 and in 1917–20.

aspects of the purely decorative art. The builders were beginners, but the sculptors merely changed their scaffolds.

The builders came from the requisitioned people, the ignorant people, whom it was impossible to train, to instruct. Hence the perpetual mediocrity of their work. But the sculptors, with their superior nature and fertile imaginations, were capable of drawing inspiration directly from the sources. Hence the rare splendor of their work. A few paragraphs earlier we came to these same conclusions by different paths.

The first stone monuments were being raised in Cambodia and in India, the source of Cambodia's literature and religion, at the same time, doubtless because the two countries had long before established steady relations and blended their intelligence. What is most remarkable, however, is that the synchronism between the two peoples ends there, as I have said, and that their arts and architectural ideas diverge.

Cambodia thenceforth displayed something peculiar to itself, something personal. The Hindu and the Khmer, though different races, had lit their torches at the same hearth, at the same time, and had then gone their separate ways. There is no question that the savage race carried their torch higher than the ancient civilized race from which they were tributary. What a fine example of genius, faith — and enthusiasm!

With such a flourishing — and if we take into account all that I have summed up above — why should we be surprised to find neither method nor kinship but superior acts from the very beginning? Why be surprised at an art that seemed new but that in fact already possessed its formulas and craft when it was transferred to sandstone?

What we are dealing with, finally, is men who would scatter seed, flower, and fruit simultaneously. They would not gather their lotus stem by stem with the passing seasons. No. They had been gathering their lotus by the armful from birth.

Deft or clumsy, everyone brought along his chisel. Neither skill nor method, but genius and craft. This art is the honey of all sorts of bees. It is like a vague murmur. And if beauty can do without rules and method; if it is the essence of man's heart and soul made manifest; if it must blossom to the last bud, resisting all efforts to restrain or master it — it has found in Cambodia the vital principle, the generous air, the sunlight, and the fervent hands that it absolutely required, and that perhaps no other country has ever possessed to such a degree.

Epilogue

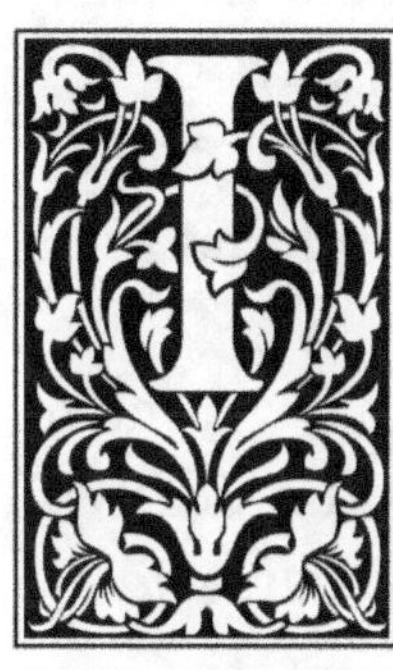I must for a time suspend the mission bestowed on me in Cambodia by the Minister of Public Education and the Fine Arts and return to Phnom Penh, to put my notes in order.

The country's current capital is so poor in the stuff with which I have tried to entertain the reader that I cannot bring myself to write another line outside the lovely solitudes of my expedition, far from the stones I so love.

It has seemed necessary to draft these pages during the actual stages of my journey, from the thick of what they describe. The general public, ill informed about Cambodian history and fascinated by Angkor alone, might welcome the resulting book as more interesting, and more moving, than those big, cold, forbidding technical tomes, or so I have imagined.

Though dispatched as an observer on a meticulous, long, and difficult job, I could not for a moment forget who truly I was. While taking a break from my labors, or after nightfall, with my schematics neatly copied and the results of my research dutifully recorded, I felt an unshakeable need for communion with that great, impartial confidant known as the public, a need to express freely the emotions of one of its children, lost amid such natural surroundings and such history.

Style has sometimes betrayed my ideas, sometimes hampered them. May my book find indulgent readers! Is it really possible to keep your head under such circumstances, when scruples bid you to ignore itchy impatience and juvenile curiosity and record the architecture, take the measure of stones, and determine differences of elevation? On such occasions it was a joy for me to break free of my strict archeological program.

Certain information in this volume will, I believe, allow the curious to form a fairly accurate picture of what Cambodia was and what is has become. My technical research and my long days of exploration and labor make but a scant appearance in this journal, but for the general ideas therein they at least provide a foundation that should not be dismissed without thorough analysis. My research either confirms certain rather vague data that have come to be regarded as fact or rebuts them. It was conducted methodically and embraced broad views, views from which the vague data did not necessarily derive.

Above all, let it be noted that Cambodia is the hospitable country *par excellence*. Its climate is hot but not infernally so. Its people are kindly. Whosoever can live a normal life of work and sobriety shall find it a perfectly healthy place. In short, it is an incomparable field of action. Here every human faculty can find grist for its mill.

The shadow of Angkor, beautiful and sweet, so alive with memories, that heroic shadow, extending so far, smiles on all artists. May they make their way to it, or plan to, and think of it often, so that it might set their imaginations soaring and drive them to study other examples of the genius of men.

George Groslier
Angkor Wat
Thursday, January 22, 1914

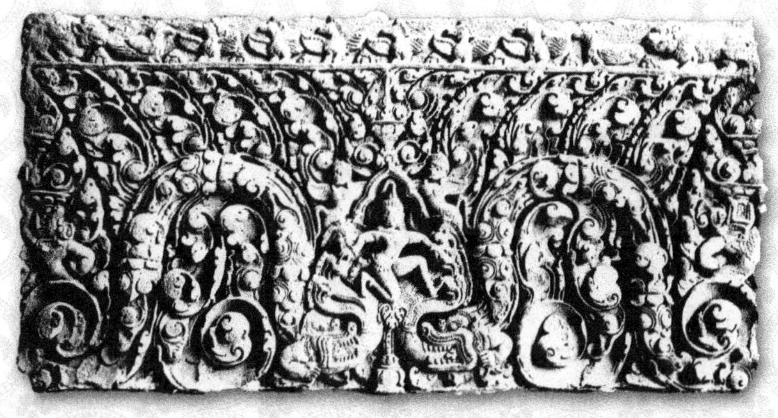

Appendices

Expedition Timeline: 1913-1914

The dates and locations below reflect the dates assigned by George Groslier for each general area.

1913	
June 6	Mekong
June 15-19	Wat Phu
July 12	Tonle Repou (river branch towards Preah Vihear)
July 25-29	Walking 50 km to the foot of Preah Vihear
Aug 2-3	Preah Vihear
Sep 2-15	Angkor
Nov 2-18	Angkor
Nov 20	Angkor Thom
Nov 23	Preah Khan
Nov 27	Dance at Angkor Wat
Nov 28	Ta Phrom
Dec 2-5	Beng Mealea (2 weeks)
Dec 11	Loley, Bakong
Dec 25	En route from Bakong to Banteay Chhmar
1914	
Jan 1	En route to Banteay Chhmar
Jan 2	Spean Top bridge
Jan 3	Banteay Chhmar (10 days of surveying)
Jan 9	Banteay Chhmar
Jan 22	Angkor Wat

Photo Index

This modern edition of *Shadow of Angkor* is enhanced with many images not included in the author's original edition. The editor is indebted to Nicole Groslier and the Groslier family for granting access to their personal collections, and to Joel Montague for contributing images from his archive, some of which are extracted from his book, *Picture Postcards of Cambodia 1900-1950*, published in 2010 by White Lotus Press. Vintage engravings from Albert Tissandier's, *Cambodge et Java Ruines Khmères et Javanais 1893-1894* and images from the DatAsia archive have also been added to improve the visual impact of George Groslier's account.

Photo Credits:
George Groslier [GG]; Nicole Groslier [NG]; *Cambodge et Java* [CJ]; Montague Archive [MA]; DatAsia Archive [DA].

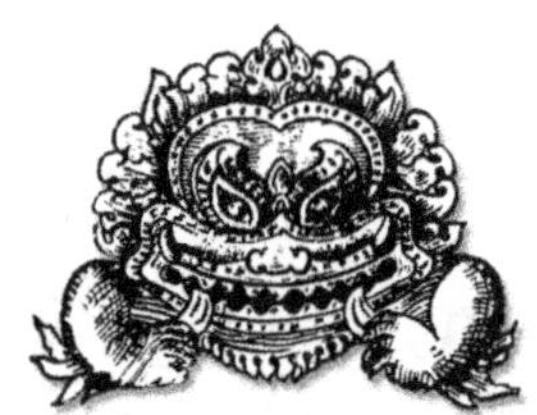

Banteay Chhmar:
First Automobile Visit by
Groslier in 1924

Darryl Collins - Independent Scholar
www.darryl-siemreap.com
All images © Copyright - The National Museum of Cambodia

In early March 1924, an automobile entourage had already passed through Battambang, Mongkol Borei and Sisophon before arriving at Banteay Chhmar. Photographs - possibly taken by George Groslier[1] (1881-1945) himself, of governors' residences, schools, a post office[2] and court witness their passage en route to Banteay Chhmar.

However, it is most likely the photograph of the arrival of the motorcade on the 9 March 1924 was restaged for posterity as a wooden glass-plate camera and tripod would almost certainly have travelled as part of the on-board luggage. Presumably the camera was positioned, and either a mechanical timer used, or someone on hand recorded this event. Parts of a glass-plate camera (possibly

---

[1] In 1924, Groslier was in charge of the then Musée Albert Sarraut (now the National Museum of Cambodia) that was officially inaugurated in April 1920.

[2] The post office at Svay Sisophon was originally among a number of telegraphic and postal services handed over by Siam to the French colonial administration at the time of retrocession of the provinces of Battambang, Sisophon and Siem Reap in 1907.

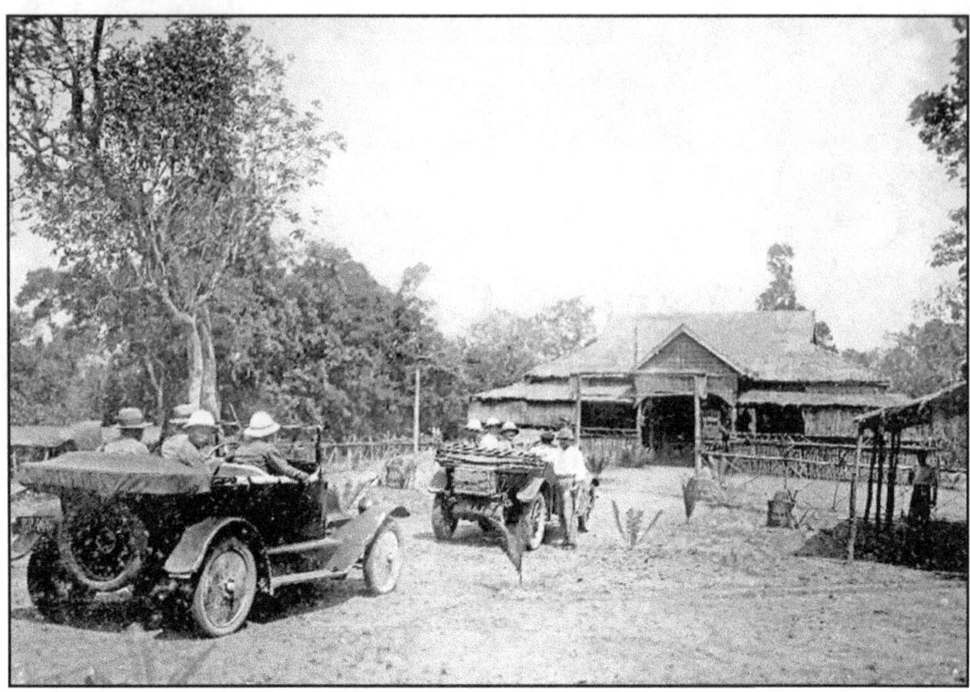

**Arrival at Banteay Chhmar, the first cars to reach the temple;
March 9, 1924.**

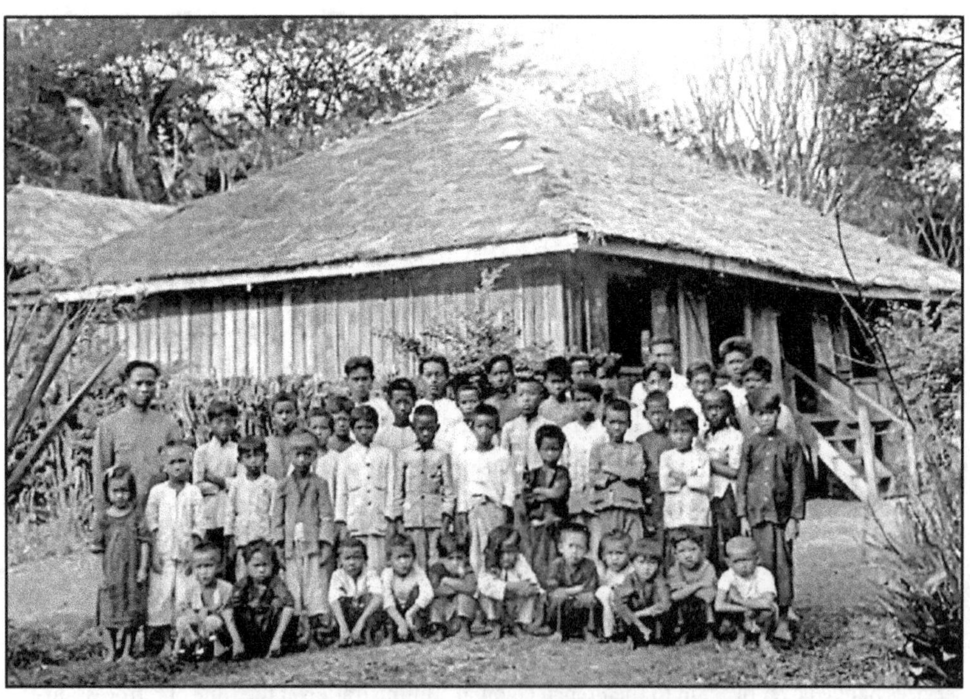

School, teacher & students at Sisophon in 1924.

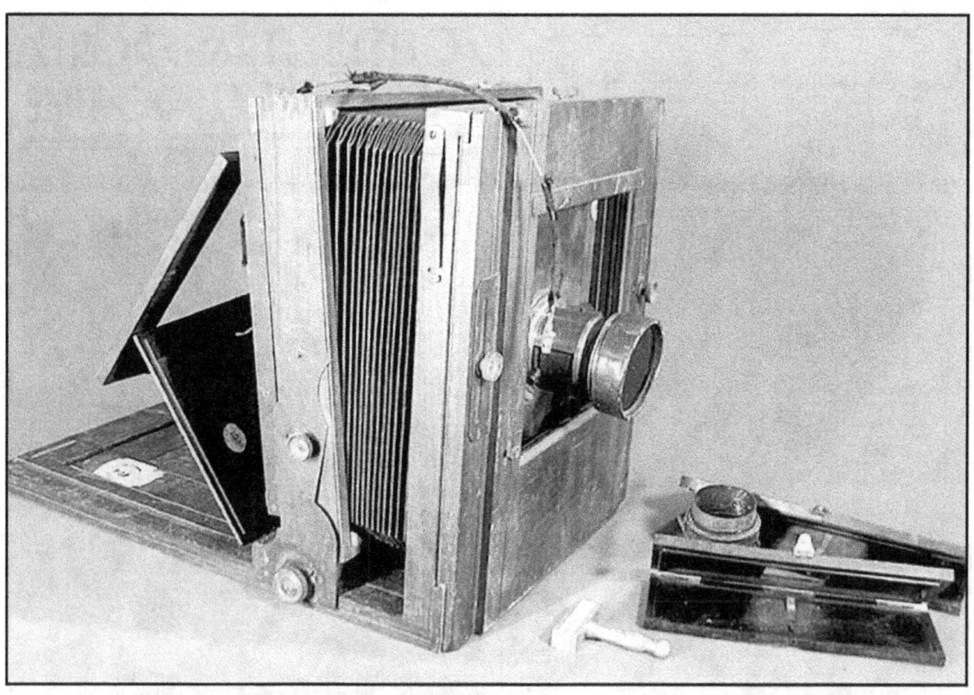

**Incomplete glass-plate camera (equipment possibly used by George Groslier)
Collection: National Museum of Cambodia.**

equipment used by Groslier), remain in the collection of the
National Museum of Cambodia.

A hand-written caption under the image states *'Arrivée à Banteai
Chhmar des premières automobiles parvenues au temple'*: stamped and
dated 'Mars 1924', is further registered as 'H181; Dim (Sunday)
9-3-1924'.

The cars display numbered licence plates: P.P.466 (rear vehicle)
and P.P.72 (front vehicle).[3] A car expert has suggested that

"the PP466 car looks to be very similar to an early 1900-29
Renault (French-made); the identifying feature being the unusual
engine bonnet, which had the radiator behind the engine on the
firewall, rather than up front behind the grill. However, I have

---

[3] P.P. presumably standing for Phnom Penh; these vehicles were most likely rented for the occasion;
automobile taxi services commence operations slightly later in Phnom Penh on 1 May 1925.

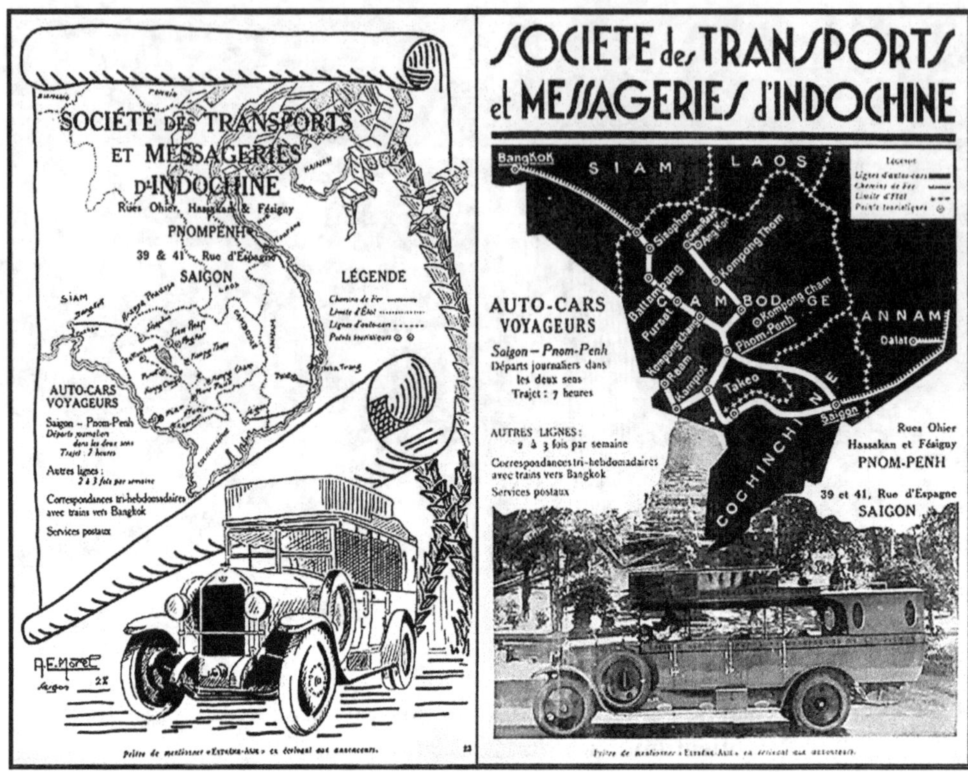

Advertisements: Sociéte des Transports et Messageries d'Indochine;
Phnom Penh-Saigon: Auto-cars voyageurs. 1928 (left) and 1930 (right).

found other French manufacturers La Buire and Clement-Bayard also used this design around this time."

Further, "on a second look at these cars I noticed that the car nearest to the camera has solid steel wheels which dates this car closer to 1924, the other with wire spokes, probably a little earlier."[4]

Advertisements for auto-cars (1928 & 1930) include maps depicting routes ex Phnom Penh via Sisophon across the Siamese border to the rail-head at Aranyaprathet. The trip in 1924 would have been a hot and arduous one, as the temple lies some 60km from Sisophon, and even today can only be reached by an uneven dirt road.

---

[4] Quotes courtesy Gordon McPherson, vintage car enthusiast, Adelaide, South Australia.

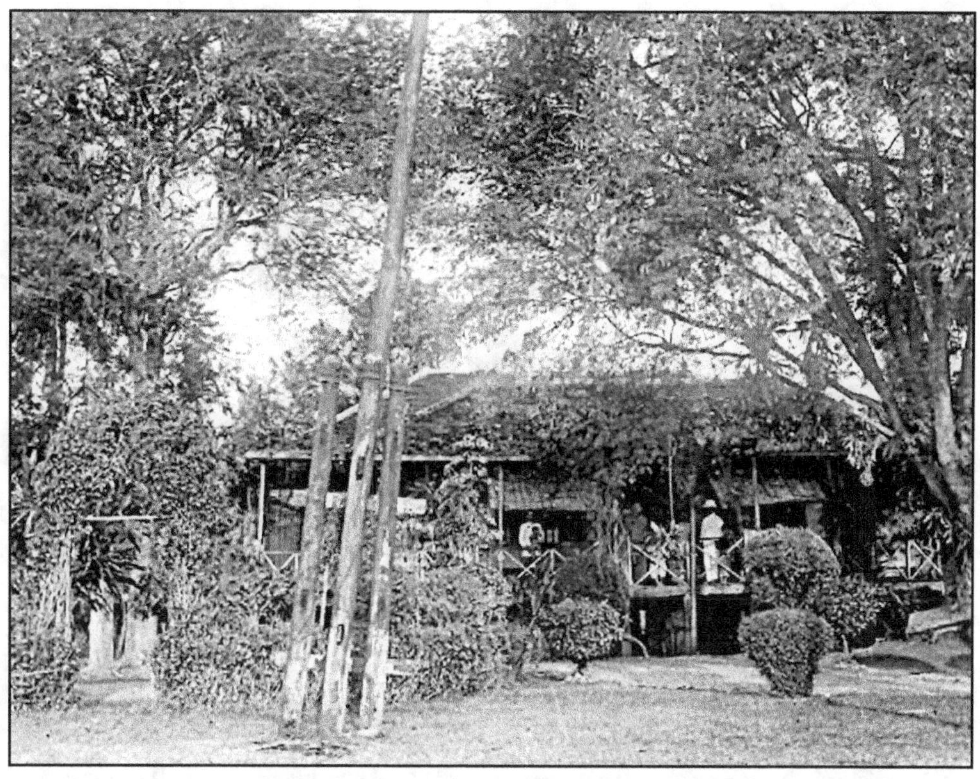

Governor's residence, Sisophon, 1924.

Personages in the photograph remain a mystery; of the eight figures in the two cars, five are almost certainly Cambodians (interpreters, guides and drivers); only three appear to be Caucasian - one in the rear car and two seated in the front car, turning to face the camera. Assuming the cars departed from Phnom Penh, together with the photographic evidence and museum interests at heart, one of the foreigners in the picture must be George Groslier.

A fourth foreign figure leaning on a walking stick, stands poised as if to welcome the group (was he resident and already working at the temple)? The sturdy wooden thatched pavilion in front of the vehicles surrounded by a fence with a decorative gate certainly lends an air of permanence to the site. Set in the dry, freshly leveled earth are three sandstone heads (*deva*) with newly planted native vegetation to provide a suggestion of a garden path approach to the *sala* (open air structure). The stone heads would have originated from the figures of

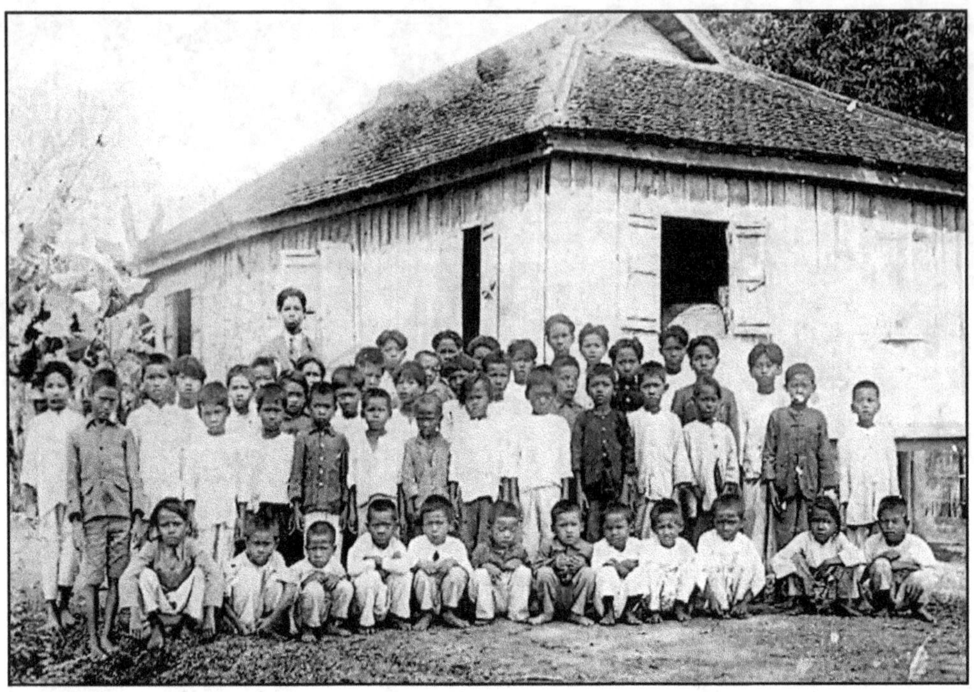

School, teacher & students, Mongkol Borei.

gods and demons grasping the serpent Vasuki that originally flanked one of the causeways to the temple compound.

The only other witnesses to this event are three shadowy figures of curious local Khmer (to the left of the vehicles) and one solitary figure under a small thatch hut to the right, viewing the arrival of the motorcade. The comparatively short shadows under the cars suggest an early afternoon arrival.

George Groslier prophetically wrote in 1924, "The collection of photographs owned by the Musée Albert Sarraut is of inestimable value. Fortunate acquisitions allowed us to gather documentation over the last 30 years or so. Most of the images are purely documentary. The conditions under which some of them were taken and the difficulties associated with their conservation in Indochina, has resulted in some low contrast prints, however, they are of sufficient quality for study."[5]

---

[5] Groslier 1924.

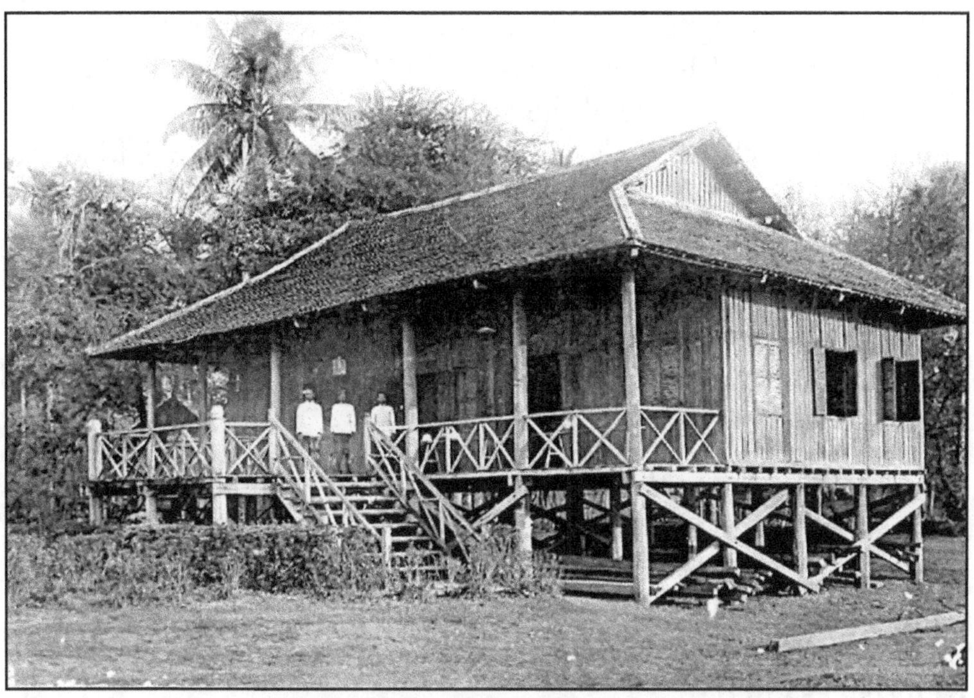

Courthouse, Sisophon, 1924

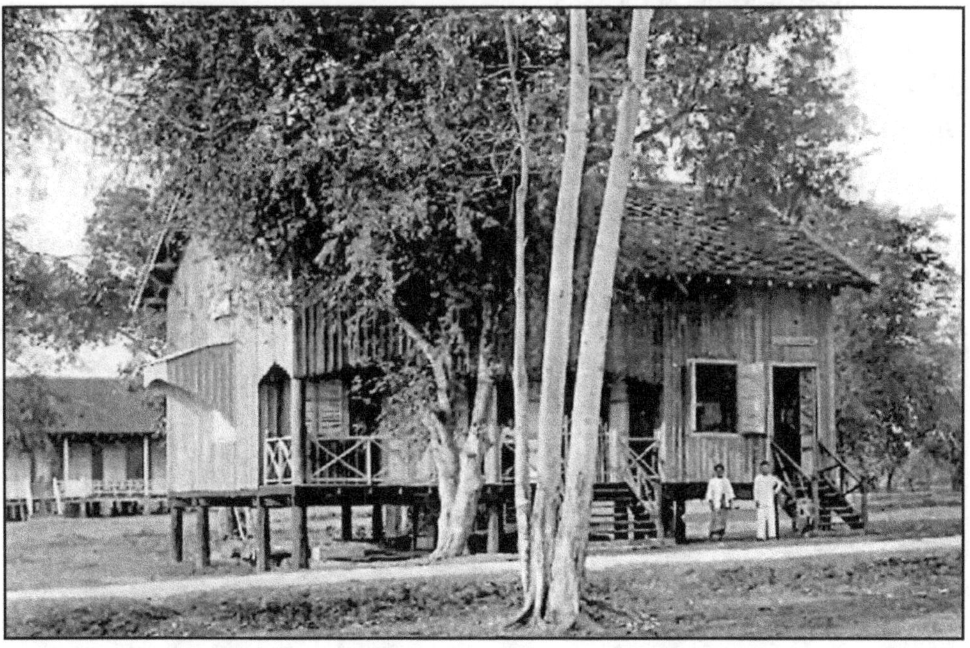

Banteay Chhmar government building, 1924.

Although photographs of the Banteay Chhmar complex were taken as early as 1914,[6] ten years later in 1924,[7] and again in 1932,[8] Groslier was not to write of the temple until some four years after in his 1936 article *"Troisième recherche sur les Cambodgiens"*[9], followed the next year by *"Banteai Chhmar, ville ancienne du Cambodge."*[10]

His son, Bernard Philippe Groslier, writing of his father, headed the tribute: 'George Groslier, French painter, writer and archaeologist: 4 February 1887-18 June 1945 (Phnom Penh, Cambodge).'[11]

In addition, could be added the terms 'museologist' and 'photographer,' for as the founding director of what is now the National Museum of Cambodia, the cataloguing and documenting of his milieu and the growing collection of masterpieces of Khmer art for public display, is arguably his greatest legacy.

References cited

Anon., undated catalogue: Musée A. Sarraut: *Service Photographique: Inventaire des Clichés*, National Museum of Cambodia.

Groslier, George, Hanoi, 1924. *Catalogue Général du Musée du Cambodge* (Musée Albert Sarraut).

Groslier, George, *'Troisième recherche sur les Cambodgiens'*, BEFEO XXXV : 159-206.

Groslier, George, Paris, 1937. *'Bantéai Chhmar, ville ancienne du Cambodge'*, L'Illustration, 3 April, no. 4909.

Various contributors, Paris, 1992. *Disciplines Croisées : Hommage à Bernard Philippe Groslier*, Editions de l'Ecole des Hautes Etudes en Sciences Sociales, Direction générale de la Coopération culturelle, scientifique et technique.

---

[6] ibid., nos. 670-716.
[7] Anon., undated catalogue, National Museum of Cambodia, L43-55; P57-63; R99-102.
[8] ibid., L86-133.
[9] Groslier 1936.
[10] Groslier 1937: 352-357.
[11] Various contributors 1992: 59.

Reprinted with permission of UDAYA - Journal of Khmer Studies

www.khmerculture.net/udaya.htm

Udaya, a new journal of Khmer studies, aims to develop understandings of Cambodian culture in both the national and international arenas. Publishing articles in Khmer, English and French, the journal is conceived as a forum for the distribution of information to all students, scholars and professionals working in the field of Khmer culture in view of promoting research and professional collaboration.

Banteay Chhmar Information Resources

Banteay Chhmar Heritage Conference Website
www.BanteayChhmar.net

Cambodia Community Based Eco-Tourism Network
www.ccben.org

Friends of Khmer Culture
http://www.khmerculture.net

Global Heritage Fund
www.GlobalHeritageFund.org

Heritage Watch International
www.HeritageWatchInternational.org

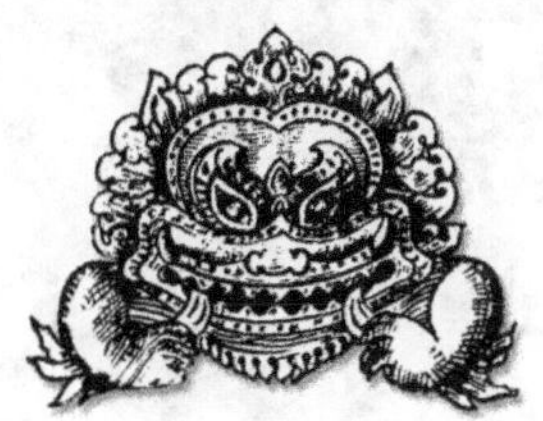

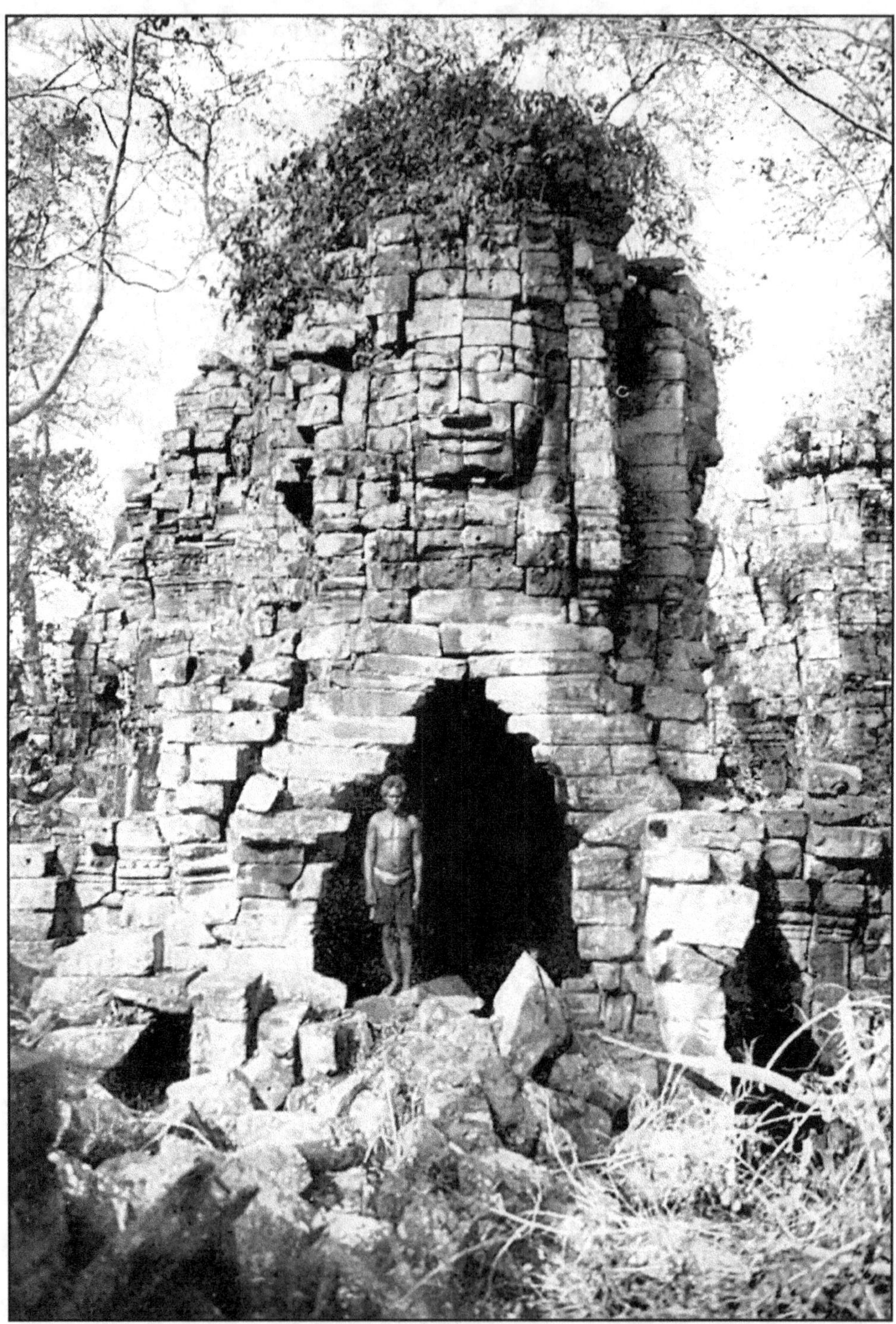

One of the towers with four divine faces at Banteay Chhmar.

A Khmer Marvel:
"Banteay Chhmar"
Ancient Cambodian City

George GROSLIER

Saturday, April 3, 1937

Advancing into the far northwest of Cambodia, one comes upon a region sealed off at right angles by the western end of the Dangrek Mountains, beyond which lies Siam. The region, some 2,000 to 3,000 kilometers square, is more or less deserted. With its soil of clay and sand, and its few rivers running dry six months out of the year, it offers the traveler nothing but a few uncultivated fields and a few measly forests, the sparse trees stunted by fire in the dry season.

Villages grow rare and finally vanish altogether. No game. Torrid heat in the summer. In the winter, violent storms that bounce off the mountains. These are the most destitute lands in Cambodia, yet here stand the ruins of an impressive set of monuments from the ancient empire, and among them the largest Khmer temple known to us (larger even than the Angkor group): indeed, *one of the largest temples in the world*. It is now called Banteay Chhmar.

What series of events led the builders some eight centuries ago, when Angkor was at its height, to settle in so godforsaken a place, long since abandoned and looking now just as it had when they found it? This is one of the most interesting questions in Cambodian history. We cannot address it here, but to understand the problem we should review a few facts. The selected lands were gradually organized. An irrigation system — whose extent we shall soon study — rendered them habitable and perhaps even prosperous.

The temple of Banteay Chhmar is today almost entirely a ruin. The two authors who have published descriptions — Aymonier in about 1883, then Lunet de Lajonquière in about 1909 — agreed that Banteay Chhmar was the most ruined, most vast, most chaotic, and most inscrutable of all the Khmer monuments they had explored. And they thus provided only summary, contradictory sketches and a few pages' worth of description. We have therefore endeavored to produce for this austere group the most comprehensive survey possible.

We were obliged to make four trips, separated by several years, because the temple is accessible only two out of every twelve months. After our third campaign we had nowhere reached

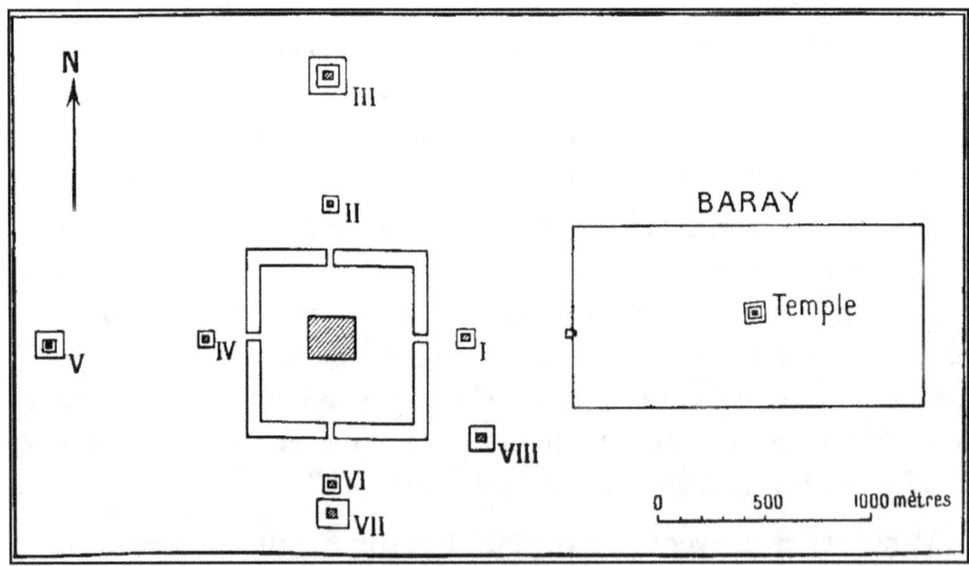

Banteay Chhmar's main temple (small grey square at left) is encircled by 8 secondary temples and a vast artificial reservoir with the Mebon temple built on an island in the center.

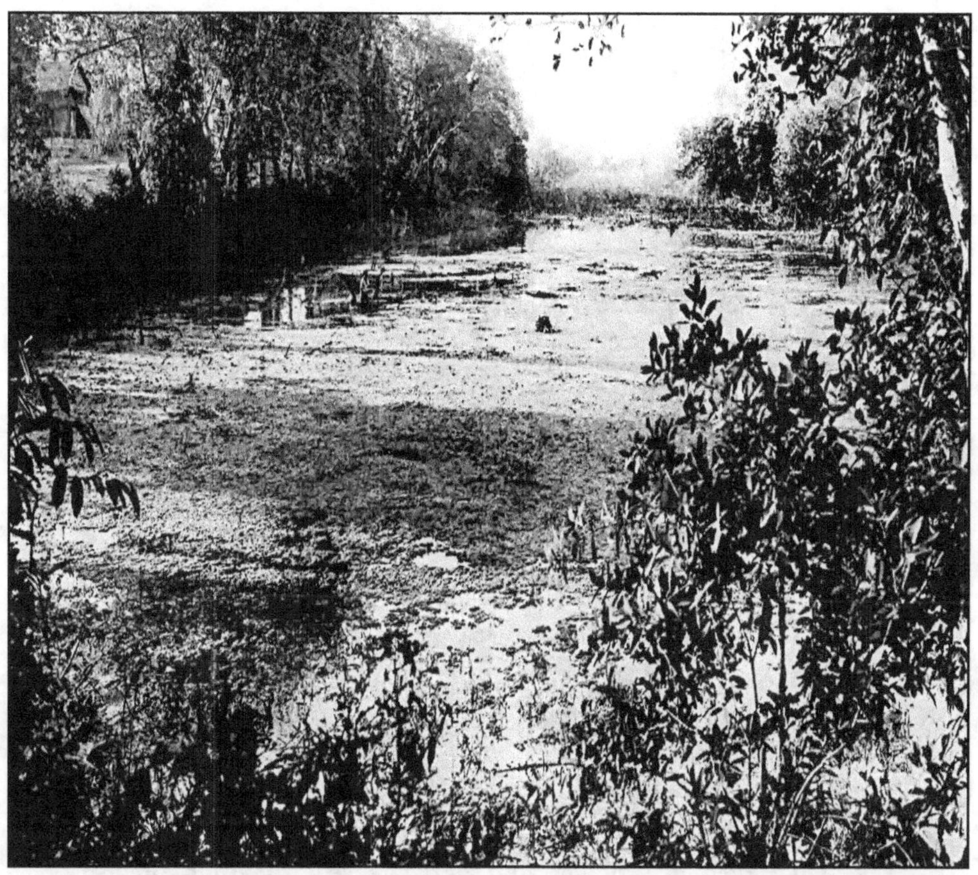

View of the south side of the moat surrounding Banteay Chhmar, with the causeway linking it to the mainland.

the flagstones of any courtyard, and it seemed that despite our dedication we would produce only a problematic survey, scarcely improving on the work of our predecessors. Enter Mr. George Cœdès, director of the Ecole Française d'Extrême-Orient, who rescued our endeavor by putting new funds at our disposal. We could now hire a team of forty coolies (who began deserting us after our second week of labor). But their efforts allowed us to plumb some thirty essential spots that had remained inaccessible during our previous investigations.

Our set of plans above shows the distribution of temples and the ancient city's surviving hydraulic systems. The Baray is a reservoir:

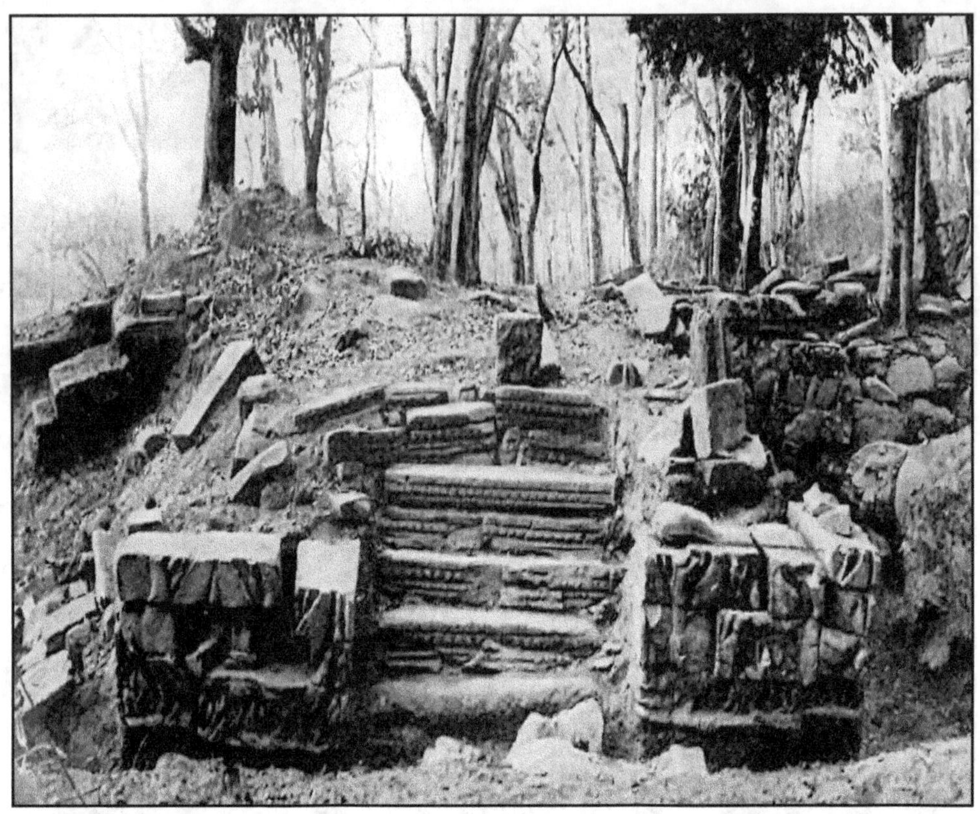

Ruins of the boat landing terrace on the Baray. Excavations by the EFEO revealed carved lotus flowers and sacred geese with wings spread.

a rectangular dyke, about three meters high on average, enclosing an area of 1,276,450 square meters. The inner walls are entirely covered with laterite steps, which made the water easy to reach. A river, now dry, once flowed into the vast reservoir, which also collected rainwater.

An artificial island was set aside more or less in the center for the building of a temple, the Mebon. On the western dyke of the Baray the Khmer erected a terraced jetty whose sub-bases, emerging from the water, were sculpted with aquatic birds, their wings spread, amid lotus. As soon as we set foot on this architectural motif its dimensions, decoration, and location (providing a view over the imposing mirror of water and its sacred island) convinced us that

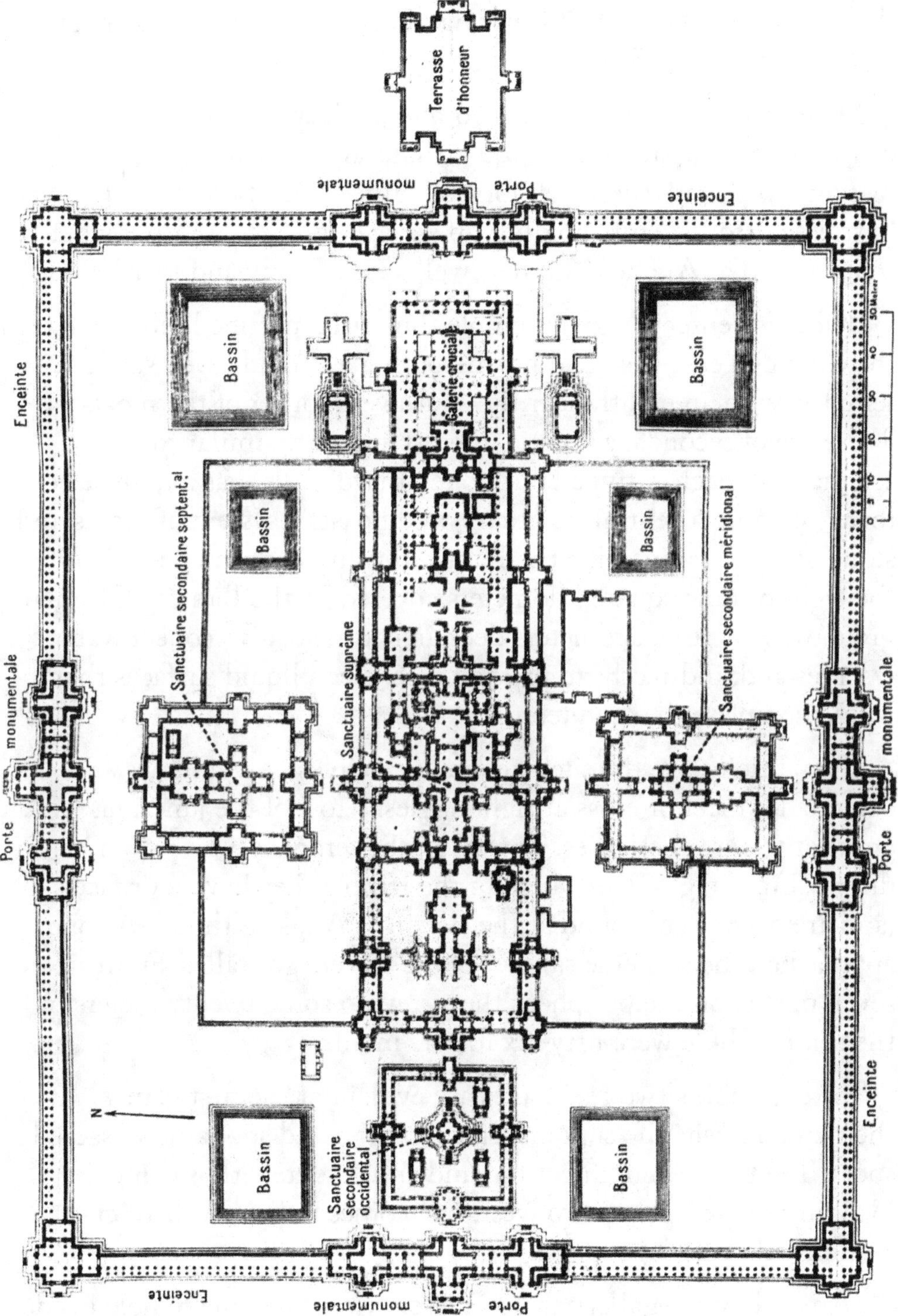

George Groslier's 1937 Banteay Chhmar temple plan.

the builders of Banteay Chhmar had had an eye for overall effect and a taste for the theatrical.

Moats 65 meters wide and 3.60 meters deep surround the central temple with a regular quadrilateral. These are crossed by four axial roadways, each formerly lined with two rows of buttressed stone giants holding up a *naga*-parapet: an ornamental motif found at Angkor Thom as well as the Baray and its Mebon.

Before we enter the great temple thus circumscribed, note that on the extended east-west and north-south axes stand seven satellite temples, with an eighth near the southwest corner of the moats. These are of secondary artistic interest and very similar to one another, but each is ringed with one or two walls, has a four-faced tower forming a central sanctuary, and boasts a system of moats and stone-stepped basins, like the Baray. Thus more than one-sixth of the eight or nine square kilometers covered by the Banteay Chhmar group was dug out, six meters deep in spots, so as to collect water reserves and, indirectly, to provide nice, clean liquid surfaces that would complete the architecture.

Here, briefly, are the site's general principles: All galleries and colonnades meet or cross at right angles. Most of the junctions occur at tower sanctuaries. Towers in the temple center rise in diminishing stages. Elsewhere in the temple they have four faces (and are of the type found at the Bayon at Angkor Thom). As one approached the supreme sanctuary the towers got taller. From six or seven meters on the periphery they grew to some twenty meters in the center. There were fifty-six towers in all.

The ensemble's two main axes are evident at the first glance. At their crossing sits the supreme sanctuary, sacred spot among sacred spots. The temple's architectural and ritual centers thus coincide. Walking the temple east to west, one comes across six distinct sections, all interdependent:

1 An outer wall–gallery that completely encloses the temple inside a rectangle measuring 250 meters by 190 meters axis to axis. It

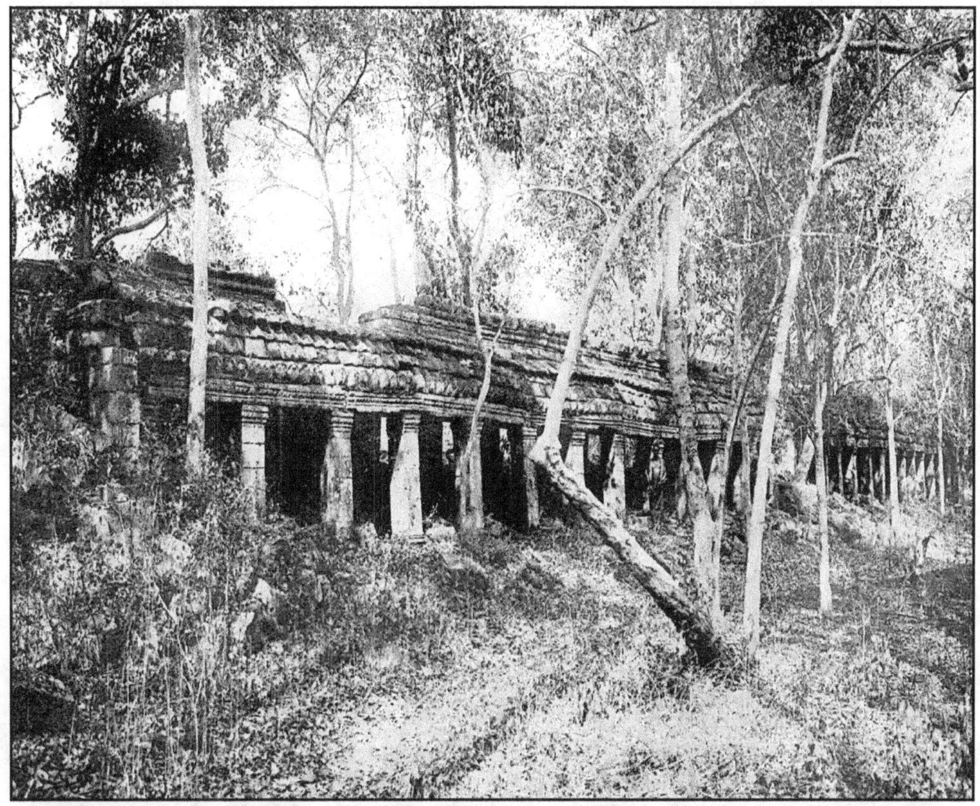

South exterior gallery of Banteay Chhmar's main temple. These galleries originally surrounded the temple covering nearly 700 meters of bas relief carvings of Khmer life.

is a vault atop a wall and pillars and flanked by a half-vault. On the wall's outer surface — a total of 1,090 square meters — is a series of bas-reliefs depicting historical and legendary scenes, which still defy interpretation. A monumental gate, with a triple opening and three towers, breaks every façade wherever the axes cross. One would reach these entrances by a court of honor ringed with *naga*-parapets, its staircases flanked with lions (our plans show only the eastern terrace).

2   A rectangular gallery circumscribes a courtyard, itself containing a cruciform gallery. This beautifully proportioned structure originally stood apart from the temple proper. In line

with it to the north and the south are two stepped basins and annex structures perched atop four-meter sub-bases. These last are flanked at a height of 1.70 meters by standing monsters that form caryatids.

3   The main body of the temple. This "grid" of galleries is itself divided into three complexes, lined up east to west like three complete temples joined end to end. Indeed, each has its own central tower-sanctuary preceded by a forward-jutting extension, its corner towers, and its monumental gates to the north and south. They are at once united and independent.

As one advances to the west the composition crowds up. Towers and jutting forward extensions multiply up to the main sanctuary. Then one is led into a wide-open courtyard, containing no more than a group of three isolated towers. The contrast is remarkably achieved. The arrangements obviously correspond to religious servitudes imposed on the architects by the many divinities served in the vast temple. But they would only have made the architectural problem thornier.

From an architectural point of view, moreover, it is interesting to see just how diverse the layout's composition is, despite the repetition of seemingly similar motifs. The long rectangle, 40 meters wide by 170 meters east to west,[1] is divided up by lines of towers. There are three here, five there. Here they're built in steps, there with four divine faces. Not a gap to be found. Nowhere does the observer's mind hesitate for a moment. Nowhere is the system of axes undergirding the whole neglected.

4 and 5   To the north and south the main body is flanked by two similar, symmetrical, independent groups. These are two sanctuaries topped with face towers and surrounded by a rectangular gallery.

---

[1] This aspect of the temple has not gone unnoticed by modern Cambodians, who have called it Banteay Chhmar, or narrow citadel.

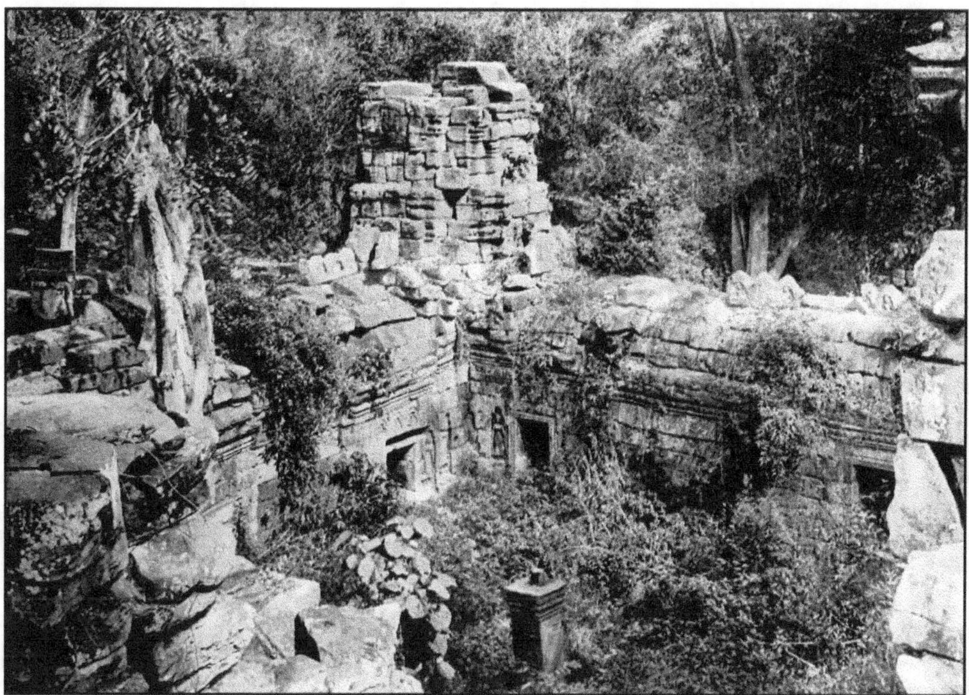

One of the courtyards of Banteay Chhmar leading to the central labyrinth.

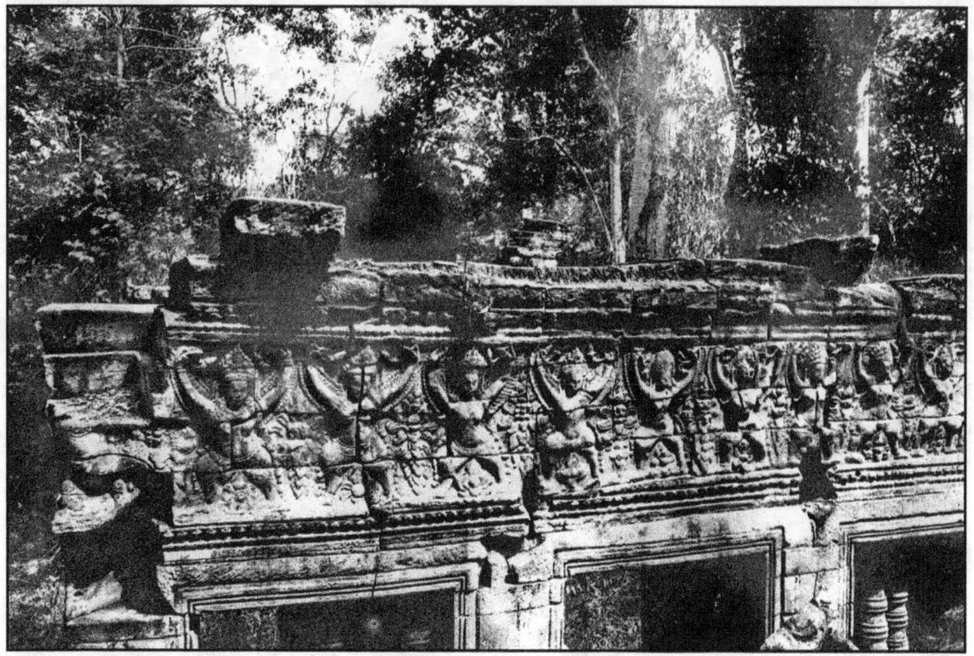

Interior structure of Banteay Chhmar's crucial gallery: winged women with arms raised holding lotus blossoms.

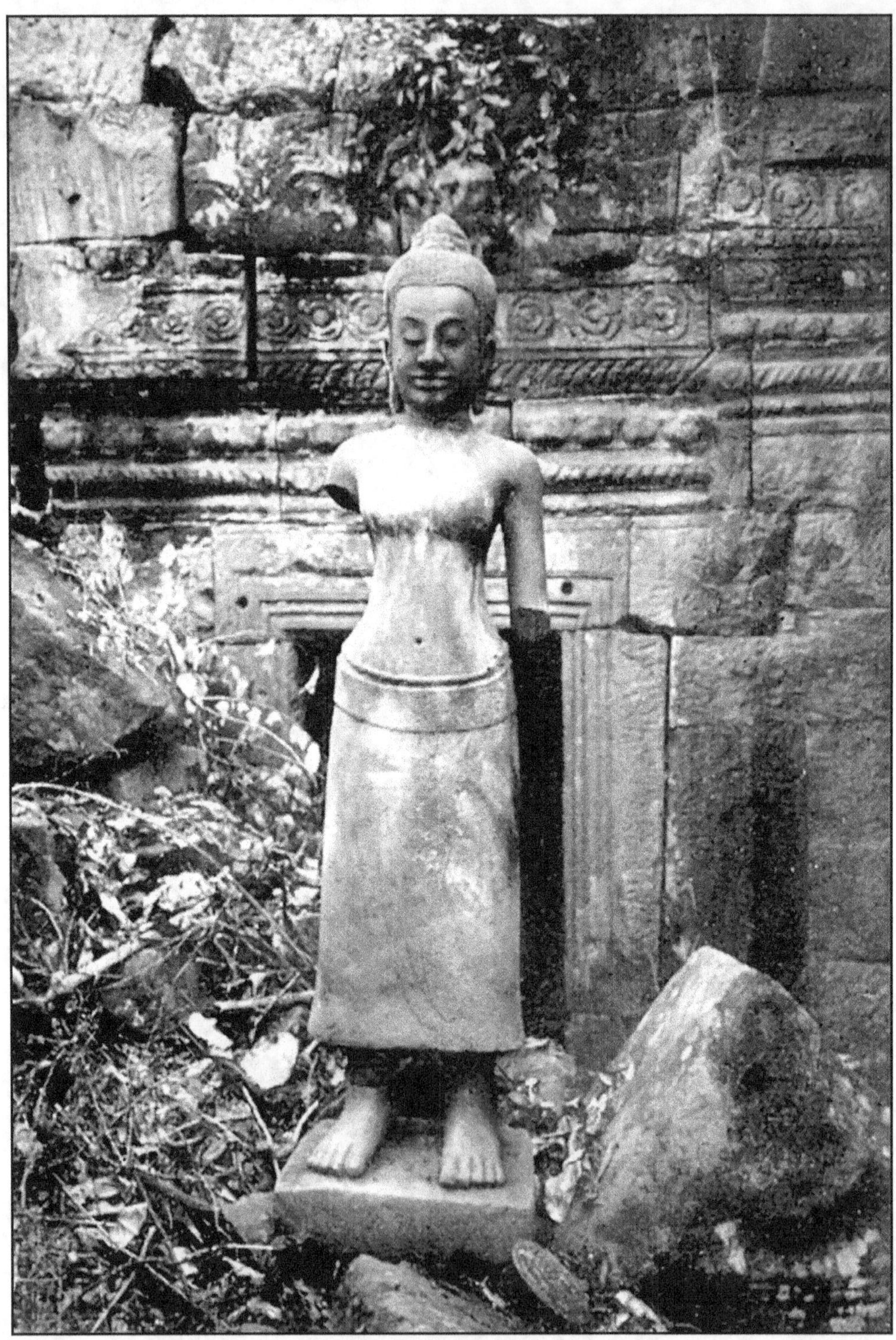

Goddess from the Buddhist pantheon at Banteay Chhmar.

6   Finally, to the far west, an ensemble of the same composition as
the two previous ones. This time, however, the central sanctuary
sits atop a sub-base 3.70 meters high, molded and toothed, and
flanked with four staircases. It thus breaks with the rest of the
temple, which is rigorously horizontal. The tallest sub-bases
so far were never more than 80 centimeters higher than the
courtyard flagstones.

The layout of Banteay Chhmar differs considerably from that
of the known great Khmer temples, which tend to be concentric
and thus present themselves as analogous in appearance and
dimension to the four cardinal points. Usually the secondary
structures were built, or added in later eras, somewhat arbitrarily,
and asymmetrically. Here, as we have just seen, the strict opposite
is true.

The layout is ex-centric, developing east to west in successive
entrenchments, without ever breaking the rigorous symmetry. The
outer wall's gallery is composed like those of the classical temples
(though it is here independent). Outside it, however, the architect
has neglected the northern, southern, and western façades of his
central group. He even masks them with independent sanctuaries.

Rigorously though the builders might have staked out their
ground, the disparity in just about every Khmer monument
between architectural design (often remarkable) and actual
construction (often mediocre) is wider at Banteay Chhmar than
at most of the other temples. With all the grinding inherent in
the stacking of stones, there were surprises when it came time to
line up three towers along axes that were only seven meters apart.
The architects had conceived this vast monument to perfection
and carefully adjusted its parts, and the teams requisitioned
for construction had built it "more or less," doing what they
could. Still, the clumsiness and impotence of the labor is usually
compensated by such resolve, by such cleverness and even daring,
that upon its completion the central temple of Banteay Chhmar
— however incapable of producing an overall effect, because of

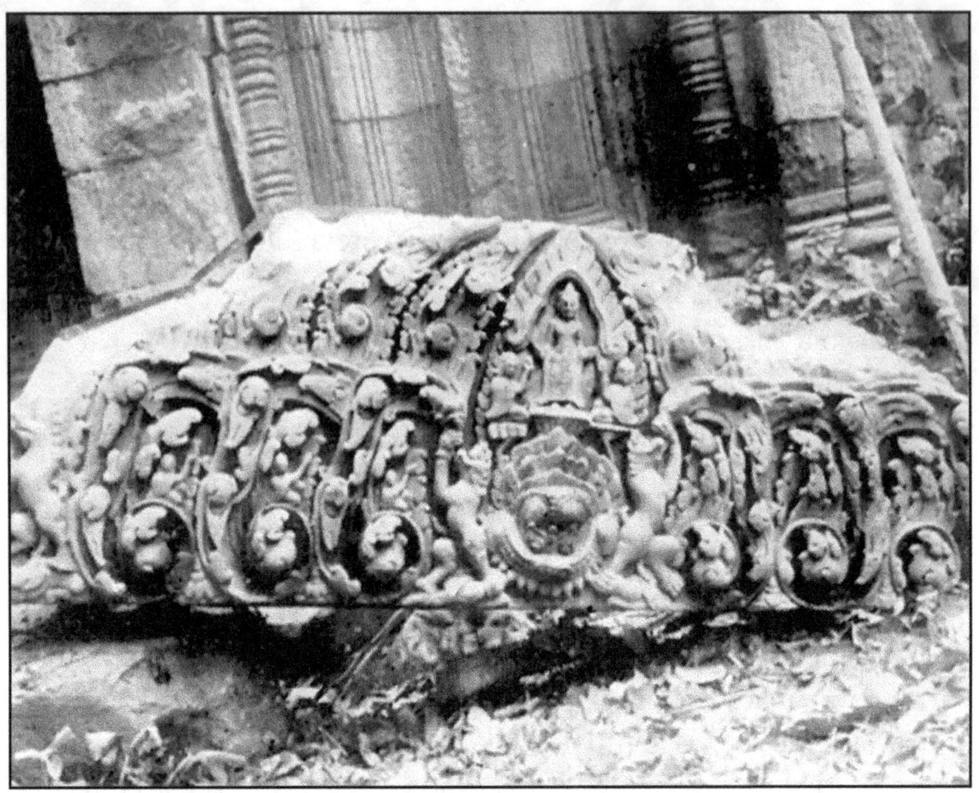

Banteay Chhmar lintel.

its horizontal layout on a single axis — must have been striking, presenting, as one walked along its length, areas where the little flaws we have just mentioned vanished to insignificance.

Our 5,000 or 6,000 measurements of these ruins have allowed us to calculate the total volume and area sculpted. From this we have been able to determine not the actual time it took to build and decorate Banteay Chhmar — that would entail too many unknowns — but the *minimum time* that such a job would require if as many workers as the site could hold were in fact to toil away there. Our result is sixty years: if, that is, nothing interrupted the work.

Moreover, inscriptions discovered there from the reign of Jayavarman VII (1180–1201) tell us when the great temple was already complete. We may therefore conclude provisionally that the ancient city whose religious center was Banteay Chhmar was flourishing in the twelfth century and that construction of its central complex, the first part to be built, was begun around 1140 at the latest. As for the religion celebrated there, the most we can say is that the temple, or at least its most recent parts, was dedicated first to Vishnu and then to Buddha. The iconography, in any case, belongs to those two religions.

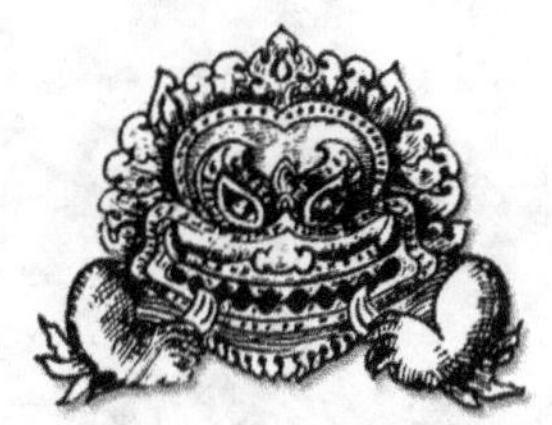

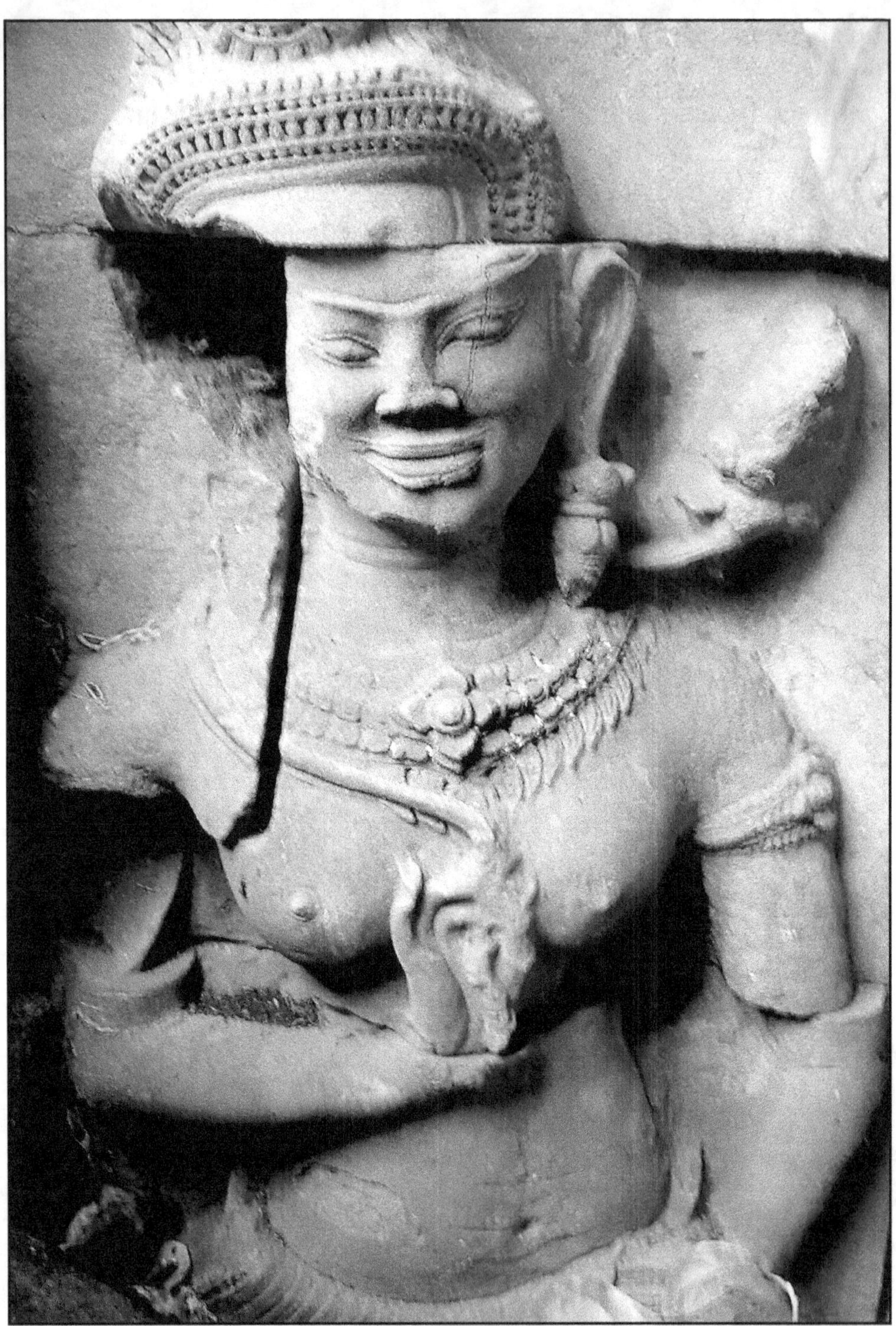

At the temple of Beng Mealea, one female image escaped the ravages of time, hidden in an alcove beneath a collapsed tower.

Death of an Angel
How antiquities theft destroys Cambodia's past… and future.

By Kent Davis

Wednesday, February 14, 2007

Her exquisite features expressed her Khmer heritage so perfectly she was chosen to become immortal.

No one had spoken her name for nearly 900 years but certainly thousands had admired her beauty; her almond eyes, the gentle cleft in her chin, her benevolent gaze, her full lips and deep smile conveyed warmth that set her apart from other women. Once adorned with a golden crown, jewelry and accoutrements this flower of the Khmers became divine. She answered her king's highest calling in the temple of Beng Mealea.

The Khmer race created some of history's most fantastic and innovative art. Their civilization emerged at the crossroads of Southeast Asia, clearly influenced by ancient Indian culture, yet the Khmer vision of religion, kingship, sculpture and architecture set them apart from any other ethnic group.

Khmer temples, their holiest of places, were actual models of heaven on Earth, ensuring balance, prosperity and fertility for their land. In the first half of the 12th century, King Suryavarman II built Cambodia's most famous monument, Angkor Wat, still featured as the central image of the country's flag.

To the southeast another magnificent structure rose from the jungle, Beng Mealea temple, incorporating many of Angkor Wat's features on a smaller scale. Experts date it to the same period, yet its builder, architect and precise purpose remain unknown.

Like Angkor Wat, Beng Mealea's designers and sponsors prominently included female deities, now referred to as *devatas* (when standing) or *apsaras* (when dancing). Balancing masculine and feminine forces in the universe was a key component of Khmer religion. Ancient accounts confirm that women held important positions in Khmer society so it isn't surprising to see women represented in temples as well.

What is surprising is the unique style of these portrayals at the peak of the Khmer culture in the 12th-13th centuries. Rather than generic images of impersonal goddesses, many *devatas* appear to be portrait carvings of actual women in divine context. These stone images show facial features, poses and personalities that imply individual women were the source of their inspiration.

The angel of Beng Mealea was one such woman.

I found her on a sweltering hot day in March 2006 while working on my quantitative analysis of Angkor Wat's *devatas*. When I heard about Beng Mealea's similar style I took a daytrip there to investigate. Despite the collapse of most of its structures, Beng Mealea is majestic in its jungle setting and well worth exploring. Sadly, most of its *devatas* were weathered beyond recognition, but when I climbed the pile of stones previously forming the northwest corner tower I had a surprising encounter.

She was hidden by vines beneath a stone overhang. Decades or even centuries ago, the tower's collapse formed a protective alcove around her. While all her sisters suffered erosion from exposure to the elements she alone remained preserved, still fulfilling the divine duties she was charged with so long ago.

My inexpensive camera didn't focus well in her compact hiding place so I already planned to return to see her again. Back in Siem Reap I saw my friend Jaro Poncar, a professor from the

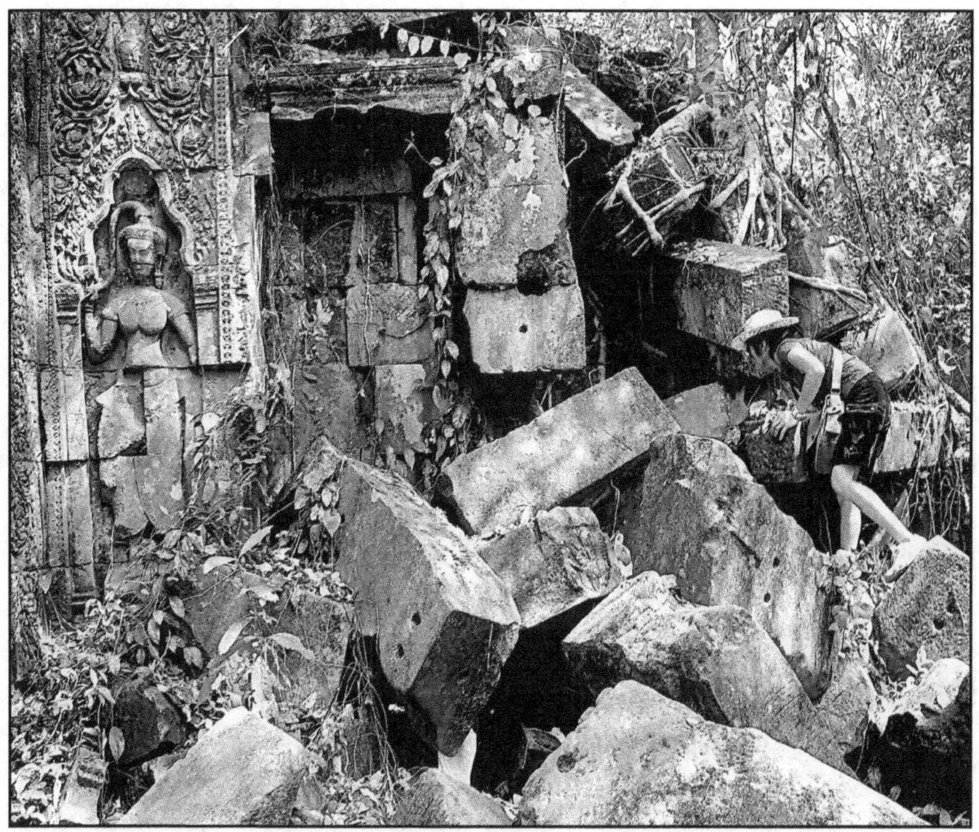

Sophaphan Davis climbing up stones from a collapsed tower at Beng Mealea to see the hidden *devata*.

University of Cologne who has been photographing Khmer structures for more than ten years. Jaro was surprised that he himself had never seen this devata before, making her discovery even more special to me.

It took me nearly a year to mount my next research trip. In February 2007 I returned to Cambodia with my wife Sophaphan and a new camera. After three days of shooting at Angkor Wat we headed to Beng Mealea and I anticipated introducing my wife to my hidden friend.

We arrived at the northwest tower and I sent Sophaphan up to look first, awaiting her shout of delight. Instead, she said, "What am I supposed to see?"

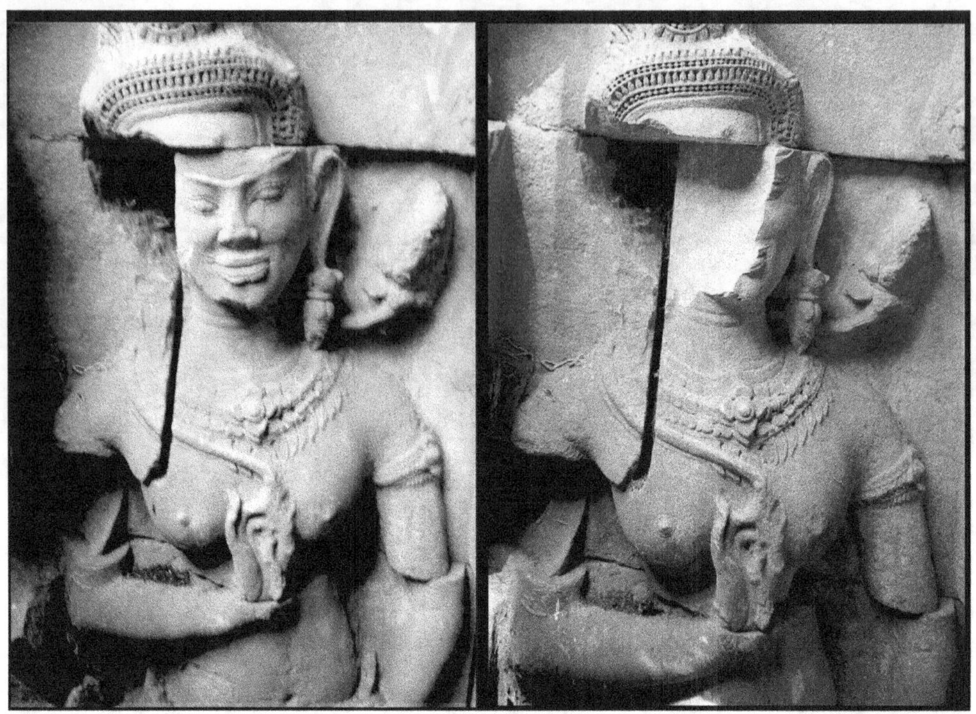

The Angel of Beng Mealea, 2006 (left) and defaced in 2007 (right).

"The *devata!* The only one here that's well preserved," I said. "Look, down in the alcove!"

"She's not there," came her reply.

I clambered up the rocks to find a faceless section of white rock. Clearly, someone had recently attempted to steal her head but the stone's stress cracks (visible in my earlier photo) caused her to break unevenly.

She, who had survived the collapse of her temple, the weather and the wars of nearly a thousand years, had been destroyed in a moment by a thief's chisel. For a few dollars, the Khmer race lost a piece of its soul. Cambodia lost an irreplaceable part of its heritage. And Beng Mealea became a bit less attractive, and less financially viable, to the Cambodian economy as a tourist destination.

I don't write these words to fault anyone. The company administrating Beng Mealea built the road that enables visitors to easily access this remote site. The Apsara Authority is charged with protecting a vast area and countless treasures on a limited budget. The Cambodian government works with legal organizations around the world to prevent the illegal sale of antiquities. But the evidence suggests that whoever destroyed this angel did so out of ignorance and probably out of economic necessity.

The best solution is education. With the help of Heritage Watch International and other organizations Cambodian leaders are teaching Khmer people that heritage is their most priceless possession. With care and preservation the Khmer legacy will support this land and its people far into the future. But this angel will not be there to see it. Her time has passed.

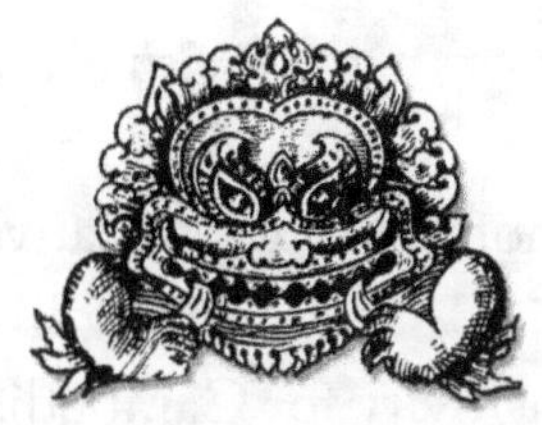

The Works of George Groslier

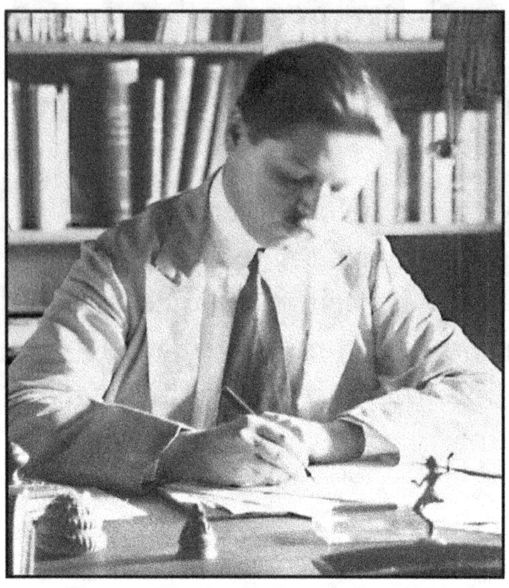

George Groslier in his study - 1922.

Creative, passionate and prolific, George Groslier was a visionary man of many talents. First trained in fine arts by Parisian master painter Albert Maignan, George returned to his Cambodian birthplace in 1911. There, he devoted his life to documenting, preserving, promoting and celebrating Khmer art, culture and history.

Groslier expressed himself visually as a painter, intellectually as an archaeologist, museum curator and essayist, and emotionally as a creative writer. He championed Khmer patrimony in every endeavor, infusing his artistic works with his unique love, respect and sensitivity for Cambodia that ensure the timeless validity of his contributions.

Modern French & English Language Editions

- ❖ *La Route du plus fort.* Paris: Kailash, 1994.
- ❖ *Le Retour à l'argile.* Paris: Kailash, 1994.
- ❖ *Cambodian Dancers – Ancient & Modern.* Holmes Beach, FL: DatAsia Press, 2010; and Phnom Penh, Cambodia: DatAsia Press, 2011.
- ❖ *In the Shadow of Angkor – Unknown Temples of Ancient Cambodia.* Holmes Beach, FL: DatAsia Press, 2014.
- ❖ *Danseuses cambodgiennes – Anciennes & Modernes.* Holmes Beach, FL: DatAsia Press, 2014.
- ❖ *Return to Clay – A Romance of Cambodia.* Holmes Beach, FL: DatAsia Press, 2014.
- ❖ *Water & Light – A Travel Diary on the Cambodian Mekong.* Holmes Beach, FL: DatAsia Press, 2014.

Books

- ❖ *La Chanson d'un Jeune.* Self-published. 1904.
- ❖ *Danseuses cambodgiennes anciennes et modernes.* Paris : A. Challamel, 1913.
- ❖ *A l'ombre d'Angkor; notes et impressions sur les temples inconnus de l'ancien Cambodge.* Paris : A. Challamel, 1913.

- ❖ *Angkor…Ouvrage orné de 103 gravures et de 5 cartes et plans.* Paris: H. Laurens, 1924.
- ❖ *Arts et Archéologie khmères, 2 vol.* Paris : A. Challamel, 1921-1926.
- ❖ *Recherches sur les Cambodgiens d'après les textes et les monuments depuis les premiers siècles de notre ère.* Paris : A. Challamel, 1921.
- ❖ *Arts et Archéologie Khmers. Revue des Recherches sur les Art, les Monuments et l'Ethnographie du Cambodge, depuis les Origines jusqu'à nos Jours.* Paris: Société d' Editions Géographiques, Maritimes et Coloniales, 1925.
- ❖ *La sculpture Khmère ancienne ; illustrée de 175 reproductions hors texte en similigravure.* Paris : G. Crès, 1925.
- ❖ *Les collections khmères du Musée Albert Sarraut à Phnom-Penh.* Paris: G. van Oest, 1931.
- ❖ *Eaux et lumières; journal de route sur le Mékong cambodgien.* Paris: Société d'éditions géographiques, maritimes et coloniales, 1931.
- ❖ *L'enseignement et la mise en pratique des arts indigènes au Cambodge (1918-1930).* Paris: Sté d'éditions géographiques, maritimes et coloniales, 1931.
- ❖ *Angkor, with 103 illustrations, 5 maps and plans. Translated from the French by Paule Fercoq Du Leslay.* Evreux: impr. Hérissey, 1933.
- ❖ *Ankooru iseki.* Japanese translation of *Angkor.* Tokyo: Shinkigensha, 1943.

Novels

- ❖ *La Route du plus fort.* Paris, Emile-Paul frères, 1926.
- ❖ *Le Retour à l'argile.* Paris : Emile-Paul frères, 1928.
- ❖ *Monsieur De La Garde, Roi: Roman, Inspiré Des Chroniques Royales Du Cambodge,* 1934, Paris: *L'Illustration.*
- ❖ *Les Donneurs de Sang, Phnom Penh et Saigon.* Saigon : Albert Portail, 1941.
- ❖ *Le Christ Byzentine,* 1953, Ellery Queen Mystère Magazine, N°69 and N°70.

Graphic Works

- ❖ *Les Ruines d'Angkor.* Indochine, 1911.

Archeological Publications

- ❖ "Objets anciens trouvés au Cambodge." *Revue archéologique,* 1916, 5e Série, vol. 4, pp. 129-139.
- ❖ "La batellerie cambodgienne du VIIIe au XIIIe siècles." *Revue archéologique,* 1917, 5e Série, vol. 5, pp. 198-204.
- ❖ "Objets cultuels en bronze dans l'ancien Cambodge." *Arts et Archéologie khmers,* 1921-3, vol. 1, fasc. 3, pp. 221-228.
- ❖ "Le temple de Phnom Chisor." Ibid, vol. 1, fasc. 1, pp. 65-81.
- ❖ "Le temple de Ta Prohm (Ba Ti)." Ibid, vol. 1. fasc. 2, pp. 139-148.
- ❖ "Le temple de Preah Vihear". Ibid, 1921-1922, vol. 1. fasc. 3, pp. 275-294.
- ❖ "Essai sur l'architecture classique khmère." *Arts et Archéologie khmers,* 1923, vol. 1, fasc. 3. pp. 229-273.
- ❖ "L'art khmèr." Paris, *Arts et Décoration,* août 1923. vol. 27. N° 260, pp. 34-40.
- ❖ "L'art du bronze au Cambodge." *Arts et Archéologie khmers,* 1923. vol. 1, fasc., pp. 413-423.
- ❖ "L'Art khmèr." Paris, *Arts et Décoration,* August 1923, vol. 1, pp. 413-423.
- ❖ "Amarendrapura dans Amoghapura." *Bulletin de l'Ecole Française d'Extrême-Orient,* Hanoï, 1924, vol. 24, pp. 359-372.
- ❖ *Angkor, Les Villes d'Art célèbres.* Paris, Laurens, 1924.

❖ *Catalogue du Musée de Phnom Penh*. Hanoï, IDEO, 1924.

❖ "La céramique dans l'ancien Cambodge." *Arts et Archéologie khmers*, 1924, vol. 2, fasc. 1, pp. 31-64.

❖ "La vie à Angkor au XIe siècle." Saigon, *Pages Indochinoises*, 15-1-1924, N.S., vol. 1, pp. 9-17.

❖ "Les empreintes du 'Pied du Buddha' d'Angkor Vat." *Arts et Archéologie khmers*, 1924, vol. 2, fasc. 2. pp. 65-80.

❖ "La région d'Angkor." *Arts et Archéologie khmers*, 1924, vol. 2, fasc. 2, pp. 113-130.

❖ "La région du Nord-Est du Cambodge et son art." Ibid., pp. 131-141.

❖ "L'Asram Maha Rosei." *Arts et Archéologie khmers*, 1924, vol. 2. fasc. 2. pp. 141-146.

❖ "L'Art hindou au Cambodge." *Arts et Archéologie khmers*, 1924. vol. 2, fasc. 1, pp. 81-93.

❖ "Essai sur le Buddha khmèr." Ibid, pp. 93-112.

❖ "Sur les origines de l'Art khmèr." *Mercure de France*, 1-xii-1924, vol. 176, N° 365, pp. 382-404.

❖ "Les influences grecques au Cambodge et l'art pré khmèr." Paris, *L'Art Vivant*, 1925.

❖ "Sur la route d'Angkor : le Prasat Phum Prasat." Saigon, *Extrême-Asie*, déc. 1925, N° 14, vol. 12, pp. 493-494.

❖ "Introduction à l'étude des arts khmèrs." *Arts et Archéologie khmers*, 1925, vol. 2. fasc. 2, pp. 167-234.

❖ "La femme dans la sculpture khmère ancienne." Paris, *Revue des Arts asiatiques*, 1925, vol. 2, fasc. 1, pp. 35-41.

❖ "La fin d'Angkor." Saigon, *Extrême-Asie*, Sept. 1925.

❖ "Note sur la sculpture khmère ancienne." Hanoï, *Études asiatiques, École Française d'Extrême-Orient*, 1925. vol. I, pp. 297-314.

❖ "A propos d'art hindou et d'art khmèr." *Arts et Archéologie khmers*, 1926, vol. 2, fasc. 3, pp. 329-348.

❖ "Les collections khmères du Musée Albert Sarraut." *Ars Asiatica*, XVI, Paris, G. Van Oest, 1931.

❖ "Les Temples inconnus du Cambodge." Paris, *Toute la terre*, June 1931.

❖ *Angkor, Les Villes d'Art célèbres*. Paris. Laurens, 1932 (English translation).

❖ "Troisième recherche sur les Cambodgiens." *Bulletin de l'Ecole Française d'Extrême-Orient*, Hanoi, 1935, vol. 35, pp. 159-206.

❖ "Une merveilleuse cité khmère. Banteai Chhma, ville ancienne du Cambodge." Paris, *L'Illustration*, April 3, 1937, N° 4909, pp. 352-357.

❖ "Les Monuments khmers sont-ils des tombeaux?" Saigon. Bulletin de la Société des Eudes Indochinoises.1941, N.S., vol. 16. N°1 pp. 121-126.

Publications on the Indigenous Arts of Cambodia

❖ "La Convalescence des Arts cambodgiens." Hanoï, *Revue Indochinoise*, Imprimerie d'Extrême-Orient, 2e sem. 1918, p. 207; 1er sem. 1919, pp. 871-890, 22 p. ill. p. 16, fig. 21.

❖ "L'agonie des Arts cambodgiens." Hanoï, *Revue Indochinoise*, 2e sem. 1918, p.207.

❖ "Question d'art indigène." Hué, *Bulletin des Amis du Vieux-Hué*, Oct.-Dec. déc. 1920, pp. 444-452.

❖ "Étude sur la psychologie de l'artisan cambodgien." *Arts et Archéologie khmers*, 1921, vol. 1, fasc. 2, pp. 125-137.

❖ "Seconde étude sur la psychologie de l'artisan cambodgien." *Arts et Archéologie khmers*, 1921, vol. 1. fasc. 2, pp. 205-220.

❖ "Royal Dancers of Cambodia." *Asia*, 1922, vol. 22, N° 1, pp. 47-55, 74-75.

❖ "Soixante-seize dessins cambodgiens tracés par l'oknha Tep Nimit Mak et l'oknha Reachna Prasor Mao, Arts et Archéologie khmers." Paris: *Société d'Edition Géographique, Maritime et Coloniale*, 1923. 331-386 p.

❖ "The Oldest Living Monarch." *Asia*, 1923. vol. 23. pp. 587-589.

❖ "La reprise des arts khmèrs." *La Revue de Paris*, Nov. 15, 1925. pp. 395-422.

❖ "Avec les danseuses royales du Cambodge." Mercure de France, May 1, 1928, pp. 536-565.

❖ "La mort de S.M. Sisowath." *L'Illustration*, Oct. 1927.

❖ "Les cérémonies d'incinérations de S.M. Sisowath." *L'Illustration*, April 1928. 86è année, n°4443. Samedi 28 Avril 1928. pp. 410-415.

❖ "Die Kunst der Kambodschanischen tànzerinn." Munich, *Atlantis*, Jan.-Mar. 1929, vol. 1, pp. 10-16.

❖ "Die Tanzerinnen des Konigs." [Miscellanea], p 16. 2 plates (1 col.) *Atlantis*, Jan 1929.

❖ "Le théâtre et la danse au Cambodge." Paris, *Journal Asiatique*, Jan.-Mar. 1929. vol. 214, pp. 125-143. (See Appendix for English translation)

❖ "Contemporary Cambodian art studied in the Light of the Past Forms." Boston, *Eastern Art*, 1930. vol. 2, pp. 127-141.

❖ "La Direction des Arts cambodgiens et l'École des Arts cambodgiens." Saigon, *Extrême-Asie*, March 1930, N° 45, pp. 119-127.

❖ "La fin d'un art." Paris, *Revue des Arts Asiatiques*, 1929-1930, vol. 6, fasc. 3., pp. 176-186; p. 184 et 251, fasc. 4, pp. 244-254.

❖ "La fin d'une tradition d'art : les pagodes cambodgiennes et le ciment armé." *L'Illustration*, January 11, 1930, vol. 175, pp. 50-53.

❖ "De Pagode en Pagode." Paris. *Toute la Terre*, July 1931.

❖ "L'Orfèvrerie cambodgienne à l'Exposition Coloniale." Paris, *La Perle*, 1931.

❖ "Rapport sur les arts indigènes au Cambodge." Congrès International et Intercolonial de la Société Indigène, Paris. 1931.

❖ "L'Enseignement et la mise en pratique des Arts indigènes au Cambodge." *Bulletin de Académie des Sciences Coloniales*, Paris, 1931.

❖ "Les Arts indigènes au Cambodge." *Exp. int. des Arts et Techniques*, Indochine Française, Paris, 1937.

❖ "Les Arts indigènes au Cambodge." 10th *Congress of the Far-Eastern Association of Tropical Medicine*, Hanoi, 1938, pp. 161-181.

Narratives

❖ "Propos sur la maison coloniale." Saigon, *Extrême-Asie*, 3° trim. 1926, pp. 2-10; March 1927, pp. 307-366.

❖ "Le Singe qui montre la Lanterne magique." Saigon, *Extrême-Asie* , Feb. 1928, pp. 347-366; mars 1928, pp. 435-450; avril 1928, pp. 499-505; mai 1928, pp. 546-554.

❖ "C'est une idylle...." Paris, *Mercure de France*, July 1929.

❖ *La Mode masculine aux colonies.* Paris : Adam, 1931.

❖ "Nos boys." Saigon, *Extrême-Asie*, August 1931, N° 55, pp. 69-76.

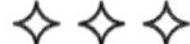

Exotic Visions of French Indochina

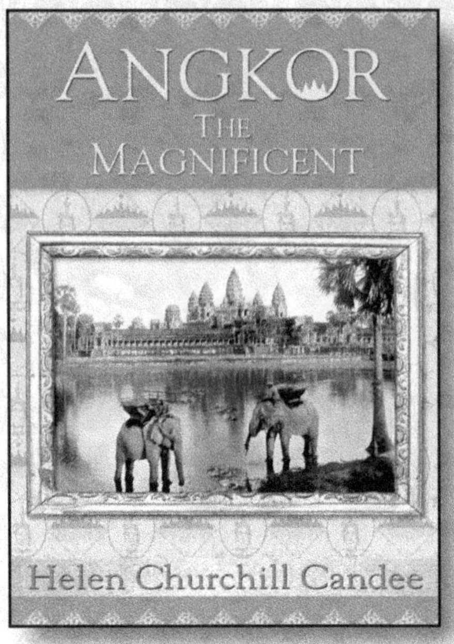

A 1925 adventure in Angkor.
ISBN: 978-1934431023

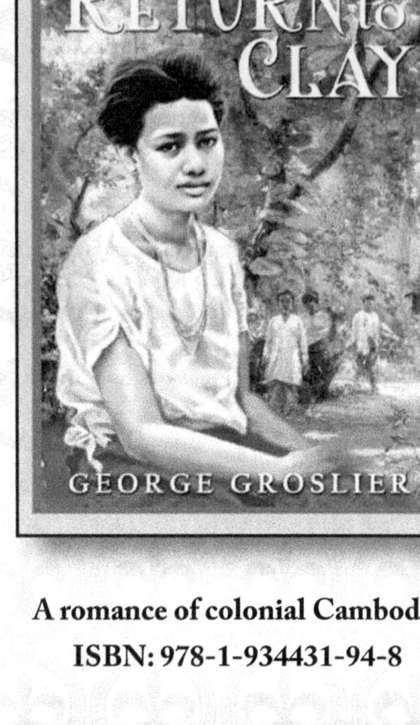

A romance of colonial Cambodia
ISBN: 978-1-934431-94-8

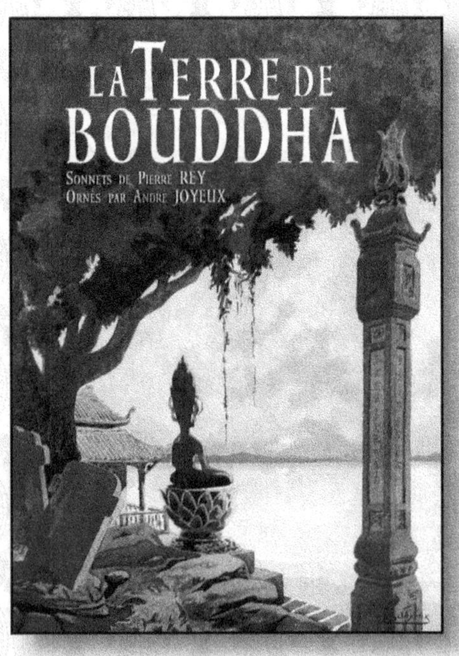

Paintings of 1920s Indochina.
ISBN: 978-1934431917

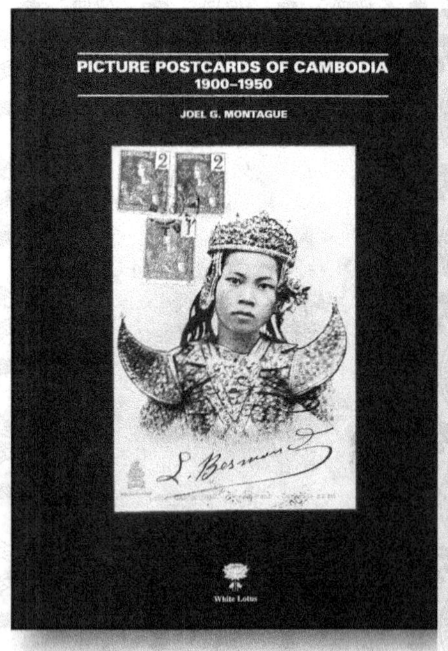

Antique postcards of Cambodia.
ISBN: 978-9744801197

Exotic Visions of French Indochina

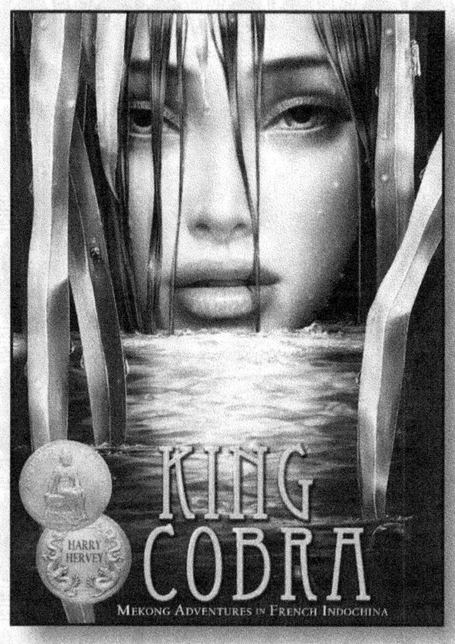

An American in 1920s Indochina.

www.HarryHervey.org

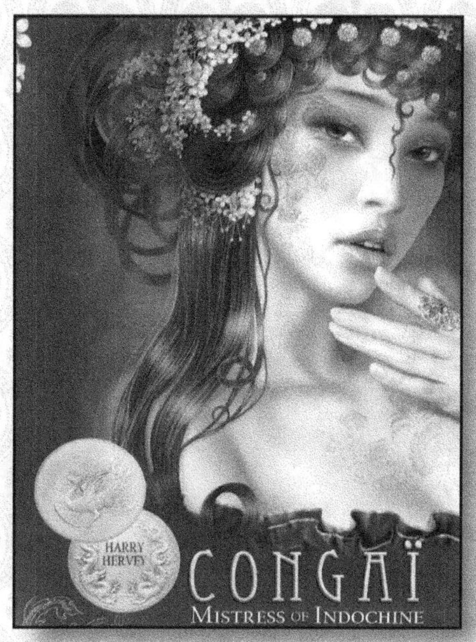

A sensual novel of East and West

www.HarryHervey.org

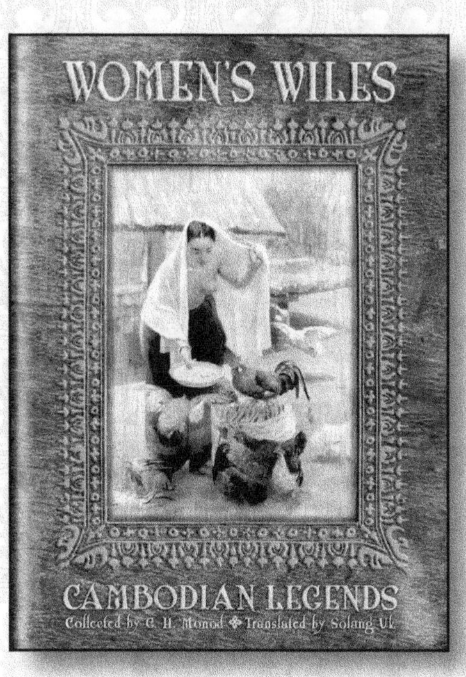

Fantastic folktales from ages past.

ISBN 978-1-934431-21-4

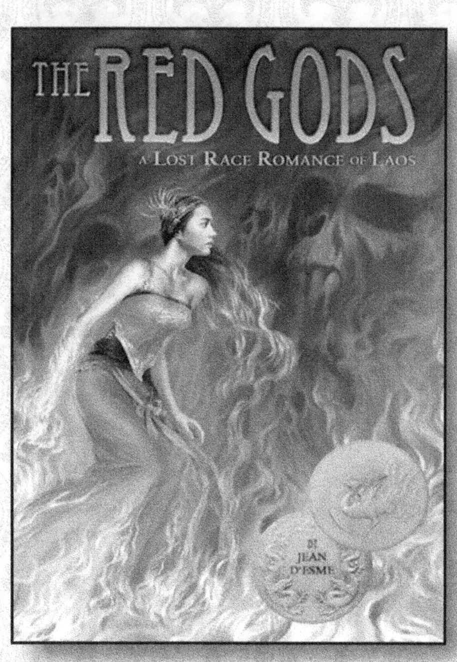

A lost-race romance of Laos

ISBN: 978-1934431764

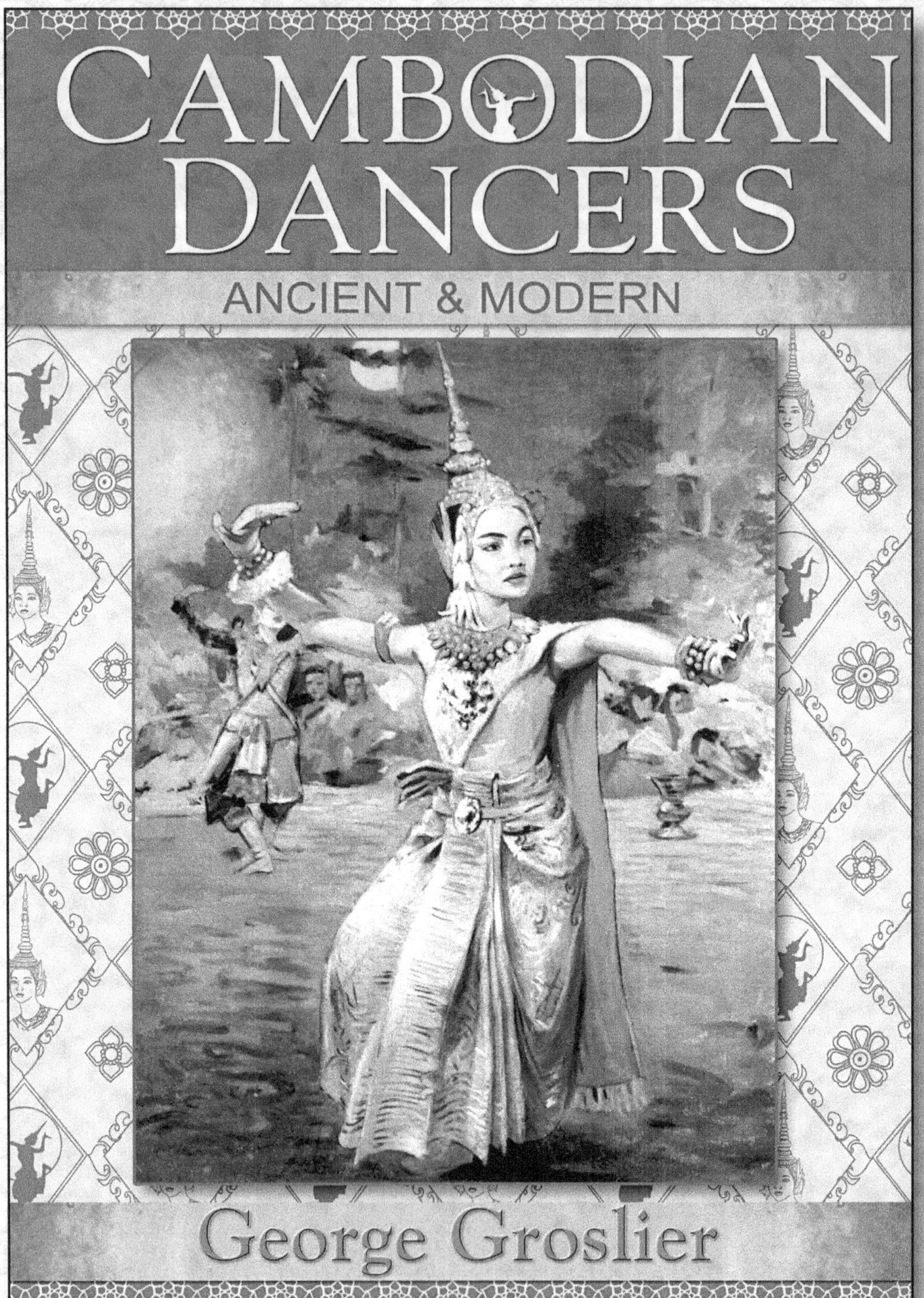

CAMBODIAN DANCERS

ANCIENT & MODERN

George Groslier

An artistic record of Cambodia's ancient dance tradition

With a foreword by Princess Buppha Devi of Cambodia, this deluxe modern edition includes the complete contents of the rare original 1913 publication, more than 250 hand-drawn illustrations and photos, an exclusive biography of George Groslier, extensive background materials, a bibliography and index.

www.CambodianDancers.com